Political Adaptation
in Canadian Theatre

KAILIN WRIGHT

Political Adaptation in Canadian Theatre

McGill-Queen's University Press
Montreal & Kingston • London • Chicago

ISBN 978-0-2280-0189-8 (cloth)
ISBN 978-0-2280-0190-4 (paper)
ISBN 978-0-2280-0323-6 (ePDF)
ISBN 978-0-2280-0324-3 (ePUB)

Legal deposit third quarter 2020
Bibliothèque nationale du Québec

Printed in Canada on acid-free paper that is 100% ancient forest free (100% post-consumer recycled), processed chlorine free

This book has been published with the help of a grant from the Canadian Federation for the Humanities and Social Sciences, through the Awards to Scholarly Publications Program, using funds provided by the Social Sciences and Humanities Research Council of Canada.

Funded by the Government of Canada | Financé par le gouvernement du Canada | Canada

Canada Council for the Arts | Conseil des arts du Canada

We acknowledge the support of the Canada Council for the Arts.

Nous remercions le Conseil des arts du Canada de son soutien.

Library and Archives Canada Cataloguing in Publication

Title: Political adaptation in Canadian theatre / Kailin Wright.
Names: Wright, Kailin, author.
Description: Includes bibliographical references and index.
Identifiers: Canadiana (print) 20200228390 | Canadiana (ebook) 20200231901 | ISBN 9780228001904 (softcover) | ISBN 9780228001898 (hardcover) | ISBN 9780228003236 (PDF) | ISBN 9780228003243 (EPUB)
Subjects: LCSH: Political plays, Canadian—History and criticism. | LCSH: Canadian drama—History and criticism. | LCSH: Adaptation (Literary, artistic, etc.)
Classification: LCC PS8169.P6 W75 2020 | DDC C812.009/3581—dc23

Contents

Tables and Figures

Tables

Figures

Acknowledgments

This research was generously funded by a Social Science and Humanities Research Council of Canada Institutional Grant and a University Council for Research Grant from St Francis Xavier University, as well as by a Social Science and Humanities Research Council of Canada Doctoral Fellowship, an Ontario Graduate Scholarship, and a School of Graduate Studies Doctoral Completion Award from the University of Toronto.

Many colleagues and mentors contributed to the preparation of this book. Mary Nyquist, who was my doctoral supervisor, went above and beyond in her honest, thoughtful, and meticulous appraisals of my work. Ric Knowles's Canadian theatre expertise and insightful questions inspired the choice of case studies and consideration of theatre's political impacts. Colin Hill not only provided essential research opportunities and training, but also advised me in numerous ways over the course of this project. I also want to thank Robert McGill and Heather Murray whose critical eyes pushed my thinking in new directions. I am especially grateful to Susan Bennett for her thoughtful feedback, which, along with her influential work on audience reception and feminist theatre, helped inspire my study of theatre audiences.

Thank you to Jonathan Crago, editor in chief at McGill-Queen's University, for his confidence in and guidance throughout this project. I am also grateful to the peer reviewers for their detailed, constructive feedback on the manuscript and its theorization of political adaptation as disidentification. Some of my earlier research on plays, including *Sinking Neptune*, *The Penelopiad*, and *Almighty Voice and His Wife*, appeared in *Studies in Canadian Literature*, *Theatre Journal*, and *Theatre Research in Canada/Recherches théâtrales au Canada*. The editors and reviewers at these journals sharpened my close readings of these key case studies.

I received valuable information from interviews and correspondence with Donovan King, Djanet Sears, and Erin Shields. Librarians helped uncover materials in archives, such as the Stratford Festival archives and the Glenbow Museum's archives. St Francis Xavier University hosted writing retreats that offered me the time, space, and collegial support to work on this manuscript.

I am also grateful to my colleagues at the University of Toronto and St Francis Xavier University, especially Amanda Baker, Christopher Byrne, Michael Cobb, Melanie East, Matthew Fellion, Alan Filewod, Nancy Forestell, Elizabeth Harvey, Kai Hainer, Linda Hutcheon, Joseph Khoury, Maureen Moynagh, Mathias Nilges, Jennifer O'Kell, Richard Plant, Marci Prescott, Cory Rushton, Laurel Ryan, and Paul Stevens. The keen editorial eyes of Tony Fong, Jennifer McDermott, Hannah McGregor, and Spencer Morrison improved early drafts of this research. I would like to offer my deep appreciation to Dean Irvine for his guidance on writing about political art in Canada and to Magdalene Redekop for encouraging me to focus on Canadian theatre. Laura Estill's endless feedback and belief in this project have been an enduring source of inspiration.

This book would not have been possible without the patience and support of my family. My husband's good humour and optimism have seen me through every stage of this work. My heartfelt thanks to my parents who instilled in me the love of literature, theatre, and the arts, and to my children for reminding me every day of the power of a story.

Political Adaptation in Canadian Theatre

Introduction

> For this is what stories do: they compete to shape the world – to impose narrative order on disparate or uncertain events – all the while prompting fresh narrative possibilities in the imagination.
> Neil Bissoondath, *The Age of Confession*

As Thomas King reminds us in his 2003 Massey Lecture, "you have to be careful with the stories you tell. And you have to watch out for the stories that you are told" (10) because "the truth about stories is that that's all we are" (2).[1] But what happens when the stories we are told – those of Shakespeare, Homer, and North America's earliest colonizers – fail to reflect, or even to acknowledge, our experiences as women, as racialized people, as queers, as Indigenous peoples, or as settler Canadians? We can choose to let the cultural dominance of those narratives make our stories invisible or distort our understandings of who we are and where we fit in the world. Alternately, we can adapt or even unsettle those stories to suit our purposes and reflect our multiple identities. The adaptation of popular narratives continues to be a leading mode of storytelling and self-definition in Canada. Canadians and Canada are continually adapting – adapting inherited stories, adapting British political systems, adapting American stereotypes, adapting old and new worlds. Adaptation, then, is more than a theatrical mode for reclaiming popular mythologies: it is a national pastime.

Canada has a long tradition of adapting stories that fail to quite fit us. The *Canadian Adaptations of Shakespeare Project* (headed by Daniel Fischlin) identifies over 600 plays dating back to 1848 that tailor the stories of Shakespeare to a Canadian context. The continued popularity of Shakespeare is not only a symptom of Canada's enduring colonial ethos and history, but it is also a sign of the ongoing critical negotiation and confrontation of this past. Today, on stages across Canada, iconic characters like Othello, Pocahontas, and Penelope are being transformed: Djanet Sears's Othello lives in present-day Harlem where he leaves his Black wife for the alabaster Mona in an attempt to fit in with white culture;[2] Monique Mojica's (Kuna and Rappahannock) Pocahontas sports a buckskin mini-dress and struggles to fit into feminist shoes; and Margaret Atwood's Penelope is a bored housewife accused of murder who tells her story from the underworld. These rewritings are part of a trend in Canadian theatre that seeks to change the political resonance of canonical works by reimagining and retelling the stories of iconic figures.[3] But despite the long-standing popularity of Canadian dramatic adaptations beyond Shakespeare, and their proliferation in contemporary Canadian theatre, little critical attention has been paid to these plays. Owing in part to the popularity and national cultural dominance of Ontario's Stratford Festival, the relatively few scholars who study Canadian drama adaptations tend to concentrate on the burgeoning field of Shakespeare adaptation studies.[4] Adaptation theory, however, warns against this exclusive focus on Shakespeare by asserting that there is never a singular, authoritative source but rather an ever-expanding corpus of diverse narratives and artistic transformations. Shakespeare was, after all, an adaptor.

This book intervenes in Canadian adaptation studies by expanding the scope of source material from Shakespeare, where Canadian adaptation studies appropriately began in keeping with the influence of the Stratford Festival, to also include adaptations of Canadian history, colonial narratives, Indigenous legends, and Greek myths. This research turns to adaptations by playwrights that identify as English-Canadian, African-Canadian, French-Canadian, French, Kuna Rappahannock, and Delaware from the Six Nations. The Canadian preoccupation with reclaiming popular narratives is not restricted to Shakespearean sources and, consequently, this project works towards representing the significant range in source material. As plays from the late twentieth and early twenty-first centuries reveal, a diverse field of political adaptations are decolonizing national stages, audiences, and the cultural imaginary across Canada.

If, as Linda Hutcheon suggests in *A Theory of Adaptation*, adaptation is repetition with difference (142) then political adaptation is repetition with announced, extended, and political difference. Political adaptation challenges the primary criterion of adaptation, that is, the adaptation's narrative fidelity to source material. Hutcheon, for instance, uses the degree of the adaptation's narrative fidelity to its source material to create a spectrum of adaptation that ranges from verbatim retellings to spin-offs (171). While adaptation is defined by its fidelity to the source narrative, political adaptation is distinguished by its infidelity to the source material's political messages. Canadian drama adapts popular narratives by revealing marginalized characters such as Othello, Pocahontas, and Penelope as reductive emblems of necessarily complex, layered gender, racial, sexual, and national identities. For instance, in an interview in which she discusses the goals of her feminist adaptation of *Hamlet*, entitled *Gertrude and Ophelia* (1992), Margaret Clarke explains:

> I have written my story between the lines of Shakespeare, and if you read the two together, it is my hope and belief that you will never be able to read Gertrude and Ophelia as minor characters again, never read them as mere appendages to male characters whose lives are without the human complexity of their wordier relatives, never read Gertrude as worse than her son, never read Ophelia as a mere weak, suicidal pawn. And if that happens, if I were to accomplish such an act with even one reader, then "adaptation" in the sense of a permanent change in one's way of thinking about the world would have truly occurred. (Interview)

Political adaptation, then, marks a change to the source material's narrative and, more importantly, to the viewer's understanding of the source and the worldview it condones. In this way, the plays subvert the iconic stories of Canada's domineering forbearers, such as Shakespeare or the French explorer Marc Lescarbot, to make room for the diverse identities and oppositional perspectives that define Canada today. In seeking to reveal and understand those complexities, Canadian political adaptations are at once popular and political as they work to engender a sense of activism in their largely mainstream and mainstage audiences.

Theatre lends itself to an examination of political adaptation because it makes manifest key elements of adaptation; repetition with difference, structures theatre productions which repeat the same performance each night without ever replicating an actor's and audience's experience. Scholars such as Marvin Carlson, Margherita Laera, and Kara Reilly highlight theatre's inherently adaptive structure and process. Illustrating the phenomenon of what he calls "ghosting," Carlson's *The Haunted Stage: The Theatre as Memory Machine* (2001) goes so far as to argue that the retelling of a story in a new context (or repetition with difference) is a unique characteristic of theatre. This, Carlson believes, is because theatre necessarily repeats specific elements, whether a familiar story, the same actor, or staging technique, but in a different context (6). Whereas other art forms repeat "individual words in poetry, tones in music, hues in painting," Carlson asserts that "the practice of theatre has been in all periods and cultures particularly obsessed with memory and ghosting" (7). In a collection of interviews, entitled *Theatre and Adaptation: Return, Rewrite, Repeat* (2014), Laera notes that theatre returns to, rewrites, and repeats histories, stories, relationships, and rules, and "in doing so" theatre "adapts itself to present contingencies and situations like animal species struggling to survive through evolution" (1). Reilly's *Contemporary Approaches to Adaptation in Theatre* (2017) similarly suggests that "adaptation is a slippery term, and like dramaturgy it alludes definition because it is so context specific" (xxi); citing famous "great playwrights *and* great adaptors," such as Shakespeare, Reilly declares that "the actual nature of the theatre is that it repeats" (xxii). For Carlson, "drama more than any other literary form, seems to be associated in all cultures with the retelling again and again of stories that bear a particular religious, social, or political significance to their public" (8). Each of these scholars highlights the necessary intermingling of the familiar and strange, or repetition with difference, in theatre performance; this makes plays ideal case studies for teasing out the ways in which political adaptors are changing inherited stories and how they are shown and told.

Political adaptation necessarily involves and calls attention to difference – a difference between the political message of the original and that of the adaptation. The necessity of this difference avoids some of the pitfalls of adaptation, which is often condemned for its changes to the original work. Like Hutcheon, Jozefina Komporaly's *Radical Revival as Adaptation: Theatre, Politics, Society* (2017) challenges the reception of adaptation with the attendant "frequent charge of 'massacre,' 'dismemberment' and other similar accusations of criminal intervention associated by critics" because adaptations' "destabilizing and deconstructive readings" of the source material "is paramount to their contemporary applicability and relevance" (5). For Komporaly, the goal of political adaptation or "radical adaptation" is "not mere artistic terrorism rooted in narcissistic attempts at reinventing the artist as an enfant terrible only content with disfiguring the canon and/or undermining cultural heritage, but a genuine desire for recontextualization within the immediacy of performance" (5). An analysis of political adaptation, then, sidesteps issues of derivativeness or expected faithfulness to the earlier work, because difference between the adapted and adaptive works is an inevitable and celebrated result of political adaptation. After all, it is through political and narrative difference that new meanings are created and exposed, and through these differences that change occurs.

Identification theory offers a discourse to understand the inherent doubleness of political adaptation that is at once popular and political, canonical and yet critical of its canonical source text. While theorists including Judith Butler, Michel Pêcheux, and José Esteban Muñoz conceive of identity in terms of performance, I treat performance as a mode of identity construction, and as a vehicle for changing the ways in which audiences conceive of and partake in cultural groups. In defining political adaptation as disidentification, I am adapting Pêcheux's and Muñoz's theory of disidentification wherein a subject can simultaneously work on and against the prevailing dominant ideology or discourse.[5] In particular, the following chapters focus on Muñoz's response to Pêcheux and his theory of disidentification.

Pêcheux defines three identificatory relationships with mainstream culture: identification, counteridentification, and disidentification. With identification, a "good subject" chooses to identify with dominant ideologies. With counteridentification, by contrast, a "bad subject" is a "troublemaker" who refuses to participate and instead functions outside dominant society (157). With disidentification, the subject participates in society but with an intention to change it from within. While Pêcheux acknowledges the dichotomy of "good" and "bad" subjects as reductive, these subject positions lend themselves to theatrical adaptations because the adaptor negotiates a relationship with a narrative that is often mainstream and highly recognizable to the public; consequently, adaptation is positioned in relation to a dominant ideology. While adaptation could represent a "good subject" that identifies with a canonical narrative, political adaptation could be perceived as a "bad subject" because it challenges these inherited stories. I argue, however, that political adaptation ultimately performs disidentification by at once retelling a narrative while challenging its political significance. Understanding theatrical adaptation in terms of identification theory helps to account for the political work of the adaptor and provides terminology for analyzing the relationship between adapted and adaptive narratives. Political adaptation simultaneously identifies with, and against, a source narrative in order to transform the dominant cultural imaginary from within. In short, political adaptation is a mode of disidentification.

Because stories often inform our understanding of individuals – and the culture, race, gender, and sexuality they represent – the transformation of these very narratives can change the way we think about marginalized and formerly marginalized peoples. The Métis playwright Marie Clements's *Age of Iron* (1993) does just this, through staging Indigenous characters and history in mainstream Canadian theatre. *Age of Iron*, Clements's first play, adapts and updates Euripides's ancient Greek tragedy *Trojan Women*, taking an Indigenous perspective, then layering ancient Troy with twentieth-century Vancouver to produce an "Urban Troy Drama" (197).[6] Mounted at Vancouver's Firehall Arts Centre in 1994, the play interweaves canonical source material with real stories of Indigenous peoples' suffering as a way to confront a popular audience.[7] The adaptation, Sheila Rabillard explains, "is highly selective and inventive":

> While some lines closely echo those of Euripides, Clements focuses on the assignment of Cassandra as a war captive (though not her prophecy concerning Agamemnon); includes a version of the death of Astyanax; omits all of the action concerning Helen; weaves these Euripidean elements into material drawn from Indigenous history and contemporary experience; and transforms Euripides's chorus of Trojan women into four groups: the System Chorus, the Sister Chorus, Apollo's Muses, and the Wall of Troy (composed of dancers/singers and some of the named characters). (1)

By layering the mythological defeat of Troy with the colonial conquest of the Indigenous peoples in Canada (Rabillard), Clements utilizes sympathies for Troy to ally the audience with the play's Indigenous characters. *Age of Iron*, then, harnesses political adaptation's inevitable mix of the familiar (Greek mythology) and the relatively unfamiliar (Indigenous culture) to challenge the way audiences conceive of Indigenous peoples as well as their knowledge of Canada's history of cultural genocide and residential schools.

Using Trojan War material as a shared cultural reference helped Clements reposition Indigenous peoples, issues, and Indigenous narratives to the theatre of a major Canadian city. As Hallie Rebecca Marshall explains, "to reach a mainstream Canadian audience, however, even if the primary intent is to discuss the experiences of aboriginal communities, the narratives need to be framed in terms familiar to theatre audiences from the western tradition, with the inclusion of voices deemed to hold authority for them" (677). Together with the Greek source material, Clements's play also draws on Indigenous stories of residential schools and the figure of the Raven in order to remind audiences of Indigenous history and mythology in the context of modern Canada. Rabillard speaks to the "ironic" doubleness of an adaptation that "stages the destructive imposition of European culture" at the same time as it engages with a classical text (118), thereby calling attention to the potential pitfall of political adaptation reinforcing the very canon it seeks to dismantle. Clements, however, avoids valorizing ancient source material by "exposing the instability of national mythologies" (Rabillard 118). As Rabillard says, Clements "rejects the mythic descent of Britons from exiled Trojans, and claims Troy for her Aboriginal-identified characters. She revises British triumphalism, and instead of prophesying Troy reborn uses setting, set, and performance to dramatize the exilic present of 'Trojans' in their homeland" (118). Clements's *Age of Iron* draws attention to the ways in which its source and consequent performance dramatize cultural histories.

Political adaptations such as *Age of Iron* invert the perspectives of earlier colonial narratives, histories, and stereotypes in order for change to take place. In this way, staged adaptations of individual characters (like Euripides's Cassandra or Clements's Raven), and their stories, can have an impact on large-scale narratives, including narratives of nationhood, race, culture, and gender. With the transformation of a dominant story, Clements's political adaptation challenges what was at the time an accepted notion of Canada's peaceful history, and recasts Indigenous peoples as exiles in their own homeland.

A study of political adaptation and of dramatists' propensities for telling borrowed stories also offers a way of engaging with Canada's from-elsewhereness. In addition to the competing narratives of Indigenous peoples and Canadian history, Irena R. Makaryk explains that Canadian literature is invested in telling stories of people from "elsewhere" as a way of speaking for Canada's population of "immigrants fleeing from somewhere else" (3). As Margaret Clarke says, "much of Canadian literature is about bringing identities formed in other places," or elsewhere, "home to a Canadian context" (Interview). "This elsewhereness inscribed in CanLit," asserts Smaro Kamboureli, "intimates that Canada is an unimaginable community, that is, a community constituted in excess of the knowledge of itself, always transitioning" (11). For

Hugh Kenner, narratives of elsewhere are cornerstones of Canadian (non-Indigenous) and Western imagination because a key to the quest for knowledge inevitably lies "elsewhere." Canadian playwrights' tendency to create adaptations of popular, international narratives is symptomatic of this very tension – of a Canadian national theatre predisposed to international contexts, writers, and cultures.

It is not surprising that adaptation is a prevalent dramatic mode and process of creation in a country so openly indebted to its Euro-colonial predecessors. Adaptation is a fitting theatrical expression of Canada's political relationship to its colonizing nations and response to the cultural imperialism of the United States. Adaptation theory helps explain the popular critiques of Canada's political and cultural derivativeness. Northrop Frye presents Canadian culture as inevitably adaptive and therefore derivative when he argues that "many Canadian cultural phenomena are not peculiarly Canadian at all, but are typical of their wider and Western contexts" (216–17). Robert Stam explains that literary adaptations are often vilified as parasites of the life-giving source texts through what Marshall McLuhan calls the "rear-view mirror logic" that "older arts are necessarily better arts" (4). Similarly, popular stereotypes present Canada as a belated version of other countries' political systems and cultural heritage, predominantly those of England, France, and the United States. Describing the "rhetoric of national identity" in Canada, Glenn Willmott says that it "paints the picture of itself as a weaker social formation self-conscious of a certain subordination and complicity, but burdened with a prophetic if terrible insight and a corresponding moral transcendence, as if created as a photographic negative, a mirror at the margin of empire" (135). The Canadian cultural imaginary, according to Willmott, is conceived as a "photographic negative" or lesser-copy of the United States despite feelings of moral superiority or "transcendence." Andrew Potter uses the language of "absorption" rather than adaptation or appropriation when he describes the national fear of "being culturally and economically absorbed by the United States" (xii); "Confederation," Potter warns, "has always seemed like a rather rickety, precarious endeavour, perpetually on the verge of … rendering to outright absorption or annexation by the United States" (x). Put in terms of adaptation discourse, non-Indigenous Canada recognizes itself as a version of the neighbours to the south and its colonial forebears, but it has a longstanding concern of being too "politically dependant" or too faithful to European source material (Potter x).[8] In claiming "New France," "New Scotland,"

and the "New World," Old World European colonizers defined Canada as a national adaptation.

Adaptation is more than a popular dramatic mode in Canada; it is an ongoing process of national mythologizing. Canada is politically organized as an adaptation – a nation-state staged as a political adaptation. Engaging with George Grant's famous argument that mainstream Canada is a nation destined to disappear and be subsumed by the United States, Potter explains that "Canada, even as understood by its own citizens, is redundant" (xxiv).[9] Whether you think about mainstream Canada in terms of absorption, appropriation, or redundancy – the argument remains the same: Canadian politics and culture are a performed adaptation. The popularity of Shakespeare's plays on Canadian stages at Stratford, Ontario, and across the country speaks to mainstream, non-Indigenous Canada's strong and continued lineage of borrowers – a lineage of borrowers that calls up Canada's settler-colonial past and its history as a national adaptation of Old Worlds. The settler-invaders of what we now call Canada have been adapting Shakespeare on a local level through plays and replicating Britain and France on a national level through borrowed political structures and figureheads. "Shakespeare," Makaryk asserts, "reigns supreme as one of Canada's pre-eminent playwrights" (5). Taking a critical stance on the fact that Shakespeare is one of the most produced dramatists in Canadian theatre Denis Salter explains that Shakespeare is often "regarded as a Canadian playwright" precisely because he is "an unimpeachable symbol of Old World cultural superiority" ("Idea" 79–80). Adaptation, then, is particularly relevant to mainstream Canada on a thematic, political, and theatrical level because it captures Canada's settler-invader narratives, colonial ties, and long-standing literary tradition of retelling European mythologies: the act of theatrical and political adaptation is a durable and prevalent mode of cultural creation in mainstream Canada. Loleen Berdahl and Tracey Raney gesture towards Canada's propensity to adapt international sources when they explain that "to be Canadian" is "to be on the world stage" (995).[10] As Berdahl and Raney say, "public opinion data suggest that Canadian's strong sense of internationalism is intertwined with their sense of national identity" (995). The politics and identity of Canada is a performed adaptation in a constant state of re-making.[11]

Canadian theatrical adaptors, however, have changed their approach to sources over time from a respectful indebtedness and method for mythologizing Canadian heritage to, more recently, a political desire for change and a critique of the inherited stories of Canada's national cultural imaginary.[12] Canadian theatre productions of political adaptations of the late twentieth and early twenty-first centuries are responding to the strong demand for representational narratives told by distinct, marginalized and previously marginalized voices. With the 1971 federal policy "Multiculturalism within a Bilingual Framework" and the *Canadian Charter of Rights and Freedoms* (1981), culture and race moved to centre stage in mainstream Canadian theatres.[13] During the 1980s and 1990s there was a pronounced critical emphasis on representational works from an authoritative point of view and so-called "firsts":[14] Tomson Highway's *The Rez Sisters* (1986) was received as part of the "vanguard" of "Native theatre artists" dramatizing their own stories for professional mainstream theatre "for the first time" (Wasserman, *Modern* 183); Sears's *Afrika Solo* (1989) was touted as the first play published by an African-Canadian woman;[15] and Guillermo Verdecchia's *Fronteras Americanas* (1993) was celebrated as the first play with a Latino-Canadian perspective.

In reaction to the growing popularity of Indigenous playwrights, Penny Petrone's *Native Literature in Canada: From the Oral Tradition to the Present* (1990) asserts that "the most exciting development in the 1980s has taken place in Drama" (170). In the 1980s, theatres were founded to produce work by and about Indigenous peoples, such as Nakai Theatre (1979) in the Yukon, De-ba-jeh-mu-jig Theatre (1981) on the Wikwemikong Unceded Indian Reserve (Manitoulin Island), and Native Earth Performing Arts (1982) in Toronto. But expectations of productions, such as Highway's, Sears's, and Verdecchia's cultural firsts, also put pressure on the authors and theatrical organizations producing them to somehow capture and represent the Canadian experience from the point of view of an Indigenous, African-Canadian, or Argentinian-Canadian person, respectively. Ironically, many Canadian plays celebrated as firsts are political adaptations or secondary retellings. These works illustrate that the mode of adaptation calls attention to the impossibility of locating a first, or original, narrative because they reveal how all stories are inherently adaptive. Using adaptation to speak from and for the margins, then, performs a self-reflexive commentary that challenges the possibility and celebration of creating the so-called first story.

Approaching political adaptation as disidentification reveals both its limitations and potential for transforming foundational narratives. This book, then, has two main goals: to define political adaptation as a mode of disidentification, and to examine how the strategies used in dramatic adaptations may change dominant yet reductive narratives of racial, gendered, and cultural identities in Canada. In *Theatre & Ethics* (2009), Nicholas Ridout compares how plays express ethical ideas through the script's rhetoric, creative process, and audience response. Similarly, Laera also applies adaptation to a "wide variety of theatrical operations," including a playwright "turning ... a novel into a play script," and "the work of directors, that of actors in performance and rehearsals, that of translators in transferring a text from one language to another, and that of audiences in co-authoring and responding to a piece" (2). The case studies I use examine how the plays' texts (metaphor, language, narrative), production process (casting, creative teamwork, advertisements), performance (staging, directing, delivery), and reception (audience dynamics, reviews) make political arguments and change the meaning of the source material. For instance, while chapter 1 focuses on the political work of the collective creation process, chapter 3 turns to plays that foreground the onstage audience in order to illustrate the political potential of the offstage spectators. My analysis focuses on: the playwrights' revisions of source material; directors' casting and staging of the political adaptations; actors' performance dynamics (delivery, socio-cultural context); and audience response. Ultimately, I investigate how political adaptation and its audience dynamics are a distinct form of adaptation in order to understand how theatre changes the way we think about and approach history (chapter 1), race relations (chapter 2), feminism (chapter 3), and Indigenous culture (chapter 4) in Canada. As subsequent chapters reveal, political adaptors share a set of theatrical methodologies for critiquing the source material that show the distinctive elements of this mode and its spectatorship. Understanding these shared tools will not only enable viewers to better recognize political strategies but will also help equip future adaptor-creators to change inherited narratives and existing cultural hierarchies.

Cultural appropriation is political adaptation gone wrong, which makes it especially important to understand the strategies of political adaptation. An unsuccessful play can result in a poor box office, whereas an unsuccessful political adaptation can engage in cultural appropriation and have grave cultural and political implications. Cultural appropriation uses stories, music, and imagery from other cultures without consent, benefit, participation, or attribution. Cancellations and protests of theatrical cultural appropriations are good reminders about the importance of examining the difference between cultural appropriation and political adaptation. In 2018, Robert Lepage's show *SLĀV* was cancelled after protests about its use of an all-white production team and largely white cast for a play that depicted African-American slavery. Kym Dominique-Ferguson, the outreach and marketing co-ordinator for the Black Theatre Workshop, responded to Lepage's plea for "artistic freedom" and said, "don't use black pain for your own profit" (Cori-Manocchio). Protests and criticisms about *SLĀV*'s cultural appropriation focused on the execution of the play, including the production team, cast, and costumes. Understanding political adaptation's effective methodologies can help artists create political work in a way that respects and involves their subject matter.

Political adaptation uses creation practices that reinforce the political goals of the play, such as an all-Black cast for a play about racism, reduced-priced theatre tickets for self-identified Indigenous patrons for a show that promulgates colonial stereotypes, or a feminist theatre company and mentor program for a work about gender-based violence. The all-Black cast of Sears's *Harlem Duet* put previously marginalized Black performers onstage at large mainstream theatre companies, including Stratford Festival, which complemented the play's consideration of racial tensions in public spaces and popular stories. Soulpepper's 2019 production of Daniel David Moses's *Almighty Voice and His Wife*, directed by Jani Lauzon, worked to include Indigenous audiences in its performance about a historical Indigenous figure: "a bus was arranged to bring people from the Six Nations of the Grand River Territory to the first Saturday matinee (both the bus and show tickets are free), and consultant Tyler J. Sloane is working with Soulpepper's outreach department to further reach out to Indigenous communities" (Fricker). Feminist theatre company Nightwood Theatre produced Atwood's *The Penelopiad* with a diverse all-female cast and the development of the show included a female artist mentorship program. Theatre is an artform of action; it is, as a result, an ideal medium for political activism, but it is also key that the form, structure, and creation reinforce the political goals. How we tell a story is just as important as who we tell it to, why we are speaking out, and what we say. This book aims to examine the intersections of the how, who, why, and what in political adaptation.

Defining Political Adaptation

Political adaptation complicates Stam's, Hutcheon's, and Sanders's adaptation theory and their analysis of narrative (in)fidelity by requiring a consideration of how political reframing of source material in these adaptations actually functions. Sanders and Derek Attridge convincingly observe that adaptation is canonical because it cites and thereby situates itself in an established theatrical and literary tradition. As Sanders states, "adaptation could be defined as an inherently conservative genre" (9) because of its engagement with the canon. What I am calling political adaptation, by contrast, is an inherently subversive form with its own particular criteria and strategies that fulfill what Sanders describes as the potential for adaptations to "assault as well as [pay] homage" (9). In this sense, political adaptation is not defined by its fidelity to the source but rather by its infidelity and "assault."

Adaptation is a potent word with many different meanings and associations. Four common, distinct definitions of adaptation capture the nuances of political adaptation as a product, a creation process, a method of change, and a strategy for biological (as well as, I would add, artistic, personal, and collective) survival (*OED*). These four meanings of adaptation gesture towards the different elements of the political adaptor's project as well as some of the strategies for changing the source material. Political adaptation as a process, product, and mode of survival prioritizes changes to, and differences from, the source in a way that is not present in adaptation proper.

By putting a premium on change, my definition of political adaptation complicates the significance of the degree of fidelity to the original in adaptations. Because adaptation is often judged based on the degree of faithfulness to the source(s), Stam explains that the language of critical commentary on adaptation is "extremely judgmental," with accusations of parasitism through the use of pejoratives such as "'infidelity,' 'betrayal,' 'deformation,' 'violation,' 'vulgarization,' 'bastardization,' and 'desecration'" (*Literature* 3). In a 2004 review of *Goodnight Desdemona (Good Morning Juliet)* (1988), Murray Bramwell denounces the play's parodic comedy and asserts, "There have been plenty of instances of scripts which use the bard as their subject – *Shakespeare in Love*, for instance and Stoppard's masterly *Rosencrantz and Guildenstern*. But intertextuality is an essentially *parasitic* business and there are pitfalls for the writer" (23; emphasis added). "In many – perhaps most – cases," Russell H. Hunt generalizes, "the theatrical adaptation remains *parasitic* on the fictional text" (emphasis added).[16] These negative assumptions about adaptation as "parasitic" have stirred recent theories of adaptation and are especially threatening to Canadian adaptations given the national anxiety of influence from its colonial forbearers and its bordering nation, the US. Like Stam, Hutcheon explains that she "want[s] to challenge that reductive, negative rhetoric – and theorizing – that see adaptations as inevitably derivative and unfaithful to the adapted works" ("From Page" 50). Sanders counters claims of parasitism by highlighting the mutually beneficial relationship between an adaptation and its source material; the adaptive process of cultural updating, after all, contributes to the survival of a source. The attacks on adaptation as "parasitic" or "derivative" are not only being taken up by theorists such as Stam, Hutcheon, and Sanders but also by adaptors themselves who anticipate and refute derogatory comparisons to their paternal forbearers within the play scripts. The critique of parasitism, however, is irrelevant in the context of political adaptation because this form of adaptation necessitates and highlights a political remove from the original. My definition of political adaptation seeks to contribute to this defence of adaptation in the face of charges of parasitism: while these criticisms of adaptation value narrative fidelity, political adaptors invest in change.

To help distinguish types of adaptation, Hutcheon charts a continuum of adaptation that ranges from fidelity to infidelity to the prior texts (see figure 0.1). As Hutcheon says, "At one end, we find those forms in which fidelity to the prior work is a theoretical ideal, even if a practical impossibility," such as translations and transcriptions (171); at the other end of the continuum, we find spin-offs, sequels, prequels, and expansions (Hutcheon 171). "Adaptation proper" is in the centre of the continuum (see figure 0.1) where "stories are both reinterpreted and rerelated" (Hutcheon 171).

Though this continuum is extremely helpful in visualizing the spectrum of types of adaptation, Hutcheon's placement of adaptation in the middle of the continuum does not reflect the fact that political infidelity is a theoretical ideal for political adaptors or that political adaptations might be faithful to the source narrative but completely unfaithful to the original political message and representations of historically marginal or minority figures. Optative Theatrical Laboratories' (OTL) *Sinking Neptune* (2006), for instance, adapts Marc Lescarbot's oceanic masque *Le Théâtre de Neptune en la Nouvelle France* (1606) in protest against Lescarbot's portrayal of *les sauvages*. As a piece of verbatim theatre, *Sinking Neptune* repeats the complete original script of *Le Théâtre de Neptune* and could thus be charted as an adaptation nearer to the repetition end of the continuum. But, aside from this fidelity to Lescarbot's script, OTL adamantly critiques *Le Théâtre de Neptune* as an agent of cultural genocide. *Sinking Neptune* thus complicates Hutcheon's adaptation continuum: the play aims to change the cultural significance and reception of *Le Théâtre de Neptune*, while at the same time repeating the original script verbatim. Charting

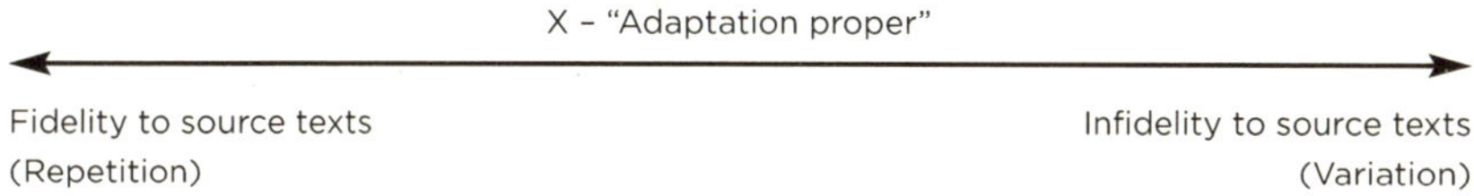

Figure 0.1 Hutcheon's continuum of adaptations.

Sinking Neptune on Hutcheon's continuum as an adaptation on the fidelity end of the spectrum is misleading because it does not capture the play's political changes and recontextualization. In short, the continuum does not reflect the complexities that emerge from turning a single text into a layered political adaptation that resonates with the earlier work as well as with new contexts and critical viewers.

Hutcheon's chart contributes a seminal organizational structure to adaptation theory, but in order to represent political adaptation, it needs to account for political infidelity. I would like to build on Hutcheon's continuum by adding a vertical axis that measures the fidelity of an adaptation to the source's political messages (see figure 0.2). The vertical axis transforms the horizontal continuum into a grid that enables a more accurate graphing of political adaptation's narrative fidelity and all-important political infidelity. The grid now accounts for *Sinking Neptune*'s political re-contextualization as well as its verbatim re-enactment of the source's script (see figure 0.2). My revised adaptation grid speaks to the paradoxical doubleness of political adaptation – that simultaneously embraces and rejects source material – because it charts political adaptation according to its simultaneous narrative fidelity and political infidelity to the source material(s).

As with *Sinking Neptune*, charting Margaret Atwood's *The Penelopiad* (2007) and Erin Shields's *If We Were Birds* (2008) on the grid calls attention to the political reframing of the sources of each play (see figure 0.2). These feminist rewritings of Greek mythology fall in the middle of the narrative fidelity continuum (x axis) because they retell the Greek myths from the female characters' point of views without changing the plot; *The Penelopiad* and *If We Were Birds*, however, would also fall close to the top of the political infidelity spectrum (y axis) because Atwood and Shields alter the sources by having disenfranchised female servants demand justice for the continued use of

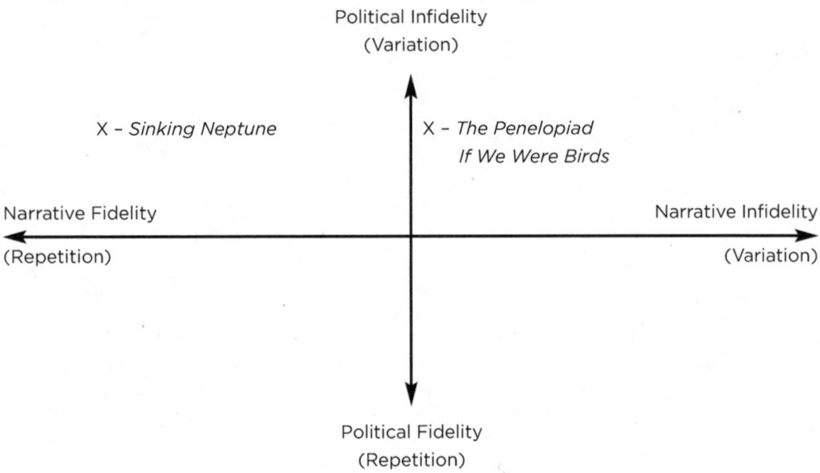

Figure 0.2 Grid of political adaptations.

rape as a weapon of war from ancient Greece to the present-day. The grid design, then, accounts for the political change that takes place in these adaptations and the ideological distance between the source(s) and the adaptation.

The grid format also helps users to distinguish political spin-offs, such as Sears's prequel to *Othello*, entitled *Harlem Duet* (1997), from the other more celebratory and commercialized spin-offs, including musicals, television series, fan fiction, and video games that focus on a specific character or element from the original work. Hutcheon credits the popularity of spin-offs to their "financial appeal" (5) because spin-offs, like all adaptations, can capitalize on the pre-established popularity of a specific story or character. There are many examples of spin-offs in popular and literary culture, but the following two demonstrate the difference between adaptation and political adaptation: Tom Stoppard's play *Rosencrantz and Guildenstern Are Dead* (1966) offers an extension of Shakespeare's *Hamlet* that focuses on Shakespeare's two peripheral death-seeking messengers; Jean Rhys's novel *Wide Sargasso Sea* (1966), by comparison, is a response to Charlotte Brontë's *Jane Eyre* (1847), a prequel that expands on the life of Bertha Mason (the mad woman in the attic). These two spin-offs differ in that *Rosencrantz and Guildenstern Are Dead* celebrates its relationship to *Hamlet* by giving back-stories to supporting characters from the source, whereas *Wide Sargasso Sea* is a postcolonial critique of Brontë's Bertha Mason. The adaptation grid makes manifest *Wide Sargasso Sea*'s overtly political differences from the source (see figure 0.3).

When political adaptation becomes successful in its transformation of dominant myths, its narrative and political fidelity to the earlier works are no longer defining factors because the adaptation displaces the source as the authoritative work. The grid for political adaptation gestures towards this distinction between plays that retell and plays that reclaim source material. How, for instance, would you chart Indigenous political adaptations of colonial fantasies, such as Mojica's *Princess Pocahontas* (1990) and Daniel David Moses's (who is Delaware and Tuscarora from the Six Nations) *Almighty Voice and His Wife* (1991), on the narrative fidelity continuum when these two plays debunk, rather than merely retell, popular legends of Indigenous heroes by settler authors? Chapter 4 argues that Mojica's and Moses's plays show the potential of political adaptation to do much more than critically reframe earlier narratives – they reclaim and replace them. The plays render the earlier versions of the two legends – namely, John Smith's letters to the queen about Pocahontas and Leonard Peterson's play about Almighty Voice – as untrustworthy reductions of Indigenous culture that use racial masquerades to serve a colonial perspective. My conclusion further develops this argument by charting these two plays on the political adaptation grid that I have developed. *Princess Pocahontas* and *Almighty Voice* illustrate the decolonization of the source material in order to foreground alternative re-imaginings.[17]

On the one hand, the success of a political adaptation can be demonstrated in the extent to which it separates itself from the source material by undermining the latter's credibility; on the other hand, however, the impact of a political adaptation can also be measured by the inseparability of the adapted and adaptive text. Whereas Hutcheon asserts that adaptation must stand on its own as an autonomous work of art that is distinct from its source(s), a political adaptation's progressive work and the playwright's ability to change popular narratives rely on the extent to which it haunts the source. In defining "radical revival" as "adaptation," Komporaly stresses that these terms "are associated with a practice that situates the newly created work in a position whereby it intervenes on its precursor(s) with an *explicit* aim to revisit, deconstruct and actualize" (3–4; emphasis added). The political adaptor often exposes a problematic element of the original – such as the racialized Othello,

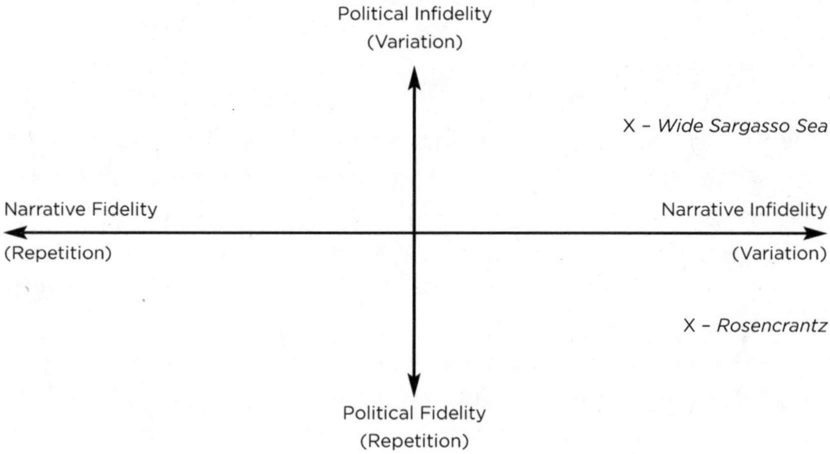

Figure 0.3 Grid of political adaptations. Charting political (in)fidelity in spin-offs.

the all-too-obliging Pocahontas, or the unrealistically faithful Penelope – thereby shedding a critical light that illuminates future interpretations of the source narrative. Unlike adaptation proper, the success of a political adaptation can be measured by the extent to which it layers the original with the new critical perspective.

My study avoids evaluating a political adaptation as a success or failure because I do not want to risk ranking the political effectiveness of radical plays, or erect a hierarchy of political adaptations (that often work to dismantle identity hierarchies). For instance, an effective political adaptation could appear at multiple points on the political adaptation grid, and the y axis is not an evaluative measure of success or failure. "On what grounds," as Sanders asks, "could this evaluation [of good or bad adaptations] be made? Fidelity to the original?" (20). Or, to apply Sanders's point to political adaptation, infidelity to the original work's politics? Political adaptation's (in)fidelity to the source material does not necessarily indicate its political effect as the political impact of a play changes depending on the production, creation process, context, and audience. For Hutcheon, Sanders, and Stam, adaptation studies are invested "in analysing process, ideology, and methodology" and "not about making polarized value judgements" (Sanders 20). I will use the plays under consideration in this study to not only define but also complicate political adaptation and its methodology.

Adaptations benefit from the source text's brand or name recognition that inevitably drives up sales of the play, book, film, video game, or theme park ride as the case may be. Yet there are also political and personal reasons that inevitably motivate the adaptor despite the critical pitfalls that so often plague any attempt to allegedly piggyback on the cultural capital of an earlier artwork. For the adaptors considered in this study, the motivation is much more political than financial. In fact, although the viewer's recognition of the source may help drive up the theatre ticket sales, many political adaptation creators avoid relying on the audience's prior knowledge by including lessons on the adapted narrative; this enables audience members to appreciate the political changes and cultural updating made by the adaptor. By including relevant information of the original version, political adaptors do not exclude their audience for a lack of prior knowledge of the source and, instead, help mitigate a hierarchy of knowing versus unknowing viewers. Timothy Findley's *Elizabeth Rex* (2000), for instance, dramatizes and instructs its audience about the impending death of Queen Elizabeth I's beloved, the Earl of Essex, in the context of the Queen's struggle to reconcile socially expected performances of feminine gender and masculine political power. Findley imagines a meeting between Queen Elizabeth I and Shakespeare on the night of the Earl of Essex's execution in the context of gender performativity. Creating a hierarchy of a knowing and unknowing audience is a common trap in many adaptations because, as Hutcheon points out, knowledge of the source enables the double pleasure of viewing the adaptation as a palimpsest (*A Theory*).[18] A palimpsest is a piece of parchment paper with layers of writing wherein previous layers may be visible in parts. Gérard Genette applies the image of a literal palimpsest to the figurative layering of narratives in literature; he argues that "the duplicity of the object, in the sphere of textual relations, can be presented by the odd analogy of the palimpsest: on the same parchment, one text can become superimposed upon another, which it does not quite conceal but allows to show through" (398–9). The adaptation's layered narrative can be understood as a palimpsest. By instructing the audience on the source's narrative and cultural resonances, political adaptors such as Findley ensure that the entire audience has access to the pleasure of viewing the adaptation as palimpsest, thereby working to flatten a hierarchy of viewers that places knowing audience members at the top of the pecking order. Political adaptations, in this way, attempt to avoid relying on the cultural capital of brand recognition or the audience's prior knowledge of the source.

By including relevant information on the source material, political adaptations can replace the audience's need to view that source material. The playwright's overt instruction on the text's source material also deters the common critical act of "spot the allusion" and invites the audience to analyze the political arguments rather than the dramatic or textual parallels between the adaptive and adapted work. The instruction on the source material, then, speaks to the doubleness of political adaptation: it teaches viewers about the source and thereby raises the source's cultural relevance, but it also decreases the audience's need to view the source and thus potentially deters the audience from returning to the source as a significant work. In short, the didacticism of the political adaptation at once underlines and undermines the canonicity of the source material.

The attempt to flatten a viewing hierarchy of knowing and unknowing audience members is fitting in works that seek to dismantle other forms of hierarchies, whether they are gendered, racial, or cultural, because the form and viewing experience reinforce the message. Moses's *Almighty Voice*, for instance, includes many references to stereotypical portrayals of Indigenous figures from Tonto to the Cigar Store Indian to Geronimo. For an audience member unfamiliar with these characters, the play makes it clear that the figures represent damaging stereotypes that reduce Indigenous peoples to "savages". An audience member who is more familiar with these references, however, may also recognize their own complicity in consuming and enjoying racist storylines and jokes. At Soulpepper's 2019 production of *Almighty Voice* (directed by Jani Lauzon) an audience of mostly highschool students audibly changed their response to the stereotypes throughout the second half of the play: the audience initially laughed at the racist jokes but then started to "boo" the white-faced Interlocutor near the end of the play.[19] In this way, Moses complicates the hierarchy of knowing and unknowing viewers by challenging the ethical responsibility of the knowing viewer and their previous enjoyment of stereotypes. The knowing audience may experience the viewing pleasure of the play as palimpsest but with it comes a heightened culpability in the transmission of the racist stories that are told about Indigenous peoples. This audience dynamic not only inverts a hierarchy of spectatorship but also calls into question any preconceived assumptions about a hierarchy of knowledge and who holds power.

Strategies of Political Adaptation

Spectatorship, creative processes, production elements, discursive form, and style all contribute to the playwrights' overarching efforts to transform the political resonance of popular source narratives. Although all theatrical political adaptors do not utilize the same set of strategies, there are eight predominant strategies and characteristics that are particular to the mode of political adaptation: (1) multiple sources; (2) identifiable politicized sources; (3) political didacticism; (4) inverted staging and cross-casting; (5) critical audience participation and metatheatricality; (6) self-reflexive discursive form, structure, and register; (7) self-declarations; and (8) collective creation and versioning. Although my analysis focuses on theatre, these eight strategies offer a model for future discussions and distinctions between political adaptation in theatre, prose, poetry, and film as the field develops.

A political adaptation often features multiple sources and intertexts, a strategy that effectively avoids the reification of a single work as the original. The title of De-ba-jeh-mu-jig's collective creation, *New World Brave* (2000), references two major sources – Shakespeare's *The Tempest* and Aldous Huxley's dystopian novel *Brave New World* – by altering Miranda's line "How beauteous mankind is! O brave new world / That has such people in't!" (*The Tempest*, 5.1.184–5). Taking on Shakespeare's vision of the savage and of encounter narratives, *New World Brave* "takes the problem of envisioning a future for aboriginal culture and addresses key issues facing aboriginal communities across Canada" (Fischlin, *Canadian*). Many political adaptations offer a list of intertexts either through paratextual materials (such as a list of works cited or a preface) or through direct references in the play script itself. In her introduction to *The Penelopiad*, for instance, Atwood explains that she adapts Homer's *The Odyssey* as well as many other Trojan War materials that include post-Homeric retellings by Ovid, Dante, Chaucer, Shakespeare, Tennyson, James Joyce, Derek Walcott, Barry Unsworth, Lewis Hyde, and others. This usage of multiple sources is a common strategy in political adaptation because the plurality of sources avoids privileging any one work as the authoritative original source.

An adaptation, as Hutcheon explains, often announces its adaptive relationship to a specific original work through the title itself, such as Julie Taymor's film *Titus* (1999), which is an adaptation of Shakespeare's *Titus Andronicus* (1594), and the television series *Anne with an E* (written by Moira Walley-Beckett,

2017) that adapts Lucy Maud Montgomery's *Anne of Green Gables* (1908), or with references to recognizable characters, such as the figure of Kurtz in Francis Ford Coppola's *Apocalypse Now* (1979), a film adaptation of Joseph Conrad's *Heart of Darkness* (1902). These adaptations celebrate their relationship to the source material and update the narratives with new settings, actors, or time periods. Political adaptations, by comparison, borrow titles and character names to indicate an overt political approach to and criticism of the source(s). The titles of Clarke's *Gertrude and Ophelia*, MacDonald's *Goodnight Desdemona (Good Morning Juliet)*, and Atwood's *The Penelopiad* gesture towards the playwrights' feminist adaptations of *Hamlet*, *Othello* and *Romeo and Juliet*, and *The Odyssey*, respectively, through their focus on the famous female characters in each work. Through the title *Beatrice Chancy* (1997), George Elliott Clarke introduces his play as an adaptation of the historical Italian noblewoman Beatrice Cenci and Percy Shelley's *Cenci* (1819), but Clarke sets the drama in Nova Scotia at the turn of the nineteenth century when slavery was legal; the Black Beatrice, as signalled by the book jacket or the embodied performance, signals Clarke's political and racial reframing of the earlier narrative.[20] While titles and character names of adaptations announce a narrative connection with the sources, political adaptations use titles, setting, names, and overt allusions to emphasize a political approach to and contextual difference from the original.

The inclusion of recognizable elements from the sources also serves a didactic purpose. Political adaptations tend to instruct the audience about the source, its critical reception over time, and the political implications of its enduring popularity. The effects of this didacticism are two-fold: it helps to flatten a hierarchical audience of knowing and unknowing viewers; and it is a key component to the playwright's political work because the adaptation reframes the audience's understanding of the original text's political messages. The didactic strategy dulls the double-edged effect of political adaptation by potentially preventing the audience's renewed investment in viewing the source material. Through these instructional efforts, political adaptations stand on their own as independent pieces of art and politics that do not require, and thereby validate, separate knowledge of the source material.

While adaptations perform an announced retelling of a source, political dramatic adaptations sometimes keep the source's main character offstage as a way of spatially inverting the relationship between the original's central and marginal characters. In *The Penelopiad*, Atwood's Odysseus only appears for the briefest of moments, enabling Penelope and her Handmaids to dominate the centre stage. Nightwood Theatre's 2012 production of *The Penelopiad* does more than shine a spotlight on *The Odyssey*'s female characters; it features an all-female cast that extends Atwood's narrative focus on female characters and leaves no opportunity for male intrusion through the use of female actors who play all the male figures (see Kelli Fox as Odysseus in figure 0.4). Similarly, Clarke battles to keep Hamlet offstage via an onstage narrator (named and playing the role of Playwright) who insists that Shakespeare's Prince of Denmark will only interfere with her focus on Gertrude and Ophelia. In these plays, the conspicuous absence of the main characters from the source's spatializes the playwright's struggle to diminish the presence of these iconic figures in the dominant cultural imaginary.

Casting, as a result, can further reinforce the playwright's political mandate and approach. Yvette Nolan (Algonquin) and Kennedy Cathy MacKinnon's *Death of a Chief* (2006, 2008) as well as Clements's *Age of Iron* adapt Shakespeare's *Julius Caesar* and Euripides's *Trojan Women*, respectively, with Indigenous casts and subject matter. The Indigenous casts and characters of these plays enact the playwrights' political agendas: to bring to centre stage those who have been previously marginalized. Similarly, Walcott's *Pantomime* (1978) critiques the racial dynamics in Daniel Defoe's *Robinson Crusoe* by dramatizing it with a Black Crusoe and a white Friday. Productions' use of cross-casting – with female actors playing Odysseus or Caesar and a white actor playing Friday – brings the margin, or marginal, to the centre while highlighting the adaptors' feminist, cultural, and racial re-framings of the sources.

Cross-casting also functions as a strategy for drawing attention to the performativity of gendered, sexualized, and racialized identities. While cross-racial casting remains controversial, Ken Gass's 2011 production of Tomson Highway's *The Rez Sisters* at Toronto's Factory Theatre experimented with casting actors from diverse racial backgrounds (see figure 0.5). This directorial choice is part of Gass's research project that tests cross-racial casting in response to Highway's complaint, in *Prairie Fire* magazine (2001), that his plays would see more productions if directors were not as concerned with casting only Indigenous actors to play the parts. Gass's production used cross-casting to make an argument about theatre in Canada and the lack of diverse casts on mainstages in Toronto.

Many productions of political adaptations also employ multiple role-play or doubling; that is, when the director casts an actor to perform more than one role. Dual roles are often a financial necessity in theatres with limited budgets and a logistical choice for productions with many smaller roles. In political adaptations, however, multiple role-play complements the works' destabilization of static identities. The use of actors playing multiple roles in *Princess Pocahontas* – two actors perform seventeen characters – bolsters the transformational structure as the actors repeatedly transform into different characters.

In order to stimulate a critically active audience, political adaptations incorporate audience involvement either by casting real audience members in specific roles, or through breaking the fourth wall with a character's plea to the audience for change.[21] When plays like *Sinking Neptune* and *Almighty Voice* cast the audience as part of a socio-political problem, they draw attention to pervasive racism and highlight the need for change. In the first scene of *Sinking Neptune*, the audience is cast in the role of news reporters who applaud celebratory re-enactments of Lescarbot's racist play. Similarly, in the second act of *Almighty Voice*, the racist Interlocutor treats the audience as "good friends" (40) who think, "the only good Indians are the dead ones" (40). In casting the audience as overtly racist onlookers, OTL and Moses emphasize potential and real complicity in continuing the narratives of Indigenous peoples as culturally and historically inferior. In a more direct request for audience activism, the opening scenes of *The Penelopiad* and *If We Were Birds* begin with the main charaters' pleas for the audience to listen to the Greek myths from Penelope's and Philomela's perspectives, respectively. In this way, the political adaptors do not cast the audience in a comfortable and congratulatory role, but instead challenge the viewers to participate in the protests against *Le Théâtre de Neptune*, stereotypes of Indigenous peoples, or idealized icons of female passivity as the case may be. Although many of these plays are performed on main stages and viewed by mainstream audience members, as political adaptations they often directly address their audiences and ask them to carry on the plays' goals of change through a transformed collective imagination.

Directly addressing an audience is just one example of how authors of political adaptations commonly use metatheatricality. *Elizabeth Rex*, *Sinking Neptune*, *Harlem Duet*, *Almighty Voice*, *The Penelopiad*, *Gertrude and Ophelia*, and *Goodnight Desdemona*, to name a few, feature an inset performance, or a play-within-a-play, that draws attention to the play's own theatricality. In each case, the metatheatricality emphasizes the performativity of prescribed racial or gender roles. *Gertrude and Ophelia* and *Goodnight Desdemona* reveal the performativity of masculinity and femininity through the use of Shakespeare's

Figure 0.4 Megan Follows (Penelope) and Kelli Fox (Odysseus) in Nightwood Theatre's 2012 all-female production of Margaret Atwood's *The Penelopiad*.

play-within-a-play method as a way to debunk the tragic, canonical Shakespearean sources and male characters as comedic subjects of ridicule. Clarke and MacDonald also show how women can combat the patriarchal readings of *Hamlet* and *Othello* by casting Gertrude, Ophelia, and Desdemona as empowered, complex characters. Further using metatheatricality to underscore the adaptation's political difference from the source material, Nightwood Theatre's 2012 production of *The Penelopiad* begins with Penelope (Megan Follows) on centre stage poised as a statue (see figure 0.6); she then breaks her statuesque pose – and with it the imagined plaster that contains her – to address the audience and challenge how she has been portrayed in art throughout the ages.[22] These political adaptations harness the performativity of racialized and gendered identities in order to de-naturalize accepted constructs of Black, Indigenous, or feminine identities among others.

Political adaptors also use discursive form, structure, and register to challenge the historical or canonical significance of source material. Adaptors sometimes change the original's high or serious register as part of the critical process and transformation of the source's literary status. A change to form

Figure 0.5 Ken Gass's diverse cast and production of Tomson Highway's *The Rez Sisters* at Factory Theatre in 2011. Left to right: Pamela Sinha, Cara Gee, Jean Yoon, Billy Merasty, Jani Lauzon, Djennie Laguerre, Michaela Washburn, and Kyra Harper.

or genre can effectively undermine the high seriousness of the original. Alternative play structures can further complement a political adaptation's rejection of inherited European traditions by modeling change. With *Princess Pocahontas*, Mojica replaces the European theatre structure of acts and scenes altogether, instead opting to organize her play by the cycles of the moon. Mojica's structure foregrounds transformation and continuity as an alternative to the linear numbered scene divisions. In refusing to use the European play structure, Mojica asks the question: whose theatre tradition are we partaking in? Mojica does not simply alter a traditional discursive form but instead presents an alternative and innovative performance structure. *Princess Pocahontas* is a good example of how a political adaptation can use its form as well as its narrative to change the popular source narrative's message (the colonial myth that John Smith saved Pocahontas by introducing her to civility) and strip the dominant version of its authority.

Anti-linear narrative serves as another method for combating the prejudice against adaptations as second and therefore secondary. A non-linear narrative is especially relevant to postcolonial works such as *Princess Pocahontas* because it rejects the premise that there can be a first or a singular beginning – a common claim in colonial rhetoric that capitalizes on so-called historical firsts. The complication of a historical first is quite pertinent to adaptations because, as I explain above, adaptations are commonly regarded as belated artistic works that are derivative of the first, "original" version. These anti-linear strategies and narratives, then, function as a critique of colonial rhetoric as well as a defense to popular denouncements of adaptations as parasitical works.

Considering that political adaptations often take up problems of individual and collective identity, it is fitting that self-definition is a recurring element that manifests itself through self-defining utterances, such as "I am" and "We are." The repetition of these climactic declarations across different adaptations creates an intertextual chorus that harmonizes the goal of self-identification. Political adaptations such as MacDonald's *Goodnight Desdemona*, Nolan and MacKinnon's *Death of a Chief*, and Nicole Brooks's *Obeah Opera* (2012) hinge on "I am" statements as a loaded refrain and marker of identity construction. MacDonald, for instance, concludes her play with Constance Ledbelly's climactic realization that "I'm the Author" (87); this moment gives authority to a young female scholar who was ghostwriting for a celebrated older male academic – a metatheatrical act that also imbues MacDonald (a female adaptor of Shakespeare) with authority. In her political adaptation of Arthur Miller's *The Crucible* (1953) and seventeenth-century Salem witch hunts, Brooks's contemporary opera features an "I AM Suite" wherein the main characters perform a series of empowering "I am" declarations in protest of racialized witch hunts (see figure 0.7). In these works, the characters' journeys of self-discovery and the larger debates over identity-construction culminate with self-declarations that capture the complexities and intersections of performed, racialized, gendered, and often othered subject-positions.[23]

As playwrights adapt the genre, narrative, and political structures of the original work, the play's creative development and rehearsal process can also contribute to the political project. The case studies will show that political adaptors repeatedly use these eight theatrical strategies on stages across Canada. Through these shared methodologies, staged political adaptations are confronting and transforming the "truth" about stories and how they define who we are because, to adapt King's statement, the truth about stories is that they reveal our political values.

Figure 0.6 In Kelly Thornton's (director) production of *The Penelopiad* (Nightwood Theatre 2011), Megan Follows (Penelope) opens the play by posing like a statue and drawing attention the many different artistic mediums and strategies for representing Penelope as a symbol of wifely duty.

Political Adaptation as Disidentification

Despite these effective shared strategies, a paradox lies at the heart of political adaptation: it is an art form that calls attention to the very narrative it seeks to undo. Put in terms of identification, political adaptation ultimately performs disidentification; it simultaneously identifies with and against a canonical story or character in order to transform its political significance from within a dominant discourse.[24] This performance of disidentification can either limit or foster the political adaptation's potential for effecting change. On the one hand, political adaptation's potential to challenge a dominant cultural narrative is constrained by its overt and extended retelling of that very story. On the other hand, political adaptation proves to be an effective strategy for changing inherited narratives because it capitalizes on the popularity and the audience's recognition of the source material. As a form for combating restrictive narratives of identity, political adaptation targets the very stories that are perpetuating damaging stereotypes. While the starting point for theatre audiences may be the political adaptation's relationship to a recognizable and even beloved source, the end point for adaptors is to render that very source unrecognizable by deconstructing its problematic power dynamics and reductive narrative. In short, political adaptation invites audiences to share in its disidentification with the source. Political adaptation, after all, is the retelling of a narrative with political and politicized difference.

While this paradox may seem to constrain the adaptor's potential to effect change, political adaptation's performance of disidentification with the source is central to its ability to transform the way we understand and talk about the source material. In offering an extended and often updated retelling of another work of art, political adaptation inevitably gestures towards the cultural significance of the source material that it aims to critique. In this way, the potential for political adaptation to transform source material can be hampered by its unavoidable entanglement with the very source it seeks to challenge. Yet, while there are limits to political adaptation's performance of disidentification its reference to a recognizable source material facilitates its revisionist project. The identification of political adaptations with popular narratives is an important element of their political potential as well as performance of disidentification precisely because the adaptation transforms the source's role and reception in the dominant cultural imaginary. In other words, the adaptors' participation in the dominant cultural imaginary enables them to effect change from within.

Figure 0.7 b current and Theatre Archipelago's 2012 production of Nicole Brooks's *Obeah Opera* (a political adaptation on the significance of race in the Salem witch trials). From left to right: Joni Nehrita, Nicole Brooks, Macomere Fifi (centre), and Saidah Baba Talibah.

Sears's *Harlem Duet* performs disidentification with its Shakespearean source by capitalizing on and disavowing the enduring significance of *Othello*. In her stirring prequel to Shakespeare's *Othello*, *Harlem Duet* imagines Othello as a present day professor in Harlem who abandons his Black (Sears capitalizes this word throughout her play and its preface) wife Billie and the hopes for a nuclear Black family in order to further his career and "White wash his life" (353) by marrying the "alabaster goddess" Mona (361). The poster for the Stratford Festival's 2006 production of *Harlem Duet* illustrates the inevitable connection between Sears and Shakespeare by presenting Shakespeare's face on the advertisement like a stamp of approval to explain that *Harlem Duet* is "Othello, the prequel" (see figure 0.8). James McKinnon offers a nuanced reading of the advertisement, suggesting that "the image of Shakespeare is a reproduction of the iconic Folio title page, and thus evokes traditional notions of Shakespeare as a universal paragon of creative achievement and dramatic authorship. Its effect is that of a seal of approval or official endorsement ('I'm William Shakespeare, and I approve this message') […] The ad uses Shakespeare to guarantee *Harlem Duet*'s high-cultural pedigree" (299). Komporaly similarly argues that any adaptation of Shakespeare carries with it a stamp of "artistic merit" and "cultural capital" because "Shakespeare is deemed beyond contestation and censorship" (24). While Stratford Festival may have embraced Shakespeare to validate the cultural pedigree of their production, *Harlem Duet* has a more ambiguous relationship to *Othello*. Billie articulates Sears's simultaneous embrace and rejection of the source when she says, "the Shakespeare's mine, but you can have it" (348). With *Harlem Duet*, Sears not only disidentifies with Shakespeare she also models disidentification as an effective strategy. *Harlem Duet*, after all, has been credited with helping to change the way performers and scholars approach *Othello*. Peter Dickinson convincingly asserts that it "forever alter[s] the way we read the 'originary' tex[t]" (203). *Harlem Duet* exposes the problematic racial dynamic of the Black-faced Moor and his interracial marriage in *Othello*.[25] In this way, *Harlem Duet* reveals the transformative potential of disidentification for changing the way we perform and imagine a particular story.

In disidentifying with the source material, the intrinsic doubleness of the adaptation – an embrace and rejection of the source – creates a politicized palimpsest that layers the source with the adaptation's retelling. As a result, the audience is a major vehicle for the potential of a political adaptation to effect change because we collectively reimagine the source after viewing the adaptation. The staged political adaptation can change the way we think about the source material, its characters, and its ideologies, but it is ultimately the audience that enacts the transformation of the cultural imaginary. This book responds to the significance of spectatorship by taking account of political adaptations' unique audience dynamics.

Theatre performances, like performances of identity, rely on a spectating "you." Theatre, after all, is derived from the Greek word "theatron," which literally means "watching place" or "place of seeing." The act of seeing and the role of the audience define theatre. Political theatre in Canada today is calling attention to the audiences' acts of watching and, in doing so, it challenges how we understand identities. Dramatic political adaptations harness the experience of theatre spectatorship by challenging constructions of individual and collective identities, thereby revealing in the process the mutually constitutive relationship of the "I" and "we." This interconnection of the individual and a collective can be understood in terms of identity theory, for instance, when Judith Butler explains that "the 'I' that I am is nothing without this 'you'" (*Giving* 82); while she is speaking about individual identity, her construct of identity can be readily applied to the mutually constitutive relationship of actor and audience. Butler unravels the tangled relationship between the self and other, speaker and listener, which, in theatre terms, also explains the interconnection of the performer and audience (*Giving* 82). Relationships inform individual identity and the process of identification, but in theatre it is not simply the relationship between an individual "I" and a singular "you" because the audience in theatre is a collective "you" that is also made up of individuals. The collective spectating "you" is inherent to the individual performing "I." Political adaptations and theatre performances foreground the importance of spectating collectives as intrinsic to the process of creating a narrative or identity. To adapt Butler, the 'I' that I am is nothing without this collective 'we' in dramatic political adaptation.

Productions of political adaptations at mainstage theatres across Canada gather a specific type of audience that is at once politically engaged and part of mainstream culture. In modeling disidentificatory strategies for the viewer, political adaptations invite the spectators to align with and against the canonical source narrative, thereby disidentifying with the sources' dominant and oftentimes normative ideologies. In this way, the audience forms a specific type of public – a dispublic – that can disidentify with and transform canonical narratives within the dominant public.[26] A dispublic participates in a dominant and normative culture but challenges facets of its popular ideologies from within. The concept of a dispublic, as a result, applies to audiences beyond political adaptation and responds to the increasingly political nature of popular spectacles today. We need look no further than Lin-Manuel Miranda's hit musical *Hamilton* (2015) to see how political adaptations can shape an audience into a politically engaged dispublic. *Hamilton*, as Lyra D. Monteiro says, "challenges" the "exclusive" versions of history that focus on white men in order to "create a world in which women's voices are no longer silenced and Black Lives Matter" (89). Proving that political adaptation is more popular than ever, Miranda's musical about the United States' first treasury secretary has been touted as "the most celebrated theatrical event of the century" (Helfman 37) and the "biggest cultural event in the United States" (Shaw 30).[27] *Hamilton* disidentifies with dominant narratives of the United States' past and, in doing so, invites the audience to disidentify with exclusionary histories that valorize whiteness.[28] While political adaptations demonstrate the political nature of mainstream performance, I argue that they also address a specific type of audience – a dispublic.

Figure 0.8 The poster for Stratford Festival's 2006 production of Djanet Sears's *Harlem Duet*.

The prevalent theoretical binary of publics and counterpublics does not reflect the nuances of theatre audiences attending productions of political adaptations: Jürgen Habermas and Michael Warner respectively define groups of viewers as either dominant publics or radical counterpublics.[29] In response to Habermas's theory of the public sphere as a vehicle of "public opinion" (194) as well as a public's ability to engage in critical debate, Warner contrasts "mass publics" (63) with "subaltern counterpublics" that are defined by their "subordinate status" (57) in order to concentrate on the making of radical counterpublics. Political adaptations' theatre audiences, however, occupy the space between these two, often-polarized groups. While Habermas acknowledges that "Sometimes the public appears simply as that sector of public opinion that happens to be opposed to authorities" (2), political adaptation's theatre audiences are simultaneously representative of "the many and the mediocre" or of mainstream authority as well as of its critical opposition (Habermas 133). As a result, Habermas's public and Warner's counterpublic do not fully capture the unique dynamics of many contemporary theatre audiences who are at once part of normative middle-class culture and yet share politically radical ideologies that challenge their own claims to privilege.

Staged political adaptations gather what I call a dispublic – a group of people that disidentify with (or simultaneously identify with and against) the source's widely accepted narrative and politics by concurrently participating in the endurance and transformation of its dominant ideologies. These audiences either share the adaptor's political affiliation prior to the theatre viewing experience or participate in this political perspective by viewing the transformation of earlier political ideologies from within the canonical source. The dispublic is popular yet political, much like the mode of political adaptation itself.

Political adaptations often gather popular audiences that are drawn to retellings of canonical works. The cultural capital of adaptation is not unique to political adaptation and Hutcheon and others explore the profit-driven market of adaptation in popular film and literature. The interconnection of politics and mainstream theatre is especially prevalent in Toronto where mid-size theatres have political mandates. Lauren Vandervoort describes in a personal communication with me, that audience demographics show that audiences of the staged political adaptations considered in this book are often affluent, with more than 50 per cent of Toronto mid-size theatre audience members reporting an annual salary of over $100,000; these audiences also list intellectual engagement as their top reason for attending the theatre (Creative Trust 15). Based on a 2010 audience survey that was emailed to over 30,000 contacts who attend midsize theatres and art productions in Toronto, theatre audience members reported "1) engaging intellectually with art; 2) being inspired or uplifted; 3) discovering new plays and playwrights" as the three most popular reasons why they attend theatre. Political adaptations cater to urban theatre audiences' desire for intellectual discourse with new and inspired perspectives by offering politicized retellings of canonical works that aim to effect real-world change. In this way, political adaptations gather a dispublic who participate in the dominant public and can therefore transform it from within.

The dispublic not only defines the audience of political adaptations; it also helps define the predominant audience in twenty-first-century mainstream theatre. As this study of political adaptations and the following chapters demonstrate, theatres successfully market performances of political intervention as mainstream entertainment. This book explores the concept of the dispublic in response to the prevalence of political adaptation as well as the political potential of dominant spectatorships (see chapter 3). Understanding political adaptation as a performance of disidentification theorizes this specific mode of adaptation and its audience dynamics, but it also helps to classify the spectatorship of popular yet political theatre more broadly.

The audience's relationship to the adaptation is a blueprint for the ideological basis of social change because the adaptive narrative presents a new, layered way of perceiving an iconic character or collective identity as well as a reminder of why this change is needed. At the end of Shields's *If We Were Birds* (2008), an adaptation of "Tereus, Procne, and Philomela" from Ovid's *Metamorphoses* (8 AD), Philomela speaks to her own personal trauma and the audience's experiences of witnessing Shields's bloody play, explaining, "the memories are forever wedged in our thoughts. / There is no escape or release" (65). This line articulates a shared goal of political adaptations: to change the way we approach inherited narratives, such as Greek mythologies of rape, by layering the memory of the adaptation with our understanding of the source. More than a form of re-narration, adaptation is a popular mode for political playwrights who seek to challenge the way we conceive of and construct normative narratives of race, gender, and culture, among others.

Cases for Political Adaptation

Through political adaptations, contemporary Canadian theatre is changing inherited histories and giving a voice to previously untold stories. The primary focus of this study is Canadian political adaptation and its audiences from 1990 to 2015. Eight playwrights serve as the subject of extended case studies: Atwood, Clarke, Lescarbot, Mojica, Moses, Sears, Shields, and the collective theatre group Optative Theatrical Laboratories. I examine their plays as both dramatic texts and as performed events. The case studies allow me to elaborate the ways in which political dramatic adaptation transforms source narratives on a contextual level with revised plots and updated historical settings as well as on an individual level with individual characters' negotiations with identificatory labels and strategies. These intersecting levels of transformation expose the relationship between individual and collective identities; they thereby reflect the plays' fundamental duality as they re-identify individual characters from canonical literature (such as Othello, Pocahontas, and Penelope) that represent reductive forms of collective identity in order to critique cultural, racial, and gender stereotypes and foster nuanced understandings of identities in difference. Taken together, the case studies reveal both the constraints and the radical, transformative potential of political adaptation.

The subsequent chapters build on my theoretical architecture by focusing on political adaptation's disidentification with source material (chapters 1 and 2), how performed disidentification has an effect on the audience dynamics and the dispublic (chapter 3), and the potential to break free from the source material by displacing it as an incomplete cultural narrative (chapter 4). The first chapter pairs *Le Théâtre de Neptune* with the verbatim retelling *Sinking Neptune* in order to consider political adaptation's potential to reinforce the very historical material it seeks to discredit. Through retelling *Le Théâtre de Neptune* in its entirety, *Sinking Neptune* offers an ideal case study for considering political adaptation's limits in changing the source material. Building on political adaptation's necessary embrace of the source, chapter 2 concentrates on the Shakespeare adaptations *Gertrude and Ophelia* and *Harlem Duet*, using them to argue that the adaptor's participation in a dominant literary tradition is an ideal position from which to change the canon. Chapter 3 turns to two feminist Greek adaptations that feature onstage choruses – Atwood's *The Penelopiad* and Shields's *If We Were Birds* – in order to examine specific contexts of audience reception and how political adaptations gather a dispublic. Both plays highlight the distinct spectatorship of political adaptation because they feature onstage audiences that instruct the real viewers on how to change the way we think about the female characters in Trojan War material, and because Atwood's play resulted in a female mentorship program. In fact, the Canadian government consulted with the cast of the premiere *The Penelopiad* production about gender issues in the arts. The final chapter and the Indigenous adaptations *Princess Pocahontas* and *Almighty Voice* demonstrate a possible radical effect of political adaptation to render the so-called original an unreliable source. Each chapter approaches political adaptation as a performance of disidentification in order to define political adaptation and explore how inherited narratives of identity change (or have failed to progress) over time.

Dramatic adaptation is a process of negotiating our own and others' identities and shared stories because, as Ric Knowles contends, "there is no better site for such a negotiation than the live, public forum that is theatre" (*Shakespeare's Mine* vi). Canadian theatre offers a unique perspective on the political performance and transformation of identities because it makes manifest the physical contexts of the theatre house as a political institution, of the audience's attendance, and of the characters' racialized or gendered bodies. With identity politics being so invested in the constructedness of the racialized, sexualized, and gendered self, drama offers the ideal opportunity to consider the performativity of identity in the context of public theatres.

Political adaptation is a category of adaptation that takes into account the subversive potential, political motivations, and cultural effects of so many adaptations – it is an artistic mode that continues to dominate stages across Canada. Canadian theatre has a long tradition of political adaptation; a tradition, as the next chapter demonstrates, that precedes Confederation, dates back to the first documented performance in North America, and culminates in the late twentieth and early twenty-first centuries. To build on a quotation from Hannah Arendt, Canadian dramatic adaptation is and has long been "political art par excellence" (188).

1 The Limits of Political Adaptation in *Le Théâtre de Neptune en la Nouvelle-France* and *Sinking Neptune*

On 14 November 2006, Montreal's Optative Theatrical Laboratories (OTL) mounted the political adaptation *Sinking Neptune*, four centuries after Marc Lescarbot's inaugural performance of *Le Théâtre de Neptune en la Nouvelle-France* (1606), the first documented play in what is now called Canada.[1] Using multiple strategies of the political adaptations outlined in the previous chapter, Lescarbot's *Le Théâtre de Neptune* adapted the European oceanic masque (traditionally performed at court) and French *réception* (performed in honour of a returning ruler) in order to welcome a French colonial leader to Port Royal, to naturalize the imperial project as a "louable entreprise," and to instruct the Indigenous Mi'kmaq viewers on how to act like dutiful "sauvages."[2] After a cast of classical gods assure the colony's leader of future success, four *sauvages* in a small canoe offer gifts and confess that "vivre toujours en ta grace / C'est tout ce que nous désirons" (*TN* 54).[3] The aptly titled *Sinking Neptune*, in turn, critiques Lescarbot's play as a colonialist "derogatory spectacle" and challenges the cultural implications of considering it as a Canadian first (King, "Sinking Neptune: Introduction" 199).[4] OTL's production sparked media interest in the quadricentennial anniversary of *Le Théâtre de Neptune* as journalists debated the historical value of such a markedly colonialist piece that depicts the Mi'kmaq nation as *sauvages*. *Sinking Neptune* is an ideal example of political adaptation's methodologies because OTL's creation process reinforced its political aims:[5] through its collective creation process, multiple sources, divergent perspectives, shifts in historical context, and interactive performance, *Sinking Neptune* frames Lescarbot's play as an imperial fantasy of intercultural harmony between the French and Mi'kmaq, challenging what has been considered the beginning of Canadian theatre history in particular, and authoritative historiography in general.

Sinking Neptune, however, also performs *Le Théâtre de Neptune* in its entirety and calls attention to Lescarbot's continued importance, thereby reinforcing the historical significance of the very play it seeks to discredit. *Sinking Neptune*, then, performs disidentification with – or the simultaneous identification with and against – Lescarbot's dominant historical narrative by underlining the relevance of the very source material it seeks to undermine. In this way, *Sinking Neptune* dramatizes the limits of political adaptation and its performance of disidentification: as a performance of disidentification, the political adaptation *Sinking Neptune* is restricted to retelling *Le Théâtre de Neptune* even as it combats Lescarbot's portrayal of *sauvages* and Canadian history's privileging of documented colonial interactions over precolonial Indigenous rituals.

Performed on the actual waters of Nova Scotia's Annapolis Basin, *Le Théâtre de Neptune* features a series of Roman gods (Neptune, Triton, Diana) and four *sauvages* who each greet the colony's returning French leader, Jean Biencourt, Sieur de Poutrincourt, and its geographer, Samuel de Champlain, with monologues of praise.[6] Controversy surrounds the material contexts of the play because *Le Théâtre de Neptune* survives only as a play script in Lescarbot's own historical writings, prompting some critics to speculate whether the masque was ever actually performed. According to Lescarbot, however, the performance of the play was instrumental in establishing Champlain's *L'Ordre de Bon Temps* (the Order of Good Cheer), which codified eating and entertainment, in 1606.[7] Lescarbot's self-congratulatory report indicates that the performance and the Order of Good Cheer were successful in preventing another winter of death, scurvy, and hunger. Charles William Jefferys's twentieth-century pen-and-ink drawing of "The First Play in Canada" (see figure 1.1) offers an imagined reconstruction of the event with French and Mi'kmaq performers in canoes, a reconstruction that continues to shape readers' conception of the performance as it appears on the cover of Jerry Wasserman's timely 2006 edition, *The Spectacle of Empire: Marc Lescarbot's Theatre of Neptune in New France*.

Although some scholars contend that the Mi'kmaq people played the *sauvages*, there is no consensus as to whether this was the case or whether the play was enacted with an all-French cast, as Lescarbot's script suggests. Jefferys's 1942 drawing, Alan Filewod explains, is the only evidence to support the claim that the Mi'kmaq people portrayed the *sauvages*; however, some historians, such as Eugene Benson and L.W. Conolly, accept the sketch as historical fact, suggesting that both the Frenchmen and Mi'kmaq people participated

Figure 1.1 C.W. Jefferys, drawing, *The First Play in Canada* (1942). *The Picture Gallery of Canadian History* 83 (Library and Archives Canada C-106968).

in the performance (Filewod, *Performing* xiv). Wasserman dismisses the controversy altogether and states that the Indians were "surely Frenchmen in Native costume, not the Mi'kmaq themselves as has sometimes been speculated" (36). In *Sinking Neptune*, Lescarbot's *sauvages* are white actors in redface, presenting as embodied colonial fantasies. If the *sauvages* speak in French rhyming couplets, as Lescarbot reports, it is reasonable to believe that Frenchmen performed these roles in the original *Théâtre de Neptune* performance. But how does this uncertainty surrounding the casting of the masque affect its significance? On the one hand, if the Mi'kmaq people performed the lines of the *sauvage* characters verbatim, they contributed to the creation of reductive stereotypes that model ideal behaviour. On the other hand, the Mi'kmaq people's involvement potentially destabilizes the *sauvage* stereotypes contained in the script. If the Mi'kmaq people participated, their lines may not have been delivered in the French rhyming couplets that Lescarbot documents. Their involvement, then, would undermine the veracity of Lescarbot's script but also reinforce his assertion that the performance successfully brought together the French and Mi'kmaq in a shared event. The controversy over how *Le Théâtre de Neptune* was performed gestures towards the indeterminacy of its script and to the larger, encompassing issue of the limits of archival research. While it is possible to question whether *Le Théâtre de Neptune* was performed, I examine it as a lived event as supported by the documented evidence.

Despite its unknown, and potentially unknowable, performance context, *Le Théâtre de Neptune* undeniably erects a racial hierarchy that legitimates French rule as natural. But the strategies of the two Neptune plays are not as different as one might initially expect. *Sinking Neptune* simultaneously recuperates and deconstructs Lescarbot's play, exemplifying political adaptation's disidentification with source material and the nuanced process of historiography. In disidentifying with Lescarbot's production, *Sinking Neptune* inevitably ties itself to *Le Théâtre de Neptune*, its historical context, and its colonial dynamics, thereby interconnecting the dramatic techniques and cultural relations of these two politically oppositional plays. Put another way, *Sinking Neptune* tests the limits of political adaptation as a performance of disidentification.

Sinking Neptune is a model for how dynamics of disidentification and shared methodologies operate through political adaptations, as outlined in the previous chapter, as well as for political adaptations of historiography. These dynamics and methodologies include the following: the play refutes anteriority, draws from multiple time periods, is a product of collective creation, resists stasis by being consistently updated with every performance, and avoids constructing a hierarchical dichotomy of knowing and unknowing audiences. In keeping with the genre of political adaptation – a politicized retelling or re-dramatization of an earlier narrative – *Sinking Neptune* serves as a corrective to Lescarbot's early modern colonialism, but only through the problematic double gesture of simultaneously rejecting and reinscribing *Le Théâtre de Neptune*'s status as the first play in Canada. This disidentification with the source is a defining element of political adaptation and its ability for effecting real-world change. After all, *Sinking Neptune* relies on its overt and extended relationship to the source material in order to change the way audiences understand *Le Théâtre de Neptune*'s role in the colonial history of what we now call Canada.

Critical Reception

Celebrating *Le Théâtre de Neptune* as a historical first transforms Poutrincourt's return into a historic moment and fails to acknowledge earlier Indigenous performances, thereby celebrating Canada as a nation that begins with colonialism and privileges documented over oral or performative art. The refusal to acknowledge precolonial Indigenous performance is a symptom of the cultural genocide of Indigenous peoples in Canada and the long-standing denial of this violent history. In addition to a commemorative plaque at Port Royal and the designation of the fort as a Canadian National Historic site, historians have celebrated the performance of *Le Théâtre de Neptune* as a monumental event in Canadian theatre. Stratford's centennial report describes Lescarbot's play as "the first theatrical happening in Canada" (*100 Years* 1); Laurent Lavoie cites *Le Théâtre de Neptune* as the beginning of Acadian theatre (451); Ann Saddlemyer credits Lescarbot's spectacle as the first "marine masque" (10); and Frederick Lewis Gay even claims it to be the "first American play" (136). The continued significance of *Le Théâtre de Neptune*, as further demonstrated by Wasserman's edition and *Sinking Neptune*, fulfills Lescarbot's goal of "Le renom immortel" ("Théâtre de Neptune" 51).[8] Celebratory histories and monuments of *Le Théâtre de Neptune* contribute to Lescarbot's colonial project by effacing the Indigenous performance history and culture that preceded the French masque; the erasure of a community's history and tradition is, after all, an agent of cultural genocide.

Historical context and site are integral to both Lescarbot's and OTL's political projects of claiming and discrediting colonial firsts, respectively, further demonstrating the oppositional plays' shared strategies. Lescarbot's masque pays homage to many courtly French theatre traditions and borrows from conventions of court festivals (*fête*) – another example of Canada's history of adaptation – but Lescarbot uses a real ocean, replacing the French nautical masque's painted seascapes and props with the Bay of Fundy itself and functioning boats.[9] Because the masque occurs outdoors rather than in a theatre or court, the performance subsumes the land as part of the spectacle. In this way, the landscape – like the spectators – becomes part of the colonial project and the historic event.

The productions of *Sinking Neptune*, by comparison, culminated with a performance at King's Theatre in Annapolis Royal, Nova Scotia, on 14 November 2006, overlooking the waters where Lescarbot mounted his play four hundred years earlier. Much like Lescarbot's use of landscape, OTL's anniversary performance reclaims the Annapolis Basin as a site of cultural genocide rather than French rule. The media attention and heated talkback following the King's Theatre production further illustrates the efficacy of *Sinking Neptune*'s performance site and date.

In 2006, the four-hundredth anniversary of *Le Théâtre de Neptune* was rung in with commemorative newspaper reports and performances. Musique 400 and Theatre 400 were created specifically for the event and planned full-scale dramatizations of the play.[10] Nova Scotia journalist Carolyn Sloan heralded the "400th anniversary of theatre in our nation," calling *Le Théâtre de Neptune* "Canada's first play." Although this and other reports gesture toward an inclusive group – uniting readers in celebration of "theatre in *our* nation" (Sloan; emphasis added) – they define a Canada and a theatre history that begins with colonial settlement and thereby excludes Indigenous tradition. Citing *Le Théâtre de Neptune* as an example of colonial drama in Canada, Helen Gilbert and Joanne Tompkins explain that "when Europeans settled a colony, one of the earliest signs of established culture/'civilisation' was the presentation of European drama, which according to official records, obliterated for many years any indigenous performance forms" (7–8). The historicization of *Le Théâtre de Neptune* as "Canada's first play" ultimately threatens to reinforce Euro-colonialist theatre traditions that obscure the Mi'kmaq people's pre-colonial performative rituals.

Countering *Le Théâtre de Neptune*'s historical significance as a Canadian "first," OTL's poster for *Sinking Neptune* alters Jefferys's sketch to highlight Lescarbot's reductive portrayal of Mi'kmaq people and the play's participation in cultural genocide (see figure 1.2). Conceived at the turn of the millennium to promote a new form of twenty-first-century performance activism (OTL, "Mandate"), the Montreal theatre company mounted *Sinking Neptune* in November 2006 to protest the anniversary celebrations for Lescarbot's play, performing at Les Artistes du Toc Toc in Montreal, King's Theatre in Annapolis Royal, and The Bus Stop Theatre in Halifax.[11] *Sinking Neptune* is a piece of verbatim theatre – a documentary genre linked to oral histories of ordinary people whose typical features include quotations from multiple sources, such as interviews, performances, and news reports (Paget 317).[12] Working within this genre, *Sinking Neptune* enacts *Le Théâtre de Neptune* in its entirety but interrupts the original script with quotations from contemporary sources, such as a character based on and named after theatre

Figure 1.2 OTL, poster, *Sinking Neptune* (2006).

scholar Alan Filewod, as well as quotations by Indigenous writers and artists. The opening projected slides, for example, feature quotations by Daniel Paul, Lisa Mayo, and Floyd Favel.[13] *Sinking Neptune* also begins and ends with a press event for the quadricentennial anniversary of Lescarbot's inaugural masque, which forms a frame narrative. In addition to framing *Le Théâtre de Neptune* as an act of imperial conquest and of imagined cultural superiority over *sauvage* supplicants, *Sinking Neptune* exemplifies Gilbert and Tompkins's definition of postcolonial performance: OTL's play responds to Lescarbot's imperialism, voices Mi'kmaq people's experiences of colonization, and critiques histories of Canadian drama that begin with Lescarbot's colonial performance and the arrival of the Europeans.[14]

While OTL contributes to an ever-growing field of scholarship on Lescarbot's play, there has yet to be substantial critical work on *Sinking Neptune.* Filewod laments that Wasserman's seminal four-hundredth-anniversary edition of *Le Théâtre de Neptune* ignored OTL's response to the play. Although Wasserman does not include a script for *Sinking Neptune*, he does frame his introduction with a discussion of OTL's play, even quoting King's postcolonial criticisms of Lescarbot's work. Filewod's edited collection, *Theatre Histories* (2009), however, presents the only print edition of *Sinking Neptune* as well as an introduction to the play written by OTL's Donovan King.[15]

The productions of *Le Théâtre de Neptune* and its political adaptation, *Sinking Neptune*, are both events in history and histories unto themselves.[16] *Le Théâtre de Neptune* establishes a narrative of French colonial discovery in the New World that posits the French colonists as benefactors of the Mi'kmaq nation who, in Lescarbot's version, are eager to welcome the returning French leader. *Sinking Neptune*, by contrast, critiques the very notion of a cultural "beginning" that excludes the Mi'kmaq people's pre-colonial culture. OTL offers a different historical narrative that challenges Lescarbot's appropriation of Mi'kmaq language and feast rituals in order to establish a French rule. *Sinking Neptune*, ironically, was also the primary cause of *Le Théâtre de Neptune*'s recent media attention. In effectively updating the 1606 play for contemporary audiences, *Sinking Neptune* contributes to the survival and historical relevance of Lescarbot's masque – a consequence of political adaptation and its disidentification strategy.

Le Théâtre de Neptune

Lescarbot's oceanic masque reminds us just how effective and powerful theatre can be as a vehicle that ushers in political change. Wasserman fittingly titles his edition of Lescarbot's play *Spectacle of Empire*, but *Le Théâtre de Neptune* not only performs a spectacle *of* empire but also enacts spectacle *as* empire: the play does not merely represent the empire but is a constitutive extension of it. Robert Wallace, in *Theatre and Transformation in Contemporary Canada*, conceives of politics and theatre in a dialogic relationship because "art both responds to and constructs social and historical conditions" (11) just as *Le Théâtre de Neptune* simultaneously reflects and constructs colonial conquest. Instead of a colonial flag or cross, it is Lescarbot's theatrical performance that claims the land and establishes racial hierarchy. Accounts of cross-cultural encounters and imperial settlers are often, as Christopher Balme explains, "drawn from theatre" and are "almost invariably [described as] a 'scene' or 'spectacle'" (1). Lescarbot begins the sixth book of *Histoire* by noting the pervasive theatricality of life and death that affects the French and Mi'kmaq alike:

> L'Autheur du livre de la Sapience dite de Salomon nous témoigne une chose trei-veritable, qu'*une pareille entrée est à tous à la vie, & une pareille issuë*. Mais chacun peuple a apporté quelque ceremonie apres ces choses accomplies. Car les uns ont pleuré, de voir que l'homme vinst naitre sur le theatre de ce monde, pour y estre comme un spectacle de miseres & calamitez.[17] (651)

Lescarbot, like many settlers before him, here uses theatre as a metaphor for life and the essential similarities of different cultures. Life, according to Lescarbot's *Histoire*, is a theatrical stage – one that shows itself to all nations. In *Le Théâtre de Neptune*, by contrast, theatre functions as much more than a poetic vehicle: the relationship between cross-cultural exchange and theatre is not merely one of metaphorical likeness. Lescarbot's spectacle is the intercultural act itself. In other words, the play does not perform a colonial narrative but rather is the colonial project: Lescarbot's spectacle is an empire.

Even the process of creating *Le Théâtre de Neptune* contributed to the colonial conquest. Because the French colony had been struggling during the long winters, Poutrincourt went on an expedition to Armouchiquois country in the hopes of discovering a warmer place for settlement. Lescarbot was put in charge during Poutrincourt's absence and documented the colony's perils in *Histoire*. *Sinking Neptune*'s Filewod character explains that Lescarbot decided that "his men needed … bread and circuses, so he collected the first for a feast and wrote the second himself, a 'masque,' or symbolic pageant, to welcome back the governor with song, dance, and declaimed verses. He called it 'The Theatre of Neptune,' and set the little colony rehearsing to occupy its time and raise morale" (6).[18] According to Lescarbot, the play succeeded in distracting the Frenchmen from their privations as winter approached and from their mutinous sentiments, while also encouraging a peaceful relationship between the Mi'kmaq tribe and the French colony.

Despite the goal of engaging the Mi'kmaq tribe in the imperialist production, the play's dramatic conventions threaten to marginalize the viewing experience of the Mi'kmaq by rewarding the French audience's knowledge of European courtly theatre traditions. The play, for example, abides by the conventions of a *réception*, or triumphal entry, wherein "the more important residents" greet a returning ruler or royal figure (Fournier 3). Working within the conventions of *réceptions*, it is significant that the Frenchmen greet Poutrincourt on the water because this symbolizes the superiority of the colonists over the Mi'kmaq people, who are believed merely to have watched from the shore. Only in their fictionalized, ideal French-speaking form – as scripted *sauvage* characters in Lescarbot's play – do the Mi'kmaq tribe fall under the category of "important residents." As a "visible sign of a contract between ruler and subject town" (Fournier 3), the *réception* both commemorates and also creates a pact of political hierarchy in the eyes of the French audience. The very act of witnessing the performance implicates the Mi'kmaq people in a contract with the returning leader. Lescarbot even scripts this compact, as the Première Sauvage expresses his immediate and future devotion: "*Sagamos*, si en nos services / Tu as quelque devotion, / A toy en faisons sacrifices / Et à ta generation" (TN 54).[19] Lescarbot's "nautical *réception*," Wasserman asserts, "celebrated the successful transition of the colony from leaderless, near mutinous contingency to god-blessed safety and stability" (36). In this way, the creation process and the dramatic form of *réception* reward the French and help to establish the colony. Like many political adaptations, OTL similarly uses the creation process and form for their postcolonial political arguments, as examined below, gesturing towards the shared strategies of colonial drama and postcolonial adaptation.

Further reinforcing theatre's ability to enact politics or claim land, Lescarbot borrows from the conventions of mock sea battles and court festivals but the painted seascapes and props of the nautical masques are replaced with the Bay of Fundy itself and with functioning canoes. Through Lescarbot's changes to traditional masques, the landscape – like the spectators – becomes part of the spectacle. The European theatre conventions at work in creating *Le Théâtre de Neptune* at once connect the Frenchmen to the Old World, while also politically grounding them in the New World.

For its French viewers, the production of *Le Théâtre de Neptune* replaces the staking of the colonial flag, claiming Port Royal and its Mi'kmaq inhabitants by performance. Filewod explains how Lescarbot "established the principle that the colonialism of spectacle is the necessary precondition of imperial invasion" (*Performing* xv). I argue that Lescarbot's production is not merely a "precondition of imperial invasion," but a figurative act of invasion itself. The Première Sauvage, for example, speaks on behalf of all the Mi'kmaq people in homage to the fleur-de-lis flag:

De la part des peuples Sauvages
Qui environnent ces païs
Nous venons rendre les homages
Deuz aux sacrées Fleur-de-lis

> Es mains de toy, qui ton Prince
> Representes la Majesté. (*TN* 54)[20]

The French audience could have interpreted this performance of the Mi'kmaq people's imagined devotion as an actual alliance of the two cultures. The Première Sauvage's speech, along with the play as a whole, aims to colonize the imagination of its audience members with tropes of imperial conquest, classical allusions to Roman gods, and performative utterances that naturalize Poutrincourt's superiority.

The play's didacticism works along ethnic lines, separately targeting and dividing the French and Mi'kmaq audiences. Lescarbot evokes the ritual of gift exchange to portray the *sauvages* as poor hunters in need of the colonists' generosity and grace. The first three *sauvages* offer Poutrincourt various gifts, such as a quarter of a moose, beaver skins, and bracelets, but the fourth and final *sauvage* is unable to "presentant à toy" due to unsuccessful hunts (55).[21] The Première Sauvage heightens this sense of failure through his confession that "noz moyens sont un peu de chasse" (54).[22] The absence of a gift is the best gift of all because it demonstrates the Mi'kmaq people's lack of survival skills and their need of the French. In this way, the play assures the French colonizers that they will better the *sauvages*' lives. The Mi'kmaq viewers, by contrast, are instructed to speak in French verse and to offer specific gifts to the Europeans.

Theatre historians often concentrate on the masque's European influences, but Lescarbot borrows both from the Mi'kmaq custom of gift giving and also from that of ceremonial feasts.[23] He revises the traditional European masque (Orgel 33) by replacing the final dance with a celebratory feast that integrates actors and audience. In fact, the feast was an integral part of marriage ceremonies, funerals, and hunting for both the French and the Mi'kmaq, making it a shared tradition that further reinforces the cross-cultural bond.[24] With this communal structure, the feast functions on the premise of equality, but it is still executed in the play as an instrument of French rule, meant to help establish peaceful relations with the *sauvages*. Lescarbot uses spectacle, namely the Mi'kmaq people's participation in the masque and subsequent feast, to cajole as well as enact their willingness to accept a peace agreement.

With Lescarbot's marked investment in the Mi'kmaq people's manners and customs, *Le Théâtre de Neptune* operates on what Richard White cites as the four elements of the "middle ground" of intercultural encounters: "a confrontation between imperial or state regimes and non-state forms of social organization, a rough balance of power, a mutual need or a desire for what the other possesses, and an inability of one side to commandeer enough force to compel the other to do what it desired" (xii). *Le Théâtre de Neptune*, in short, performs the integration of the European and Mi'kmaq people as well as their respective cultures, but it does so without physical force. In performing the "middle ground," according to White, an imperial power engages in what they perceive to be Indigenous customs as a method of negotiating a peace or trade agreement. When the Première Sauvage expresses his immediate and future devotion to Poutrincourt, calling him "*Sagamos*" (54), this acts as a type of naming ceremony that hails Poutrincourt as not only a French leader but also a Native chief. Although both *Le Théâtre de Neptune* and *Sinking Neptune* engage in cross-cultural performances, there is one significant difference: where Lescarbot attempts to establish French rule at Port Royal, OTL aims to decolonize the so-called "birthplace of drama and poetry in the New World" (Posner).

As a performance of a successful return, an assurance of future prosperity, and a promise of peaceful *sauvages*, *Le Théâtre de Neptune* is a play that "makes happen what it celebrates" (Schechner 17). Not simply an idealized reflection of peaceful cross-cultural relations, this performance was an embodied contract that ensured "god-blessed safety and stability" in the eyes of the French (Wasserman 36). OTL, however, is much more interested in the masque's meaning in the eyes of the Mi'kmaq people. Despite their oppositional political perspectives, OTL engages in many of the same dramatic techniques and strategies as Lescarbot.

Sinking Neptune

Sinking Neptune's non-hierarchical creation process and dramatic form challenge Lescarbot's performed fantasy of diplomatic intercultural relations, offering a methodology for political adaptations of history. As a piece of "verbatim theatre," *Sinking Neptune* is composed of quotations from multiple sources, such as interviews, performances, and news reports (Paget 317). In "'Verbatim Theatre': Oral History and Documentary Techniques," Derek

Paget explains that words from "'ordinary' people" are collected and performed "in the context of research into a particular region, subject area, issue, event or combination of these things" (317). Paget's emphasis on the use of "ordinary people" as sources gestures towards the political resonances of OTL's theatrical process. OTL aims at inclusivity and rejects artistic or political hierarchies, as demonstrated by the theatre's mandate:

> Optative Theatrical Laboratories is a non-hierarchical dramatic collective whose mandate is to "theatrically challenge hegemonic thinking and oppressive systems." Its community-based project is both activist and theatrical, occupying the unique transformative space between the two fields […] The word *optative*, defined as "the dramatic expression of a wish, desire or choice," drives the collective in its theatrical explorations, experiments, and cultural interventions.

These goals are especially evident in *Sinking Neptune*. Speaking on behalf of OTL, King explains that *Sinking Neptune* "was created as an anti-racist project to deconstruct the play [*Le Théâtre de Neptune*], critically engage the Eurocentric process of re-enactment and commemoration, and expose it all with a twenty-first century spotlight to stimulate critical reflection" (Introduction 199). OTL's methodology and *Sinking Neptune*'s script work together to destabilize *Le Théâtre de Neptune*'s narrative of French authority.

Sinking Neptune draws attention to the very dramatic and theoretical structures that inform its creation – political adaptation, verbatim theatre, and postcolonialism. After four slide projections of "Native Quotations," the play begins with a self-reflexive emphasis on the pervasiveness of its own theatricality with the "*spectacular*" news conference (4). The opening scene presents the 2006 news reports and plans for a commemorative "musical on the Order of Good Cheer" as spectacles of an empire (5). An actor portraying Ken Pinto (director of Theatre 400) greets the news reporters, just as Lescarbot greeted Poutrincourt, updating the colonial *réception* to a contemporary setting. By layering Lescarbot's play with Pinto's re-enactment, *Sinking Neptune* suggests that the past and present inform each other, thereby refuting Pinto's argument that we must approach *Le Théâtre de Neptune* in its pure historical context and refrain from applying a postcolonial lens. *Sinking Neptune* braids together two parallel narratives – the early modern masque and its present-day responses – in a way that dramatizes their inseparability.

The play's use of time and its sequencing of events exemplify a key strategy of political adaptation introduced in the previous chapter: in order to challenge the significance of a national "first," *Sinking Neptune* disrupts the chronological order of history and the three unities of time, place, and action. The quick shifts in time (from the seventeenth century to the present) and in perspective (from Lescarbot to Indigenous artists) undercut sequential history, and, as a result, lessen the importance of a "beginning." OTL also critiques the recent re-enactments and anticipates the excuse that Lescarbot's work was merely a product of the seventeenth century by merging Poutrincourt with Pinto. The same actor performs the roles of both Poutrincourt and Pinto, suggesting that the 2006 director engages in the same colonial rhetoric as the 1606 leader.

In keeping with its multiple historical contexts and perspectives, *Sinking Neptune* avoids propagating a single source or dominating voice.[25] *Sinking Neptune* reproduces *Le Théâtre de Neptune* in its entirety (see OTL's enactment of Lescarbot's Neptune and Tritons in figure 1.3), but OTL's adaptation foregrounds responses from Indigenous artists, directly quotes from the press releases about the quadricentennial celebrations, and includes Filewod as a character, thereby refusing to privilege Lescarbot's script as the primary source of national history. As a verbatim piece, *Sinking Neptune* does not change the words in Lescarbot's text but instead alters the original's political significance and reception. *Sinking Neptune*'s verbatim script, as a result, further reinforces the importance of distinguishing between narrative and political (in)fidelity when charting political adaptations.

In deconstructing *Le Théâtre de Neptune* as merely one of many intertexts, OTL pointedly foregrounds Indigenous artists's responses and writings (Paul, Mayo, Favel), scholarship on Lescarbot's work (namely by Filewod), and recent commentary broadcast by CBC and *Halifax Herald* reporters. Paget speaks to this recuperative element when he describes verbatim theatre as a genre that "involves nothing less than the continued reclaiming and celebrating of that history which is perennially at 'the margins of the news'" (336). The form of *Sinking Neptune*, then, at once deconstructs the hegemonic *Le Théâtre de Neptune* and reclaims narratives of "the margins" that seek to displace Lescarbot's historical status.

Further interconnecting theory and practice of OTL's political adaptation, King's dramaturgical note about *Sinking Neptune* emphasizes the "flexibility" of collective creation. King sees the work as a counter-measure to the authority

Figure 1.3 Photograph from *Sinking Neptune*'s inset performance of *Le Théâtre de Neptune* with George Mougias (Neptune) and Natalie Gural (Triton) (14 November 2006).

of *Le Théâtre de Neptune* as a documented text and as a means of fostering change: "There is no playwright, but rather a flexible team of researchers and editors." Because "a deconstruction is always a work-in-progress, the text is flexible and can be altered with new or other pieces of source text" (202). As a work-in-progress that accommodates continual revisions, *Sinking Neptune* demonstrates one of Salter's strategies for postcolonialist theatre historiography by "destabilizing structures" and resisting "the temptation to closure" (120). The constant updating and collective creation process, together with the verbatim theatre genre, avoid erecting a singular authorial voice. "Generally speaking," as King explains in a personal communication with me, "the entire cast is involved in the creation of the script, based on the source materials that are found." Moreover, OTL makes these source materials available to the public online. Underscoring the dangerous relationship between authorship and authority, an opening projection quoting Hanay Geiogamah warns, "If you don't do it, then the white people will do it for you … They'll tell your story for you. They'll tell you who you are. They'll tell you what you are if you let them" (SN 4).[26] This projection targets Lescarbot's scripting of the Mi'kmaq people and argues for the importance of self-narration and historical adaptation. The process of collective creation, wherein there is no singular authorial voice, contrasts with Lescarbot's creation process, which was all about authority – the authority of Lescarbot as interim leader and playwright as well as Poutrincourt's supremacy as the returning leader.

Sinking Neptune disidentifies with *Le Théâtre de Neptune* by retelling the source's narrative while still managing to alter its political significance. Through staging and casting the actors in multiple roles, for example, *Sinking Neptune* reinforces the artificiality of the *sauvages* in *Le Théâtre de Neptune*. During the Première Sauvage's speech, one of the journalists, Van Gorder, transforms into a "savage" providing a visual commentary on the effect of Lescarbot's script: Gorder "*assumes a 'savage' posture. Over the course of four 'Savage' monologues, he becomes more and more scantly* [*sic*] *clad, 'redfaced' and stereotypical of Natives*" (10). Gorder's transformation points out the potential of performance to turn anyone into a "savage," but, together, the Première Sauvage's speech and Gorder's parodic transformation undermines the credibility and plausibility of Lescarbot's renderings of the *sauvages*.

Keeping with political adaptation's strategy of using discursive form to reinforce its political critique, *Sinking Neptune*'s play structure also speaks to its mission. As an alternative to a traditional play structure that organizes the dramatic action with a series of acts and scenes, *Sinking Neptune* uses "units," including a final unscripted one that engages the audience. These "units" resemble teaching units and thereby foreground the production's didactic and pedagogical intentions. OTL's concluding "Talk back" unit – effectively a question and answer period between the audience and actors – emphasizes the play's open structure by encouraging critical dialogue. Like Lescarbot's feast, OTL's "Talkback" unit breaks the fourth wall and integrates actor with audience. King describes the "Talkback" units as "fruitful discussions," and he invites viewers to "decide for yourself about what approach [to Lescarbot's play], if any, you feel is best" ("Sinking Neptune: Introduction" 199–200). While Lescarbot's feast aims to recruit the Mi'kmaq people as participants in the French colonial production, OTL's "Talkback" involves viewers in an open and unscripted discussion of a postcolonial play.

In 2005, *Sinking Neptune* was performed at Halifax's OneLight Theatre forum on the "Canadian Theatre Identity Crisis: Challenging Eurocentricity through Aboriginal Myth and Ritual." The forum topic, like OTL's play, was selected in response to Theatre 400's plan to re-mount *Le Théâtre de Neptune* (Campbell 225). In a personal communication with me, King explains that the conference attendees, "including Mi'kmaq and other First Nations present," were "invited to participate in the 'meta-performance.'" OTL then incorporated the attendees' involvement in future productions. In this way, the unpredictable "Talkback" unit and ever-changing script literally reinforce *Sinking Neptune*'s project of speaking back to an original.

Providing another platform for responses from politicians, writers, and artists, the slide projections frame and punctuate *Sinking Neptune*. After the six Tritons deliver their speeches in Lescarbot's play, a quotation from Daniel Francis's *The Imaginary Indian* appears on the screen, which describes *sauvages* as merely an "invention of the European [colonizers]" viewed "through the prism of White hopes, fears, and prejudices" (as cited in *SN* 9). OTL here applies Francis's theory of "the imaginary Indian" to suggest that Lescarbot's racial fictions support French sovereignty. The projections comment on Lescarbot's masque and disrupt the audience's viewing experience by calling attention to the script's racial rhetoric and wishful dramatization of the submissive Indian.

In emphasizing the fictionality of Lescarbot's play, *Sinking Neptune* also reminds the audience that we can never know what the Mi'kmaq tribe thought or felt about the oceanic masque. After the first *sauvage* declares devotion to the French King, the Filewod character concedes that "We don't know [what the Mi'kmaq thought] because of course, nobody asked them" (10), which establishes a level of uncertainty about the historical event and introduces the slide-projected quotations as only hypothetical responses. A quotation by Paul suggests that the Mi'kmaq audience "thought the white man and his customs strange, but, being such gracious hosts, they would not contradict them, even though they thought them loco" (10). With these interjections, *Sinking Neptune* dramatizes as well as modernizes the process of witnessing and responding to *Le Théâtre de Neptune*. The slide projections represent possible viewpoints of the Mi'kmaq people and the French colonists through a twenty-first-century lens. *Sinking Neptune* critiques *Le Théâtre de Neptune*'s historical significance and offers a more pluralistic view of the historical event, but what is equally important is its performance of how some cultural attitudes toward Indigenous people, imperialism, and racial minstrelsy have changed since 1606.

Narrowing the Gap? Identifying with and against Colonial Performance

In dramatizing postcolonial responses to *Le Théâtre de Neptune*, *Sinking Neptune* speaks from the gap between the French and Mi'kmaq audiences' perspectives that occurred during the 1606 performance. But what does it mean to speak from the Mi'kmaq people's imagined perspective and for their untold experience? Despite the contradictory political aims of the two plays, the dramatic techniques of OTL's *Sinking Neptune* and Lescarbot's *Le Théâtre de Neptune* have some commonalities. Though the goal of exposing *Le Théâtre de Neptune* as an agent of the French colonists' "cultural genocide" of the Mi'kmaq people is laudable, *Sinking Neptune* also takes on the difficult task of dramatizing the seventeenth-century Mi'kmaq audience's unknowable perspective, much as Lescarbot did four hundred years earlier. Interrupting the inset performance of Lescarbot's play, a quotation by Favel appears on a slide projection: "[The] unsubtle message in the European languages is human superiority over nature, man over woman, man over the birds and bees and the beast, and all brown, black, and yellow folks" (SN 8). In the midst of the re-enactment, Favel's words read as a critical response to the masque; however, in dramatizing the gap in perspectives between the French and Mi'kmaq audiences, *Sinking Neptune* also risks colonizing this gap and ventriloquizing the Mi'kmaq people. Whereas Lescarbot uses transliterated Mi'kmaq vocabulary – *Sagamos* (chief, 54), *adesquidés* (friend, 51), *Matachiaz* (sashes and bracelets, 79), *caraconas* (bread, 56) – to gain authenticity, OTL uses quotations by Indigenous writers to gain cultural authority. *Le Théâtre de Neptune* and *Sinking Neptune* demonstrate conflicting political perspectives, but Lescarbot's and OTL's similar dramatic strategies and shared script complicate the binary categories of colonial and postcolonial drama. The mutually used techniques and scripts help to destabilize the racial (French/Mi'kmaq) and theoretical (colonial/postcolonial) polarities entrenched in any discussion of *Le Théâtre de Neptune* and *Sinking Neptune*.

Comparing Lescarbot's and OTL's dramatic techniques reveals the similar methodologies involved in colonizing and decolonizing the audience's imagination, such as the performances of racial hierarchies, Mi'kmaq culture, and interactive elements. These commonalities do not suggest OTL's failure to challenge the original – no one could argue that *Sinking Neptune* reifies *Le Théâtre de Neptune* – but rather underline how a political adaptation is a performance of disidentification that can effectively critique source material even though it involves an identification with the earlier work through re-enactment and shared techniques. *Sinking Neptune* may have been the primary reason for the media attention on the anniversary of "Canada's first play," but it also reframed discussions of *Le Théâtre de Neptune* with critical responses from academics and Indigenous artists.

I see *Sinking Neptune's* disidentification not as a liability but as a postcolonial feature and an essential paradox of political adaptation. *Sinking Neptune*'s ever-changing script illustrates the impossibility of excavating a stable historical account of a performative event: we can never know what the audiences thought on 14 November 1606. *Sinking Neptune*'s diverse inset responses to Lescarbot's masque avoid colonizing the audience's imagination with a single conception of the Mi'kmaq people's experience, and speak to the relative unknowability of that nation's participation. What is certain, however, is that *Sinking Neptune* uses disidentification and performance as tools for reclaiming the cultural imaginary, that is, the shared historical narratives of a culture.

Sinking Neptune does more than attack *Le Théâtre de Neptune* for its racist portrayal of *sauvages*; it challenges Canadian history as racist. By injecting Indigenous voices in Canada's theatre history, *Sinking Neptune* asks non-Indigenous audiences to consider Canadian historical moments from an Indigenous perspective. If we take on OTL's challenge for more nuanced national memorials and histories, then Champlain and Lescarbot should be treated as complicated historical figures that contributed to the cultural genocide of the Mi'kmaq peoples. Recent nation-wide protests against monuments of historical figures that contributed to the cultural genocide of Indigenous peoples are another example of OTL's political argument. In 2018, for instance, Halifax removed an Edward Cornwallis statue due to his scalping proclamation that rewarded the killing of Mi'kmaq people.[27] Political adaptations indicate how Canadian histories, and with them celebratory plaques, statues, and performances, are somewhat changing.

As *Sinking Neptune* illustrates, political adaptation is a performance of disidentification that calls attention to and debunks its own source materials. The next chapter builds on this definition by examining Margaret Clarke's *Gertrude and Ophelia* and Djanet Sears's *Harlem Duet* as plays that promote political adaptation as a mode of resistance. While *Sinking Neptune* tests the limits of political adaptation, *Gertrude and Ophelia* and *Harlem Duet* foreground the potential of political adaptation as a performance of disidentification that effects change from within by critiquing identification and counteridentification.

2 Political Adaptation as Disidentification in *Gertrude and Ophelia* and *Harlem Duet*

Margaret Clarke's *Gertrude and Ophelia* (1992) and Djanet Sears's *Harlem Duet* (1997) are self-reflexive plays that advocate political adaptation as a strategy of disidentification and a mode of surviving within patriarchal and racist institutional systems.[1] Clarke retells Shakespeare's *Hamlet* from the perspective of two main female characters, whereas Sears adapts Shakespeare's *Othello* by focusing on the titular character's marginalization as a Moor and the ramifications of his interracial marriage to Desdemona. Clarke's and Sears's plays denounce identification and counteridentification as extreme strategies for existing within and outside a dominant system, respectively; through these critiques the plays reveal why political adaptation, as an act of disidentification, is an effective strategy for transforming Shakespeare's characters and stories. While I used Optative Theatrical Laboratories' *Sinking Neptune* in the previous chapter to test the limits of political adaptation's unavoidable connection to its source material, this chapter turns to Clarke's *Gertrude and Ophelia*, and Sears's *Harlem Duet*, in order to examine the benefits of political adaptation's position within the very tradition it seeks to challenge. *Gertrude and Ophelia* and *Harlem Duet* are ideal case studies for showcasing the radical potential of disidentification with dominant sources through political adaptation; this is because both plays dramatize characters' failed acts of identification and counteridentification.

The narrative structures and casting reinforce the plays' feminist and racial political goals. Clarke's political adaptation uses a frame narrative to dramatize the making of an all-female production of Shakespeare's *Hamlet*, which the character "Playwright" titles "Gertrude and Ophelia." Although Clarke's play-within-the-play focuses on Shakespeare's two main female characters (Hamlet's mother Gertrude and his suffering love interest Ophelia), the metatheatrical frame interrupts the inset feminist production and consists mostly of heated exchanges between the female Playwright and the male Actor as they debate the ramifications of an all-female cast. The playwright character, then, offers didactic commentary on the scenes between the maternal Gertrude and the naive Ophelia. The "Gertrude and Ophelia" play-within-a-play follows *Hamlet*'s narrative arc: Hamlet drives Ophelia insane and accuses Gertrude of a murderous alliance with Claudius. The Playwright's version, however, ends with Gertrude mourning Ophelia's death and begging forgiveness for failing to help the young girl. The play-within-a-play's ending of fractured female relationships contrasts with the frame narrative's conclusion; in the final moments of *Gertrude and Ophelia*, we see a respectful partnership of female artists as the actor playing Ophelia leaves the theatre with Playwright, assuring her that "everything will be fine" (52). Clarke shifts the focus of *Hamlet* from male madness and paternal hauntings to issues of maternity, pregnancy, marriage, and female relationships. *Gertrude and Ophelia* encourages the audience to consider the significance of Shakespeare's female characters by developing their interiority and suffering.

Clarke and Sears stay relatively faithful to the original plots of Shakespeare's *Hamlet* and *Othello*, respectively, by offering nuanced interpretations of actions and characters rather than changing the narrative events themselves. *Gertrude and Ophelia*, for instance, quickly establishes that the onstage Playwright is taking a markedly "feminist" (2) approach to Shakespeare's *Hamlet* where Gertrude is no longer the implied co-conspirator of King Hamlet's death. In fact, Clarke's Gertrude marries Claudius in order to ensure Hamlet's claim to the throne, and she is the one who is taken aback at the Mousetrap when she realizes that Claudius "reigns with my husband's blood on his hands" (23).[2] From the opening scene of *Gertrude and Ophelia*, Clarke's Playwright makes it quite clear that she aims to change the way we think about Shakespeare's notorious maternal figure. Clarke further complicates our understanding of the mother figure with a graphic scene where Ophelia struggles with the end of her own pregnancy. Although it is unclear whether Clarke's Ophelia experiences an abortion or miscarriage, both Shakespeare's and Clarke's Ophelia reference famous abortifacients such as the herb rue (*Gertrude* 25, 42). Fittingly, Clarke also alters our conceptions of Shakespeare's father figure, King Hamlet, by casting doubt on the paternity of the Prince and by suggesting that Gertrude had relations with Yoric. When Ophelia longs to "build a shelter in the woods and live there together" with Gertrude, the Queen hints at her intimate past with the fool and recounts that "Yoric used to talk such foolishness to me" (15). The

Queen later concedes, "the jester was more father to [the Prince] than [King Hamlet]" (20), which is why the fool was sentenced to death; as Gertrude laments, "We cried together my son and I for the loss of our … fool. It was the only time that I defied my husband" (20). Clarke's reimagining of Gertrude and Yoric's affair alters Shakespeare's graveyard scene in *Hamlet* from a pinnacle moment of Hamlet's philosophical self-reflection to one of a son mourning the undeserved death of his father, Yoric. But, as Playwright reminds us, the identity of Hamlet's biological father "doesn't matter, not in terms of the mess these women are in" (22). This is because Gertrude's maternal relationship with Ophelia and Ophelia's pregnancy steal the play's focus: Ophelia's madness is as much a result of her pregnancy loss and of Gertrude's betrayal in Clarke's play as it is of Hamlet's "get thee to a nunnery" dismissal in Shakespeare's version (3.1.122).

Harlem Duet, by comparison, is a "rhapsodic blues-tragedy" that features an all-Black cast and tells the story of Othello's relationship with his first, Black wife, Billie, whom he leaves for the white Mona (Shakespeare's Desdemona) (Sears, "NOTES" 14). As counterpoints to the present-day main narrative, the two subplots concern the characters HIM and HER in 1860 as well as HE and SHE in 1928 in which HER/SHE seeks murderous revenge on HIM/HE when he announces that he is in love with a white woman. In all three of *Harlem Duet*'s narratives, a Black man leaves his Black lover for a white woman, thereby dramatizing issues of racial hierarchy and miscegenation in different time periods. The two counterplots feature the same actors that play Billie and Othello. From the earliest narrative thread to the present-day plotline, the characters progress from grammatical objects of speech (HIM/HER), to subjects (HE/SHE), and finally, to proper names (Othello/Billie) – a fitting progression that reinforces their historical development from enslaved property to citizens with rights. Although Othello and Billie have arrived at proper names, they still grapple with self-identification. In this way, Clarke and Sears call attention to the difficult matter of marginalized characters' self-identification in a story that is not their own – Ophelia's selfhood is crushed under the weight of the Prince of Denmark, while Billie and Othello struggle with preconceptions about racial difference established by Shakespeare's famous Moor.

Whereas Clarke retells *Hamlet* with a renewed focus on the female characters, Sears offers an addendum set in the present day that paradoxically comes before the narrative actions in *Othello*: a present-day prequel. In *Har-*

lem Duet, Sears devises Shakespeare's *Othello* as a miscegenation narrative that exemplifies a history of racism and anachronistically recasts Othello's marriage to Desdemona as his intentional embrace of a dominant white American culture. Like Clarke, Sears alters the roles of the characters, and their motivations, in Shakespeare's original play. Through *Harlem Duet*, Othello's marriage to Desdemona becomes tainted with the destruction of Billie and the rejection of Black Harlem culture. As a stereotypically shrill faculty wife, Desdemona is undone as the heroine and the strawberry-spotted handkerchief is now Billie's wedding-day present that Othello merely re-gifts to Desdemona. Sears, in fact, makes Billie responsible for putting a spell on the handkerchief and thereby prompts Desdemona's ultimate death in Shakespeare's *Othello*. In this way, Sears dethrones Iago as the vice figure because *Harlem Duet* poses racism and Billie's spell as the catalysts of Othello's enraged downfall.

Ultimately, Clarke and Sears highlight political adaptation's strategy of disidentification by using the main characters to enact the limitations of identification and counteridentification with gender and racial expectations. While Gertrude and Othello articulate strategies of identification, Playwright and Billie attempt to counteridentify with dominant white patriarchal ideologies. Neither of these two strategies, however, is successful. Identification fails: Ophelia tries to identify with feminine gender roles but goes mad in the absence of Hamlet and her father; Gertrude ironically debases the very patriarchy that she so desperately tries to support; and Othello always already fails to align completely with white American culture. Likewise, counteridentification also fails: Playwright's refusals to participate in mainstage theatres or in an androcentric canon recede as she eventually gives into the demands of the male director; Billie's rejection of white culture inevitably reinforces the racial dichotomy that plagues her by enacting inverse racism. In his analysis of the interracial child in *Harlem Duet* and *Othello*, David Huebert underscores Billie's troubling racism:

> As *Othello* demonstrates, the fear of the sexualized black male entering white communities and reproducing therein has been a cause of severe racial phobia since the early seventeenth century. Billie's anxiety about interracial coupling, then, is both understandable and problematic: understandable insofar as for her racial mixture carries the weight of historical trauma, problematic insofar as her discomfort

> with the relationship between Othello and Mona threatens to recapitulate historical prejudice and stereotypes. (43)

Billie's counteridentification perpetuates the same type of prejudice that she longs to eradicate – a structural weakness that José Esteban Muñoz warns about in his discussion of counteridentification. The failed acts of identification and counteridentification, in turn, draw attention to the flimsiness of identity as an all-too-simple performance.

Iago's famous "I am not what I am" speech from Shakespeare's *Othello* best encapsulates political adaptations' disidentificatory relationship to their source (1.1.69).[3] His confessional aside sets up a binary of identificatory categories, "I am" and "I am not," only to merge the two. With "I am not what I am," the second "I am" carries with it a now tacit "not." Iago recasts his performances of honesty as acts of mischief, providing a new code of behaviour that layers truths with fictions and creates a nuanced and complex experience for the audience: at this point in the play, the other characters (mainly Othello) perceive Iago's performances as truthful, whereas the extra-diegetic audience understands them to be dishonest. In other words, Iago's speech acts succeed according to the play's onstage audience and fail according to its offstage audience.[4] After the "I am not what I am" aside, Iago's subsequent declarations perform a transformative doubleness – an "am" and "am not" – that speaks to political adaptation's disidentificatory relationship with its source material.

An adaptation announces its relation to its sources in terms of "am" (repetition) and "am not" (difference), and it is this convergence and divergence that creates meaning. Just as political adaptation aims to transform the source by working with and against it, disidentification "is a strategy that tries to transform a cultural logic from within, always labouring to enact permanent structural change while at the same time valuing the importance of local or everyday struggles of resistance" (Muñoz 12). Clarke's and Sears's political adaptations realize the political potential of disidentification by working with and against Shakespeare to re-signify the identities of his marginalized characters. The plays "labou[r] to enact permanent structural change" in the way Shakespeare's Othello, Gertrude, and Ophelia are performed, but they also celebrate the value of changing the significance of the characters within the adaptations themselves. As Clarke's Playwright says, "we're supposed to identify like crazy with Hamlet and his pals, feeling our ever-so-neat fear and pity, because all the nasty bits have been displaced into her. Well, I'm here to tell you it's a crock. I identify with Gertrude and I don't like the bad press she's been getting" (2). *Gertrude and Ophelia* and *Harlem Duet* effectively transform the major characters from within the canon. These two plays, then, further reinforce my argument that political adaptation performs disidentification.

Adaptors and theatre scholars point to the inherent doubleness of political adaptation. Clarke herself draws on the doubleness of political adaptation when she explains in an interview with the *Canadian Adaptations of Shakespeare Project* (CASP) that "I try to practice a 'both/and' art rather than an 'either/or' oversimplification" in *Gertrude and Ophelia*, and "I hope that I critique and honour at the same time." In "'Redescribing a World': Towards a Theory of Shakespearean Adaptation in Canada," Linda Burnett further speaks to how political adaptations simultaneously "critique and honour" and provides a helpful overview of racial and feminist transformations in four plays: Ann-Marie MacDonald's *Goodnight Desdemona*, Clarke's *Gertrude and Ophelia*, Ken Gass's *Claudius*, and Sears's *Harlem Duet*. Burnett suggests,

> what is really significant about these playwrights' endeavour is their refusal to start a new picture from scratch. Instead of painting over Shakespeare's work, they touch it up some places and in others add their own representations to stand beside his. In so doing, they are engaged in the […] project that [Salman] Rushdie calls "redescribing a world." And by adding to the cultural canvas those perspectives previously left out of the picture, they are, again in Rushdie's words, taking the "necessary first step toward changing" a world. (9)

While Clarke and Burnett discuss the doubleness of these works – that "critique and honour" (Interview) and both "pay tribute to" and "sabotage" Shakespeare (Burnett 5) – I seek to further complicate this doubleness by approaching Canadian political adaptations as a disidentification with (or identification with and against) Shakespeare.

Clarke's and Sears's plays disidentify with Shakespeare and the mainstages that house his work, but they also promote disidentification as an effective strategy for dealing with a canonical storyteller. In this chapter, I consider how the plays disidentify not simply with Shakespeare but also with Canada's theatre industry. In doing so, I contextualize the critical understanding that Shakespeare's presence in Canada speaks to the (non-Indigenous) nation's from elsewhereness. Furthermore, I argue that Shakespeare's role in Canada is defined by the same doubleness that structures political adaptation: a performance of difference and sameness. Canada is a nation to which Shakespeare does and does not belong; just as *Gertrude and Ophelia* and *Harlem Duet* are plays to which Shakespeare's protagonists do and do not belong. Canada's long-standing disidentification with Shakespeare sets the stage for more recent political adaptations that disidentify with his plays. The failed performances of identification and counteridentification gesture towards the potential of disidentification as a mediating strategy in these plays. In short, I approach *Gertrude and Ophelia* and *Harlem Duet* as theorizations of political adaptation's performance of disidentification.

Disidentifying with the Theatre Industry

Historical portraits of theatre in Canada have often been Janus-faced, with mainstage theatres like Stratford Festival on one side, and smaller alternative theatres on the other. Although Canadian theatre is no longer as stratified, this double-sided image reflects two recurring definitions of Canadian theatre as either theatre in Canada or theatre by Canadians, respectively. The Stratford Festival is the largest classical repertory theatre in North America. Though critics have celebrated the Stratford Festival as Canada's most internationally renowned theatre, the company concentrates on Shakespeare's works and has a history of employing artists from abroad. With the boom of Canadian literary arts and theatre houses in the 1970s, Canada's theatres and dramatists redefined mainstream conceptions of theatre and dedicated themselves more and more to using Canadian playwrights, actors, and directors. Canadian political adaptations such as *Gertrude and Ophelia* and *Harlem Duet* go so far as to challenge mainstream theatres as a platform for canonical works that marginalize diverse storytellers and performers. Many mid-size theatres stage political adaptations and have political mandates, such as Nightwood Theatre (Toronto's oldest professional feminist theatre company), Buddies in Bad Times Theatre (invested in queer theatre), and Native Earth Performing Arts (devoted to Indigenous works). Yet when playwrights adapt Shakespeare for a politicized purpose, the two profiles meet. Bringing together these two facets of Canadian theatre, Clarke's *Gertrude and Ophelia* and Sears's *Harlem Duet* perform disidentification by simultaneously capitalizing on and disavowing their Shakespearean sources as well as Canadian mainstage theatres.

Both plays premiered at smaller alternative theatres while also paying tribute to Shakespeare and the mainstages that his work tends to occupy. *Gertrude and Ophelia* was, as Clarke explains, "successful at a local level because word of mouth alone filled the theatres in which my play was produced with packed houses every night the play was performed" (Interview). Since its conception as a student performance at Winnipeg's The Gas Station Theatre produced by the Black Hole Theatre Company in 1987, *Gertrude and Ophelia* has been performed at Calgary's Pumphouse Theatre (1992) and at Victoria's City Theatre (1993). Maenad Productions – a feminist theatre group in Alberta (1987–2001) – produced the 1992 show and advertised the play as a "feminist revisioning" while also relating it to Stoppard's canonical play *Rosencrantz and Guildenstern Are Dead* (the spin-off of Shakespeare's *Hamlet* that focuses on two male courtiers). In a newsletter, Maenad Productions announced that "Rosencrantz and Guildenstern are dead, but what about Gertrude and Ophelia? Both are very much alive in GERTRUDE AND OPHELIA, Margaret Clarke's feminist revisioning of Hamlet's women" (File 18).[5] If there was any doubt about Clarke's feminist approach, the poster for Maenad's production features their logo of a maenad (see figure 2.1, top right) as well as an image of a woman (see figure 2.1, centre). The name "Maenad Productions" references the maenads, the "raving women" (literal translation of their name) who were the followers of Dionysus, the Greek god of theatre, and his Roman counterpart, Bacchus: this production of *Gertrude and Ophelia* dramatizes a female response to male-created drama. The advertising for *Gertrude and Ophelia* positions Clarke and her characters in relation to Shakespeare much like the maenads' relation to Dionysus. The Maenad theatre company and Clarke's show promote an announced political "feminine vision" (Newsletter) that reframes this tradition by focusing on women with the goal of "reinstat[ing] the maenadic wild women of Greece to their rightful place in the theatrical spectrum" (Maenad Theatre Productions fonds). The 1992 production of *Gertrude and Ophelia*, then, disidentifies with the Shakespeare theatre tradition through the script, the producing theatre company, and its advertisement.

Gertrude and Ophelia was greeted with full theatre houses during its amateur productions, but professional theatres were not interested in staging the play, according to Clarke: "when I offered this play to various professional theatres across Canada, the fact that it would attract audiences gave it no advantage. It was called 'non-theatrical' or unsuitable for production" (Interview). For Clarke, then, the production history of *Gertrude and Ophelia*

Figure 2.1 Maenad Theatre Productions' poster for the 1992 production of Margaret Clarke's *Gertrude and Ophelia*.

gestures towards the power of mainstages to exclude and marginalize certain voices. As Clarke explains, "the risks of speaking truth to power are no different today then they ever were" because "the people can like your art, but the gatekeepers of artistic power have to also like your art if it is to be widely available" (Interview).

Although they premiered only five years apart, *Harlem Duet*'s production history, tells a different story about political adaptations' place on Canadian mainstages. The popularity of Sears's political adaptation, which found a home at the iconic Stratford Festival in Ontario, suggests that it was not necessarily cultural gatekeeping that kept *Gertrude and Ophelia* off the mainstage. Just as likely, *Gertrude and Ophelia*'s graphic and extended dramatization of an on-stage pregnancy loss may have deterred professional theatres from picking up the play. Clarke's point about pleasing cultural gatekeepers, however, remains: Clarke and Sears both use Shakespeare as a shared canonical reference point from which to critique theatrical tradition.

Sears's *Harlem Duet*, as did *Gertrude and Ophelia*, had its premiere with a small alternative theatre – opening at Toronto's Tarragon Extra Space theatre in 1997 (20 April to 18 May) and produced by Nightwood Theatre. But in contrast, Sears's play was welcomed by mainstage theatres precisely because it represented marginalized perspectives on race and involved an all-Black cast. The Canadian Stage Theatre mounted *Harlem Duet* the very same year it premiered (27 October to 29 November 1997) and it was later performed at Halifax's Neptune Theatre (2000), New York City's Blue Heron Arts Centre (2002), Royal Holloway University's RHUL Studio (2002), and Ontario's Stratford Festival (2006). While *Gertrude and Ophelia* has been credited as "the only contemporary Canadian dramatic revisioning of *Hamlet* by a woman" (Knowles, *Shakespeare* 125), the 2006 production of *Harlem Duet* was celebrated as Stratford's first show with an all-Black cast.

Harlem Duet's production at Stratford drew attention to the festival's history of staging white Canadian and European plays. Margaret Jane Kidnie observes that "For the audiences watching the history-making Stratford production in 2006, the challenges of sight, race, and the continuing production of Othello within the Canadian theatrical establishment were perhaps not resolved, so much as further deepened" (*Shakespeare* 87). Despite the landmark production with the first all-Black cast at Stratford Festival, the festival still marginalized the Black actors to "Black plays" or small parts:

> At the 2006 Stratford Festival, black actors could star in black plays, but were otherwise relegated to minor roles. In *The Duchess of Malfi*, the *Harlem Duet* cast played such juicy roles as "understudy," "Malateste," "Doctor," and "Madwoman," which arguably undermines Stratford's project of improving records of ethnic and racial representation. In 2012, there were no black playwrights, but black actors played leading roles in *Elektra* and *Cymbeline*. (McKinnon 315)

Examining Stratford Festival's 2006 production of *Harlem Duet*, James McKinnon convincingly suggests that "the production's publicity paratexts used Shakespeare to encourage spectators to read the production as an emblem of African Canadian culture, to encourage intercultural engagement, and especially to promote a vision of the Stratford Festival as a (newly) inclusive, multicultural institution" (292). While Kidnie and McKinnon, among others, point to the work that remains to be done in creating a diverse Stratford Festival, McKinnon offers an optimistic interpretation of the 2006 production.[6] Examining the production as an event that attracted Black actors and audiences to the otherwise white streets of Stratford, Ontario, McKinnon argues that "*Harlem Duet* worked productively towards Sears's vision of a world in which black spectators can always find a play that appeals to them, and white spectators realize that not everyone can take this privilege for granted" (312). *Harlem Duet* worked in, on, and against the politics of Stratford Festival's mainstage in order to transform it into a place that joined a diverse set of spectators – even if only for one season.

Clarke's and Sears's scripts as well as their production histories disidentify with mainstage theatre houses and the politics of whose stories get told on mainstages across Canada. In addition to challenging the Canadian theatre industry and re-identifying previously marginalized characters, both plays banish central canonical figures to the physical margins of the stage: Clarke's Playwright refuses to allow Hamlet into her play and rejects the patriarchal demands of mainstage theatres, just as Sears denies Desdemona access to the stage and critiques productions of *Othello* that fail to change the original. Yet neither *Gertrude and Ophelia* nor *Harlem Duet* escape the force of the sources they seek to revise, as Hamlet and Desdemona haunt the political adaptations. No matter how hard Clarke and Sears try to challenge Shakespeare's canonical renown and the popular representations of Gertrude as a hyper-sexualized succubus, or of Othello in blackface, their plays cannot undo their Shakespearean counterparts. Owing to their unavoidable dependence on Shakespeare's *Hamlet* and *Othello*, *Gertrude and Ophelia* and *Harlem Duet* disidentify with mainstage productions of Shakespeare's virgin-whore duo (Ophelia and Gertrude, respectively) and famous Moor (Othello).

The history of Shakespeare's plays in Canadian theatre helps to account for Clarke and Sears's simultaneous embrace and disgrace of their renowned source materials and the mainstage theatres, such as Stratford Festival, that celebrate them. As is the case for many theatres worldwide, a persistent belonging and unbelonging govern Shakespeare's role in Canadian theatres despite dramatists' best efforts to appropriate Shakespeare as Canadian. The *Canadian Theatre Encyclopedia*'s entry on Shakespeare, for instance, heralds him as the "most produced non-Canadian playwright" in Canada. Irena Makaryk's celebration of Shakespeare comes with a fitting provision when she explains that "the phrase 'a world elsewhere' is an apt metaphor for the position of Shakespeare in Canada" because it alludes "to difference and sameness" (3). Shakespeare is embraced as a sign of "Canadian theatre," but fulfilling Judith Butler's definition of disidentification, it is a sign to which he does and does not belong. Further reflecting the pervasive disidentification with Shakespeare in Canada, Clarke notes that "we are good at honouring Shakespeare, witness everything from the Stratford festival to our typical high school curriculum and good at deflating bardology, witness everything from Wayne and Shuster's old TV skits to the ongoing genre of 'adaptations' [and political adaptations] which offer various new, and subversive, readings of old materials" (Interview). Shakespeare's role as a "Canadian playwright," then, is characterized by a simultaneous appropriation and disassociation. As Sears's Billie pointedly says, "the Shakespeare's mine, but you can have it" (52).

Although there is no doubt about Shakespeare's prominence in Canada, the relevance of Shakespeare productions to a Canadian theatre culture has been especially controversial since the inception of the Stratford Festival. Beginning as a national theatre in 1957, Ontario's Stratford Festival was founded by a British director (Tyrone Guthrie) and has been criticized for relying on American and British artists (actors, directors, playwrights). In historicizing the problematic relationship between Shakespeare and national theatre in Canada, Margaret Groome explains that "this tension was manifested in theatrical discussions that stressed the importance of developing a national dramatic canon while simultaneously favouring the English model of theatre and making a decided turn to Shakespeare" (109). Ontario's Stratford Festival has received critical backlash for its homage to Shakespeare and its efforts to replicate England. "With the growth of Canadian nationalism during the 1970s," Makaryk explains, "Shakespeare and Stratford came increasingly under attack from some quarters, since both were perceived as enshrining Canada's colonial dependence" (25). These attacks consider the Stratford Festival's productions of Shakespeare to be anti-nationalistic and derivative of a colonial mentality. Clarke and Sears's adaptations, therefore, speak to a national, and even transnational, controversy over Shakespeare's cultural importance.

Though the popularity of Shakespeare in Canada has garnered mixed responses, political adaptations of Shakespeare can play to both sides of the debate by working with and against Shakespeare's canonical renown. These adaptations often target Shakespeare from a specific political perspective in order to transform canonical representations of marginalized identities. For instance, Ken Mitchell and Humphrey and the Dumptrucks' production of *Cruel Tears* (1975) addresses class issues in a populist version of *Othello*;[7] Tibor Egervari's "*Le Marchand de Venise*" *de Shakespeare à Auschwitz* (1977) sets *The Merchant of Venice* in Nazi Germany and highlights the original's anti-Semitism;[8] MacDonald's *Goodnight Desdemona (Good Morning Juliet)* (1988) engages with feminist-queer issues while adapting *Othello* and *Romeo and Juliet*;[9] and Timothy Findley's *Elizabeth Rex* (2000) uses the cross-dressing in *Much Ado About Nothing* as a catalyst for considering the performativity of gender and queer sexuality.[10] Knowles compares *Othello* adaptations – *Cruel Tears, Goodnight Desdemona*, and *Harlem Duet* – from three consecutive decades (the seventies, eighties, and nineties) as representative of the shifting political concerns from class, to feminism, and finally, to the intersectionality of class, feminism, and race. Each adaptation, as Knowles says, "is very much a product of its place and moment and, at the same time, productive of its own and subsequent moments as a marker of, and site for, the negotiation of social change around specific issues" ("Othello" 39). As these examples show, there is a standing tradition of Canadian Shakespeare adaptations that reflect their political environment while voicing the need for certain changes.

Gertrude and Ophelia comments on the Shakespeare industry in Canada, and more specifically, on Canadian mainstage theatres. Clarke uses gender politics to frame her critique of mainstage theatres, satirizing the popularity of Shakespeare and Stoppard as the current arbiters of a gender hierarchy that marginalizes female characters and writers in the theatre. *Gertrude and Ophelia* features a female Playwright who warns, "it's a world with many seductions, including the mainstage" (48). For Clarke's Playwright, mainstage theatres are mainstream, hegemonic theatres. Because the "eternal male script" and mainstage theatres are mutually constitutive in Clarke's play, Playwright must reject both. In a metatheatrical moment, Actor warns:

> ACTOR: Your play will wear itself out on little stages like this … what is this place … a gas station, a fire hall?
> PLAYWRIGHT: A pumphouse.
> ACTOR: Whatever. This play is never getting onto a mainstage without a Prince Hamlet. (48)

Clarke acknowledges the real Pumphouse Theatre venue as a symbolic consequence of her concentration on only female characters and her refusal to foreground Hamlet's character. Located in Calgary, the Pumphouse Theatre's mandate "is committed not only to providing a high-quality venue for the arts but also to keeping that venue affordable for Calgary's arts community" (*Pumphouse*, "Virtual Tour").[11] The staging of *Gertrude and Ophelia* there suggests that the small Pumphouse Theatre venue's mandate inevitably goes hand in hand with the play's political rejection of a phallocentric canon because mainstage theatres, such as Stratford Festival Theatre, privilege the male characters and would not be interested in a feminist staging of *Hamlet*. In fact, the metatheatrical moment challenges other theatre venues to produce a version of *Hamlet* without the Prince of Denmark himself. With one foot in and one foot out of Shakespearean theatre tradition, Clarke uses the play to reflect on the theatres that will and will not house her political Shakespeare adaptation.

Gertrude and Ophelia calls attention to and works to reject the tradition of an all-male cast (including boys playing female roles) in Shakespeare's theatre through her fight for an all-female cast. In this way, Playwright's feminist adaptation not only critiques Shakespeare's male-dominated script but also the all-male performance dynamics that brought it to life originally. Playwright speaks to the play-within-a-play's disidentification with Shakespeare's theatre tradition when she explains that she is "writing inside" of *Hamlet* in order to "write myself *out* of the world that Shakespeare had to live *in*" (48; emphasis added).

While *Gertrude and Ophelia* attacks commercial and patriarchal demands on the theatre, *Harlem Duet* critiques racial inequality in universities, theatres, and other institutions. In the main plotline, Sears's Othello works as a professor at Columbia University, or "Harlumbia" as his landlord calls it, where he encounters racism and must "White wash" his race by mimicking the behaviour and attitude of his white colleagues in order to advance (353). The scene of Othello putting on white shaving cream visually draws attention to his desire to don a white mask (see figure 2.2). The whitefaced Othello, however, also inverts the history of white actors in blackface who have performed the role of Othello. In the 1928 narrative thread, for instance, HE is an actor who struggles with the minstrel tradition as he longs to be "of Ira Aldridge stock" and perform Shakespearean roles without blackface (363). After reading Sears's foreword to *Harlem Duet*, it is not surprising that the play targets universities and theatres as propagators for racial stereotypes: Sears explains how

"Shakespeare's Othello had haunted me since I first was introduced to him. Sir Laurence Olivier in black-face" (14). Clarke and Sears use their political adaptations both to revise the original plays and to challenge some of the very industries and institutions – academia and theatre – that house them.

Gertrude and Ophelia: Failed Counteridentification with the Male Script

Gertrude and Ophelia and *Harlem Duet* are fitting companion plays to study because Clarke keeps Hamlet and the male director off-stage in order to foreground the female characters Gertrude and Ophelia, while Sears keeps the white Mona (Desdemona) offstage in order to concentrate on Othello and Billie. Yet, both plays also feature an on-stage criticism of these gender or race reversals as a problematic form of counteridentification. The plays, for instance, counteract the omission of Hamlet and Mona with many discussions of the two absentees. Clarke and Sears may relegate Hamlet and Mona to the physical margins of the stage, but the canonical figures haunt both works. Hamlet and Mona's ghost-like presence personifies what Muñoz describes as the "phantasm of normative [identity]" that cannot be undone because of the illusive promise of accepted normalcy (4). The failure to counteridentify with Shakespeare's Hamlet and Desdemona results in a performance of disidentification: Clarke and Sears's plays simultaneously identify with and against the source's famous protagonists by rejecting them while at the same time reinforcing their enduring significance and spectral presence.

In *Gertrude and Ophelia* the male director figure embodies the phantasm of normative gender: he is never seen but his "male directorial voice" (27) can be heard from off-stage and the male Actor relays the director's desire for "something to represent the men who are missing from the action" (3) of the inset play. In this way, the male director and Actor defend and thereby give a presence to Hamlet. The Playwright and Actor's overarching discussion over whether to include the tragic Prince parodies Hamlet's "to be or not to be" dilemma in Shakespeare's version, making the debate all the more significant. At the end of *Gertrude and Ophelia*, Hamlet makes an appearance when the male Actor finally gets to perform the role of the Prince of Denmark. The play is structured by the male Actor's constant interruptions and by Playwright's repeated directives to "Get out of my play" (6, 16) and "get out of

Figure 2.2 Karen Robinson (SHE) and Nigel Shawn Williams (HE) in Stratford Festival's 2006 production of *Harlem Duet*.

here" (11), which playfully appropriate Hamlet's "get thee to a nunnery" in Shakespeare's version (3.1.122). These disruptive episodes mark scene breaks for the inset play, and also function as a type of dumb show about the Playwright's and Clarke's political struggle with a patriarchal theatre tradition. As a result, the failed attempt to remove Hamlet from the inset play structures the play proper, effectively dramatizing that a political adaptation can never divest itself completely from its troubled source material

Clarke's Playwright refuses to appease the male director and overtly counter-identifies with Shakespeare, Stoppard, and an androcentric canon. In rejecting Hamlet and the mainstage, Playwright explains that she wants Gertrude and Ophelia's obsessions "on the stage, not his, not his body on the stage, his flesh invading my play" (48). Playwright even performs the role of Gertrude in the play-within-the-play, and when Playwright breaks character she refuses to comply with popular representations of Gertrude as an emblem of female subordination. In a scene following Ophelia's death, Playwright performs the role of Gertrude but refuses to wear a veil because it emblematizes female silence and passivity: "If you expect me to play this melodrama at least let me play it with out [*sic*] having my mouth stuffed with lace. Talk about silencing the female voice!" (46). Playwright, however, eventually acquiesces to the male director's requests and rehearses a scene with Hamlet that adds a "male presence" and "a little relief from all that female realism" (29). Doomed from the start, Playwright's feminist production of *Hamlet* does not counteridentify fully with Shakespeare's original work.

Clarke's Gertrude, by contrast, chooses to work within the patriarchal codes of female duties and marriage in order to protect Hamlet's right to the crown. By marrying Hamlet's uncle, Gertrude ensures that "there can be only one heir – my only son" because she "cannot conceive […] a legitimate heir" for Claudius (10). The Queen further explains that her "marriage [to Claudius] is the best thing for everyone" (11) and that women must always make sure that their husbands "succeed" (13). Gertrude advises Ophelia that "Men are not the hot goats they all pretend to be and if they fail at love … they always find a way to blame that failure on the woman […] So it is important, when you come to wed, no matter what it means for you, he must succeed" (13). Highlighting the sheer performativity of sexualized gender roles, Gertrude's instructions to Ophelia advocate strategies that identify with and support stereotypes of the virile man and submissive woman. Gertrude pointedly explains to Ophelia, "You did right to obey your father and your King" (17). Even after Hamlet rapes Ophelia, Gertrude instructs her to "*act* as if nothing happened" and to "be your usual gentle self" in order to lure Hamlet into marriage (15; emphasis added). For Gertrude, Hamlet and Ophelia have simply consecrated their marriage without "the words of the church" because "the same blood would come to you on your wedding night" (15). Commenting on Ophelia's discussion of the rape in the 1992 Pumphouse production of *Gertrude and Ophelia*, Clarke explains:

> The director of the Maenad production, Joyce Doolittle, made a wise choice when she had Gertrude in bed as the scene begins, and had her take Ophelia into bed with her, as a mother might a young child. I once remarked to Barbara Campbell-Brown, the actor who played Gertrude in the Maenad production, that this was her hardest scene since she must establish the opposites of Gertrude's situation, her love and her political scheming, her divided loyalties, her strength and her ultimate helplessness. Having, in the past, played Gertrude in Shakespeare's play, Campbell-Brown asked me if I had ever counted the scenes in which Gertrude stands silent in Hamlet, in which the woman playing her part must act only with her body, never her voice. She said it was wonderful to finally have words to work with!

In the scene after Ophelia's rape, Gertrude frames femininity in terms of a conscious performance of submissiveness for male onlookers, and she preaches identification with gender stereotypes and patriarchal notions of wifely duties as a survival strategy. Clarke, however, offers a violent warning against Gertrude's identification with meek feminine roles by giving the female characters a voice and by staging Hamlet's rape of Ophelia. *Gertrude and Ophelia*, then, undermines the Playwright's performances of counteridentification with the "male script" as well as Gertrude's identification with submissive femininity.

Ultimately, it is in performing the role of Gertrude that Playwright most successfully destabilizes Prince Hamlet's role as protagonist. Despite the Playwright's efforts to focus exclusively on the female characters, she eventually gives in to the male director and rehearses a scene between Hamlet and his mother; but as Gertrude she unravels the Prince's tragic role through comedy. While the inexperienced male Actor plays the role of Hamlet, Playwright performs the role of Gertrude and effectively "*upstages him for comic effect in all the subversive ways that an experienced actor can*" (46). Gertrude quite literally takes over for Hamlet as she recites his lines:

> ACTOR: "Shall I lift this veil ..." (*realizes there is no veil on the now sweetly smiling face of "Playwright" and throws up his hands*). Damn!
> PLAYWRIGHT: (*prompting*) and show the world's corruption in the face of a woman? Gosh, I know your scene better than you do. (47)

With this interruption, Playwright both upstages and replaces Hamlet; Clarke's Gertrude is "better" than Hamlet (47). The Actor's performance of Hamlet fails, and the frame instructs the audience of this failure: as Actor complains to Playwright, "You are ruining my scene. You are doing it deliberately" (48). Playwright then asserts, "We cannot have your scene, because your scene is Prince Hamlet's scene and I will not have him in my play" (48).

In addition to Playwright's superior acting abilities and refusal to accept Hamlet's scene in her play, sexual innuendos further render Hamlet's originally serious speech comedic. Following Gertrude's story about Claudius's shortcomings in the bedroom, Actor performs the role of Hamlet and recites the following monologue:

> I do not hate you mother. I love you. And hate myself bitterly that I can not [*sic*] stop loving such a woman. To be such a man! To love such a woman as you! I thought I had hardened my heart against you, but while I was away I softened and felt once again as I did when I was a child. Then you were my angel-mother. I forgot your recent sins. Forgave your frailty. Then my first sight when I return is you like some black spider, crouched over her grave, strewing flowers like poison venom on her sweet body. (47)

With a "hardened" and "softened" heart, the sexual symbolism is overt in this scene: Hamlet is emotionally and phallically "soft" in the absence of his mother but longs for her as he did as a child, which, as Freud suggests, is a very sexual longing. Throughout the scene, as the stage directions explain, "Playwright overplays the lines, presenting the most 'Freudian' of Gertrudes" (46). This comic performance of the Freudian mother usurps Hamlet's tragic speech, transforming it into a parody of the many psychoanalytic treatments of *Hamlet.* According to Freud, Oedipus and Hamlet share the same "basic wish-phantasy of the child" (257): "the death of the father" and, as a "complement" to this wish, the desire to have "sexual intercourse with one's mother" (257). Clarke's sexual innuendos purposefully echo Freudian psychoanalytic interpretations of Shakespeare's original play. Yet the performance of this speech renders masculinity, not femininity, as "frailty." The earlier "not-so-wedding night" scene about Claudius's failed sexual performance with Gertrude places the "softened" Hamlet among a cast of men who fail to perform in both the sexual and the theatrical sense.

Whereas Shakespeare pins our empathy to Prince Hamlet and suggests that Gertrude helped orchestrate the death of King Hamlet, Clarke pointedly rejects "Shakespeare's Gertrude" (2) and defends the Queen. In Clarke's play, Gertrude gains the audience's sympathy over Hamlet because she is not the virago that we expect:

> PLAYWRIGHT: as "The Mother," Gertrude is like an ideological sponge. The crap and piss left over from shaping the play, is sucked up into the Gertrude character, where we can safely feel all the disgust and contempt we want. Then we're supposed to identify like crazy with Hamlet and his pals, feeling our ever-so-neat fear and pity, because all the nasty bits have been displaced into her. Well, I'm here to tell you it's a crock. I identify with Gertrude and I don't like the bad press she's been getting. (2)

From this opening scene, Playwright clearly informs the audience, and the male Actor, of her "feminist" (2) reinterpretation of Shakespeare's *Hamlet* and desire to flesh out the character of Gertrude as a more sympathetic character. Further aligning the audience with the female characters, Hamlet's Freudian speech and the women's songs point to his harmful duplicity towards Ophelia. Hamlet is not only "hardened" and "softened" (7) but also, as Gertrude's songs warn, "frost and fire" (16).[12] As well as critiquing Hamlet's treatment of Ophelia and Gertrude, Clarke thematizes the Prince's ambiguity towards Ophelia and indecision through binaric imagery, which parodies popular understandings of *Hamlet*'s women as virgins or whores. Clarke adapts the virgin-whore binary and applies it to the male characters who are cast as either "soft" or "hard," "frost" or "fire." Hamlet's failed sexual performance in the inset play as a "softened" man and as Ophelia's romantic companion, together with Actor's inability to perform the role of Hamlet adequately in the play proper, are central to Clarke's critique of Shakespeare and point to her play's disidentification with its source.

While the inset Playwright aims to restore Shakespeare's female characters by completely excluding the tragic prince, Clarke's political adaptation, in turn, completes this restorative goal through disidentification by simultaneously including and excluding Hamlet. In *Gertrude and Ophelia*'s only scene with Hamlet, Gertrude undermines Hamlet's tragic role through her ironic performance, parodies Freudian interpretations, reduces him to a binary, and after all tragic tenor has been robbed from his role, she pillages his speech by performing his lines. Instead of ending with bloodshed, Playwright (Gertrude) and Actress (Ophelia) conclude the play proper. Ophelia is not revived but the actor who plays her is, when Playwright and Actress cordially leave the stage together and Actress promises that "Everything will be fine" (52). Clarke's play as a whole disidentifies with the androcentrism that Gertrude submits to and Playwright tries to eradicate. As Mark Fortier says, "Clarke's play, after all, unlike the Playwright's, includes a scene from *Hamlet*, even if it is to be played suspiciously or ironically" ("Undead and Unsafe" 351). Illustrating the central characteristic of political adaptation, Clarke's play disidentifies with *Hamlet* because it calls attention to the struggles of at once heeding to and countering the canonical source and its scholarly significance.

Robert Stam argues that adaptations are often denounced because of logocentrism, or, the love of words and text: as Stam explains, adaptations usually take a visual form (such as theatre or film) and are seen as a lesser version of their documented source texts. Clarke's handling of the sensitive issues of abortion and miscarriage tackle the inability of words and text to capture performed identity. Ophelia's howl interrupts her madness monologue and does what Shakespeare's words cannot: it expresses her interiority, grief, and self-loss. *Gertrude and Ophelia*, then, dramatizes the limits of *Hamlet* as a logocentric source through the embodied pain of its female characters.

Gertrude and Ophelia exemplifies political adaptation and its act of disidentification through failed instances of identification with Shakespeare's material. Illustrating the mutually constitutive relationship of addresser and addressee or of actor and audience, Ophelia loses her sense of an "I" because of her inability to define herself as a "you" after Hamlet has unintentionally killed her father and she has then lost both parents, brother, and the Prince.

In Clarke's "Ophelia's Bower" scene (32), Ophelia's loss of relational identity and her inability to self-identify lead to her madness. As neither daughter, sister, nor lover, Ophelia quickly shifts from a playful game to a serious question of self:

> He loves me. He loves me not. He loves me … me … me … who is this 'me.' I know her not. Her father is dead. Her mother is dead! Her brother is far away. Her lover … My love is gone gone … gone sailing […] I will make words, like you, and be the victor … over (*she mouths words which have no sound. Finally giving into the pain, sound does come from her in the form of a long howl and then as the spasm subsides, she pants*). She had a love once. But he is gone. She had a brother once. But he is gone. She had a father once. But he is gone. Such wise heads! All, all, gonc … There was a lady once, who loved me. (Sings) " … your child … a feather … roof and robe and safety." Gone. Gone. But I shall make words. Words. Words. And be the winner over pain. (33)

This soliloquy begins with Ophelia plucking petals from a daisy to determine whether Hamlet loves her. Yet the juvenile "He loves me. He loves me not" game speaks to Hamlet's hurtful ambivalence towards Ophelia in both the source play and Clarke's adaptation. Ophelia's contemplation of "this me" in relation to Hamlet's affection gestures towards the gendering of the addresser and addressee in their wooing scenes, wherein the male pursuer and female object of desire perform masculine and feminine identities. Ophelia, in her conversations with Gertrude, makes it quite clear that she does or says very little in her interactions with Hamlet: when Hamlet "put his hands under [Ophelia's] skirt" she "did nothing" and "spoke no words" (5); and when he forces her to have sex with him she is similarly "quiet" (14) and succumbs to his violent actions. Ophelia is merely the object on which Hamlet acts – she is a grammatical object (me) to his subject (he). Both Gertrude and Ophelia define themselves according to their relations with male characters. For instance, Gertrude's "I" is merely the possessive object of the King as she asks, "whose Queen am I?" (23). Clarke's Ophelia suffers from a loss of self-knowledge when she does not know what Hamlet expects from her because Ophelia's identity is in large part predicated on their relationship. Without Hamlet, Ophelia does not know how to be a "me." Put another way, Clarke suggests that Shakespeare's Ophelia has been emptied of meaning because the interpretations of her character are reliant on the male protagonist for significance. Ophelia is the casualty of scholars' and mainstages' focus on Hamlet.

Clarke disidentifies with Shakespeare's Ophelia by referencing the source material's flowers and herbs from Ophelia's madness scene and retelling her decline in order to implicate Hamlet and Gertrude as causes of her madness. In addition to losing her Father and being raped by her beloved, Clarke's Ophelia feels betrayed by Gertrude her mother figure, and sole solace, throughout *Gertrude and Ophelia*. Ophelia is most emphatic when mourning the loss of the maternal Gertrude, or "a lady" (33): Clarke uses an exclamation mark after "Her mother is dead!" (whereas her father, brother, and lover get no such emphasis in the script) and Ophelia performs the hyperbolic "All, all, gone" after her description of Gertrude's abandonment (33).

"Ophelia's Bower" scene performs the double loss of Gertrude as a maternal figure and of Ophelia as a mother herself. In *Hamlet*, Ophelia sings of abortifacients through the code of various flowers and herbs. Clarke develops these references by suggesting that Ophelia is pregnant. Throughout a climactic scene in *Gertrude and Ophelia*, Ophelia has "*very painful uterine contractions*" and, while it is unclear if it is a miscarriage or abortion, she experiences a pregnancy loss (32). "Ophelia's Bower" scene is a reaction to and enactment of the loss of the maternal. With her howl and "words without sounds" (33), Ophelia's pregnancy loss is marked with inarticulateness and an absence of a subject – a powerful scene that exposes what Shakespeare's play leaves out; that is, the painful consequences of Hamlet's behaviour and some context for Ophelia's death. While psychologists report that abortion can cause feelings of self-loss, pregnancy loss is not merely a catalyst but an act of self-loss and a future in Clarke's play. Mary Frost and John T. Condon explain that the end of a pregnancy is often experienced as a crisis of self-identity: "the baby is experienced as part of the mother. Thus, the loss of part of the self in miscarriage results in an abundance of confused feelings" (56). This causal relationship between miscarriage or abortion and self-loss is reversed in *Gertrude and Ophelia* when Ophelia's mental breakdown precedes her self-induced abortion. Ophelia sings of daisies and rosemary at the end of act 1, and her mental breakdown culminates in the second act with the abortion: as the stage directions note, "Ophelia's Bower" scene takes place with "*Ophelia on her knees, legs apart, her body slightly rocking. The basket is directly in front of her. The front and back of the skirt is visibly stained with her blood as are her hands. She is having very painful uterine contractions intermittently throughout this scene*" (32). These painful contractions punctuate her soliloquy on the loss of her mother figure, father, brother, Hamlet, and most importantly, of Ophelia's "me" (33). Her loss of self is at once dramatized as and heightened by the abortion or pregnancy loss.

Ophelia's rape and pregnancy are a symbolic undoing of her selfhood because they effectively invalidate her archetypal role as "virgin." While Shakespeare's Hamlet directs sexual innuendos at Ophelia, Clarke's Hamlet violently rapes her. In *Gertrude and Ophelia*, Ophelia's pregnancy is a physical sign of her loss of virginity and a bodily reminder of Hamlet's rape. Although the exact cause of the pregnancy loss remains ambiguous, Gertrude suggests that Ophelia tried to "abort" the baby by using "plants" and "potions," which is why I refer to it as an abortion (33).[13] She was not in control of her impregnation through rape, but with the abortion, Ophelia seems to enact some agency. The pregnancy loss completes Ophelia's descent into madness, but because the abortion is self-induced, she arguably chooses this self-disassociation as she extricates herself from the patriarchal web that Gertrude more successfully navigates. Ophelia's abortion, then, does not merely resemble or occur in tandem with her inner breakdown, it *is* her breakdown. The abortion is not a simile but a catachresis: the play conflates the literal abortion with the figurative loss of the self. As Gertrude says, "She has tried to abort herself" (33). With the abortion of her selfhood, therefore, Ophelia calls attention to the violent erasure of her agency as well as her lack of control over the literal (or physical) and figurative (or artistic) reproduction of her likeness.

In *Gertrude and Ophelia*, Ophelia's signs of madness – speaking to herself, referring to herself in the third-person, releasing wordless sounds – are all instances of the breakdown of the source text and its language. Ophelia's "*howl*" (33) in Clarke's play is the antithesis to Shakespeare's philosophical Hamlet as Ophelia's sounds and spasms manifest her inability to express herself through accepted linguistic codes.[14] Betrayed by language, Ophelia regresses to a pre-linguistic stage or what Julia Kristeva defines as the semiotic domain, which, for Kristeva, involves the maternal body and connotes female madness (*Desire*).[15] The linguistic breakdown of the symbolic, which is associated with grammar and structure, externalizes Ophelia's inner breakdown. In this void of self-narration, Ophelia is a formless howl, an "O," a zero, on which "the patriarchy" (2) has scripted Freudian interpretations of the virgin-whore dyad. In *Gertrude and Ophelia*, the performed failure to express Ophelia's interiority points to the problematic non-existence of a linguistic structure that can express self-loss or female madness. Although she works within prescribed codes of self-identifications ("who is this me") and of female madness (spasms, howl), the scene also challenges and thereby disidentifies with the codes themselves.

Clarke's Ophelia complains that she fails to measure up to Hamlet in Gertrude's heart, but she succeeds in acting as a replacement for Shakespeare's Hamlet in Clarke's play. Just before her death, Ophelia confronts her subsidiary role, realizing that "Everybody saw little Ophelia, the mouse, because the Prince saw her" (41) and that even Gertrude prefers Hamlet because he is her legitimate son. Ophelia's hatred for Gertrude replace Shakespeare's confrontation scenes between Hamlet and Gertrude: just as Shakespeare's Hamlet accuses Gertrude of lying "In the rank sweat of an enseamèd bed, / Stewed in corruption, honeying and making love" with his uncle Claudius (3.4.94–5), Clarke's Ophelia labels Gertrude a "scheming, pimping mother," and more pointedly, "Gertrude the whore" (41). In this way, the structure of *Gertrude and Ophelia* – which concentrates on developing the two female characters – responds to Ophelia's complaint that everyone is too focused on Hamlet: "With you I hear nothing but the Prince" (41).

Ophelia's madness and failed identification with patriarchal demands function as subversive acts that deflate scholarly interpretations of Gertrude as a corrupt mother and of Ophelia as a virginal madwoman. Clarke's Ophelia dies because she cannot conscientiously stand by as Prince Hamlet rapes her and kills Polonius. Ophelia fulfills the fate of her double – the "little girl" who died "perfectly shaped" (10) – in adopting a child-like manner, acting as a stand-in heir, and having an aestheticized death. It is only after Ophelia's death that Gertrude realizes that she failed as a mother to the young Ophelia. Clarke thus complicates the overly simplistic characterization of Ophelia as archetypal virgin and Gertrude as archetypal mother because both characters fail in these respects: Ophelia is undone as the virgin, and Gertrude is plagued by her infertility and inability to mother any more children.

Much like Sears's inversion of the racial dynamics in Shakespeare's *Othello*, Clarke's choice to dramatize Ophelia's madness and death on the centre stage reverses the original performance dynamics in Shakespeare's *Hamlet* by enacting what was merely glossed over and reported in the original. Clarke fights against the silencing of female madness, grief, and death through the inset (female) Playwright who refuses to reduce Ophelia's death as an aside or a "bracketed phrase" (43): "Ophelia may be dead, she may even have to die off-stage, but I will not have it passed over with some bracketed phrase – 'She should have died hereafter; there would have been time for such a word' […] Macbeth, act five, scene five" (43). In dramatizing both Ophelia's death and an abortion on the stage, *Gertrude and Ophelia* exposes the tragedy of the un-narratable and of stories left untold on mainstages.

Harlem Duet: Failed Counteridentification with Racialized Skin

Harlem Duet similarly undermines performances of identification and counteridentification, which I see as underlining the potential of disidentification. Many critics, such as Kidnie and Kate Taylor, aptly focus on Sears's all-Black cast and marginalization of Mona as a radical response to Shakespeare's original staging of *Othello*, but I argue that the play offers an embedded critique of this race change as a failed performance. Although Sears's Mona, like Clarke's Hamlet, has only a brief, albeit comic, appearance, *Harlem Duet* fails to fully marginalize Mona, and the play critiques the minstrel-like production techniques that have been used to dehumanize Othello as a racial minority. Arising in nineteenth-century America, minstrel shows featured white actors in blackface who would comically enact Black stereotypes on stage, thereby reducing African-American culture to being the subject of comic targets through the presence of Black skin. Eric Gardner describes the popular Jim Crow character from minstrel performances as a "rural, enslaved, but happy African American who sings, dances, spews malapropisms, and cracks jokes" (136). Sears makes explicit references to the minstrel tradition in her foreword to the play and with the 1928 narrative thread that presents a Black actor playing Othello in blackface. Responding to this performance history, productions of *Harlem Duet* reverse the minstrel tradition by featuring an all-Black cast, by using a Black actor to play Mona, and by poking fun at a Black actor's performance of whiteness. Although Sears's casting notes merely describe Mona as "White, 30s (an off-stage voice)" (337), all productions to date have featured an all-Black cast and have used a Black actor to play Mona's minor role; after all, it is unlikely that a theatre would cast an actor to play a minor off-stage voice that merely waves her hand in one scene. In the premier production of *Harlem Duet*, the same actor – Dawn Roach – performed the role of both Amah (Billie's sister-in-law) and Mona. While Sears's Mona does not engage in song and dance, the audience laughs at the comically brief glimpse of Mona's arm and her shrill off-stage voice. These performance techniques echo strategies in Shakespeare's play that similarly isolate body parts to signal Othello's Blackness. Characters like Iago, for instance, derogate Othello for having "thick-lips" (1.1.66) and a "sooty bosom" (1.2.70). In this way, Sears adapts Iago's strategy of anatomization as well as the minstrel tradition by reducing Mona to a white hand. In a review of Stratford Festival's 2006 production, Taylor notes that the "joke" appearance of Mona's "very, very pale white arm framed in a doorway … greatly amused [the] audience." Mona is made into a "joke" by her shrill voice, by her role as the stereotypical domineering woman, and by the overt race change. The Black actor's race change and performance of Mona does not convince the audience that she is a real "White woman" nor is it intended to. In this way, the performance fails to enact convincingly a white body, but it is this failure to embody a white woman that is most subversive and disidentificatory because it performs failed minstrelsy.

The ideal that Mona represents is illusive, unattainable, and phantom. Like Clarke's Hamlet and male director figure, Sears's Mona haunts the stage and "*we see nothing of her but brief glimpses of a bare arm and a waft of light brown hair*" (47). In all three timelines Sears evokes, Othello idealizes Mona, and as Billie tells him, "White people are always the line for you, aren't they? The rule" (55). Despite Mona's physical absence, we hear her disembodied "shrill voice" and she acts as the catalyst for the main action of the play – Othello and Billie's breakup. The audience, for example, hears Othello's side of a conversation with Mona: "Hey Mone … Mone, I'm not done yet … Mone? Mona? I'm coming, OK? I'll be right … Just wait there one second, OK? OK?" (61). Although we cannot see Mona or even hear her voice during this conversation, her impact is visible and her elliptical (" … ") presence is felt. As signalled by his stuttered delivery, Othello's attitude shifts immediately from light-hearted confidence to a more serious and apprehensive tone as he begins to apologize to the off-stage Mona. As the stage directions note, Othello's "*demeanour changes*" much to Billie's "*astonishment*" (351). His confidence and dynamism fade during this conversation with Mona, and Billie explains that

Othello is "oh so happy to oblige" the "White woman" (353). Mona is talked to, described at length, and the cause of visible "*changes*" (351). In short, Mona is "the rule … the variable of control" (349).

As a preface to *Harlem Duet*, Sears gives "32 SHORT REASONS WHY I WRITE FOR THE THEATRE" where she explains that "Othello is the first African portrayed in the annals of western dramatic literature. In an effort to exorcise this ghost, I have written *Harlem Duet*" ("NOTES," 14). Yet the dramatization of *Harlem Duet* has produced a new ghost: Mona. In her review of *Harlem Duet* at Stratford, Taylor mourns Mona's failure to appear onstage. According to Taylor, Othello is "an implausible figure who is supposed to be full of racial conscience and educated intelligence yet is leaving a woman he is clearly still in love with for a *phantom*" (emphasis added). For Taylor, Mona's absence inhibits Othello's character development and believability. While Taylor interprets Mona's absence as destructive to Othello, I suggest that it is constructive to the play because it dramatizes the illusiveness of normative whiteness and reduces the power of a racialized ideal. Although the non-dramatization of Mona transforms her into a ghost, her non-existence presents whiteness as an unarticulated entity, an ellipsis. Mona symbolizes the impossibility of embodying the phantasm of normative culture. *Harlem Duet*, therefore, does much more than reverse the racial dynamics of *Othello* as it was performed in Shakespeare's time: the structure and casting of Sears's play disidentifies with earlier productions' marginalization of Shakespeare's Moor.

Disidentification and failed performance are intimately linked in both *Gertrude and Ophelia* and *Harlem Duet*. In his discussion of types of "passing," Muñoz explains "the subject who passes can be simultaneously identifying with and rejecting a dominant form" because "one would be naïve and deeply ensconced in [n]ormative culture to consider such a performance, no matter how 'real,' as an actual performance" (108). The cross-racial performances of Mona and of Othello's identification with white culture engage in a similar negotiation with essentialist conceptions of race by revealing the constructedness of whiteness and Blackness. *Harlem Duet's* audience, no matter how real the race change, does not consider Mona an actual white woman. Because race change counters essentialist notions of gender and race, the seemingly counteridentificatory reversal of previous all-white casts has disidentificatory effects. The failure to easily transgress racial boundaries and fully enact race change is a necessary part of the disidentificatory act because a successful performance would merely reinforce gender or racial ideals: through this transparency of race change, the actors simultaneously work with and reject the accepted forms of race, thereby enacting disidentification.

As with Playwright's unsuccessful attempt to counteridentify with Shakespeare's *Hamlet*, Billie's counteridentification with the white world outside Harlem also fails. As the figure of counteridentification, Billie does not want to participate in the majoritarian society and instead retreats to Harlem with the hope that someday Harlem will serve as an all-Black refuge. Billie admits that she "love[s] seeing all these brown faces" (350) and that Harlem is a "respite [from whiteness] like an ocean in the middle of a desert" (365): she imagines a future Harlem "teeming with loud Black people listening to Jazz and reggae and Aretha" (366). Yet Sears problematizes Billie's separatist sanctuary because Billie's opposition to the dominant culture fills her with rage: "I hate. I know I hate" (369). In obsessing over race and in hating white culture, Billie reinforces racist rhetoric. In one of her lectures to Billie, Magi the landlady reveals the debilitating effects of counteridentification:

> Is everything about White people with you? Is every living moment of your life eaten up with thinking about them. Do you know where you are? Do you know who you are anymore? What about right and wrong. Racism is a disease my friend, and your test just came back positive. You're so busy reacting, you don't even know yourself. (364–5)

The counteridentification with "White people" and the reductive racial opposition of "Black" versus "White" cause Billie to lose her own identity. By contrasting Othello and Billie's identificatory practices, Sears dramatizes not only the danger of Othello's identification but also the harmful effect of Billie's counteridentification because both characters lose hold of their self-identities. The equally harmful effects of identification and counteridentification illustrate Pêcheux's and Muñoz's warnings about the two positions' symmetrical structures. As Muñoz says, "the danger" of counteridentification is "the counterdetermination that such a system installs, a structure that validates the dominant ideology by reinforcing its dominance through the controlled symmetry of 'counterdetermination'" (11). In its inversion of identification, counteridentification merely duplicates the same ideological problems and racial hierarchies as exemplified by Othello's rejection of his Black ancestry and Billie's rejection of white culture.

If Othello is obsessed with white-washing his life, Billie only wants Black. She defines herself in terms of Black culture – "We are Black. Whatever we do is Black" (349) – but even Billie is at times suspicious of this word and of her racialized skin as an identifying agent. Billie seems to have little control over the identificatory category of Black: "When someone doesn't serve me, I think it's because I'm Black. When a clerk won't put the change into my held-out hand, I think it's because I'm Black … I'm even suspicious of the word Black. Who called us Black anyway? It's not a country, it's not a racial category, its [*sic*] not even the colour of my skin" (349). In this speech, Billie imagines that others (such as the server and clerk) identify her first and foremost as Black. With these statements Billie's "I" becomes the object of external identification, prompting her to assume a selfhood outside of society. But Billie cannot escape the racialized binary of white versus Black, and her counteridentification with white culture merely reaffirms this racial polarity. In contrasting Othello's and Billie's positions, Dickinson also describes Billie in terms that echo definitions of counteridentification. "Where Othello," Dickinson argues, "like [Aimé] Césaire's Ariel, chooses to work within the system, the more revolutionary Billie, like Caliban, chooses to challenge it from without" (10). But unlike Billie, Caliban embraces his status as monster "as a site from which to curse Prospero" (Muñoz 185); Billie, by contrast, is, at least in part, paralyzed by perceived derogations of Blackness, gesturing towards the play's critique of these oppositional stances on race. *Gertrude and Ophelia* and *Harlem Duet* feature acts of counteridentification, but this strategy falls short because it merely reinforces dominant binaries.

Othello is the inverse of Billie. He identifies with English and American culture, and, as Leslie Sanders says, he is "a member of the black community who is dazzled by whiteness" (558). After fighting with Billie about the difference between white and Black feminists, Othello defines himself in a climactic soliloquy:

> I am not minor. I am not a minority. I used to be a minority when I was a kid. I mean my culture is not my mother's culture – the culture of my ancestors. My culture is Wordsworth, Shaw, Leave It to Beaver, Dirty Harry. I drink the same water, read the same books. You're the

> problem if you don't see beyond my skin. If you don't understand that I am a middle class educated man. I mean, what does Africa have to do with me […] Some of us are beyond that now. Spiritually beyond this race shit bullshit now. I am an American. The slaves were freed over 130 years ago. In 1967 it was illegal for a Black man to marry a White in sixteen states. That was less than thirty years ago … in my lifetime. Things change, Billie. I am not my skin. My skin is not me. (355)

In this scene, Othello tries to negate the significance of his skin, but the negation of Blackness merely enables him to align with a culture that he defines as "White" and "American." In assuming a misconception that "race" does not matter and is irrelevant, Othello refuses to acknowledge the power of racism or racialized history. Yet there is a logical fallacy to his denial of racism and his self-identification with mainstream white American culture because the premise that skin colour does not define identity contradicts Othello's preference for white women and Mona's alabaster skin. Despite Othello's repeated insistence that "we're all equal in the eyes of God" (355), he explains that white women are "different" (354). With "a Black woman," Othello feels that he "represent[s] every Black man she has ever been with and with whom there was still so much to work out" (355). Othello's generalizations about Black women undermine his rejection of Black male stereotypes. In HER's parable to HIM, HER suggests that Othello tries to become white through his relationship with Mona:

> Once upon a time, there was a man who wanted to find a magic spell in order to become White. After much research and investigation, he came across an ancient ritual from the caverns of knowledge of a psychic. "The only way to become White," the psychic said, "was to enter the White." And when he found his ice queen, his alabaster goddess, he fucked her. Her on his dick. He one with her, for a single shivering moment became … her. Her and her Whiteness. (361)

HER channels Frantz Fanon's arguments about race by suggesting that a Black man desires whiteness in desiring a white woman: "by loving me, she proves to me that I am worthy of a white love. I am loved like a white man. I am a white man" (45).[16] For Dickinson, it is "no accident that Billie is a psychology major" and that HER echoes the language of Fanon's *Black Skin, White Masks* (196). "The visceral, obscene language with which Her describes interracial lovemaking," Huebert explains, "mirrors Billie's own disgust at the notion" while "Her's description of the two bodies becoming one for a 'shivering moment' brings to mind Iago's image of a 'beast with two backs'" (40). White women, then, are not only "easier – before and after sex" (355), but they also enable Othello to "become White" and thereby to self-identify as a white American.

Othello's self-defining utterances aim to assert his individuality and masculinity: "I am a very single, very intelligent, very employed Black man" (355). In declaring his single status and separation from Billie, Othello renders their marriage void. *Harlem Duet* explains that when slaves did not have access to recognized wedding ceremonies they would jump over a broom as an act of marriage. In homage to this tradition, Billie and Othello jumped over a broom in their earlier days in Harlem. With Othello's departure, Othello not only leaves Billie but also refuses to acknowledge the legitimacy of the subversive marital tradition. Othello's assertion of individuality thus relies on an identification with a white collective and tradition. But the ease with which Othello negates his past speech acts and ancestral tradition gestures towards the flimsiness of self-identifications as retractable or negatable: with a single speech act, for instance, Othello proclaims, almost effortlessly, that he is "officially" engaged to Mona and separated from Billie (354). Othello punctuates his defiant monologue with the self-assertive statements "I am not minor," "I am not a minority," and most poignantly, "I am not my skin" (355). These identifications are grounded in negation, ranging from his refusal to be considered a minority to his disassociation from Africa when he says, "What does Africa have to do with me" (356). Othello pairs these negations with affirmations, proclaiming, "I am a middle class educated man" and "I am an American." These affirmative "I am" declarations, however, paradoxically destabilize what they seek to confirm – Othello's "I" – because the accompanying "I am not" negations demonstrate the instability of the very signifiers – "Black," "American," and "man" – that form his identity. Othello, then, fails to fully identify with white culture and dominant society. In Sears's play, as with Clarke's, both strategies of identification and counteridentification fail.

Othello and Billie personify strategies of identification and counteridentification, respectively. In *Harlem Duet*, these two strategies parallel assimilationist and separatist perspectives as suggested by the location of Billie and

Othello's apartment "*at the corner of Martin Luther King and Malcolm X Boulevards*" (17). Kidnie suggests that the "highly charged stand-off between Billie and Othello, turning on the question of whether to live according to a separatist or integrationist racial politics, is never conclusively resolved in favour of either side" (31). But this absence of a conclusive winner can be read as a type of resolution because it refuses to uphold a hierarchic binary that privileges separatism or assimilation. *Harlem Duet* critiques both perspectives, purposefully favouring neither assimilationism/identification nor separatism/counteridentification.

Harlem Duet steps outside "either/or" constructions of race and ideology by questioning the boundaries of Blackness and whiteness. The performed intersection of these racial identities and racial ideologies is key: the intersection offers the option of "both/and," as opposed to a binary "either/or" structure. The setting of the play – at the junction of Martin Luther King and Malcolm X Boulevards – spatializes the joining of these two positions. The meeting point of Martin Luther King (a figure associated with American assimilation) and Malcolm X (a figure of racial separatism) Boulevards gestures towards the fallibility of choosing either separatist or assimilationist politics and also towards their similarity as ideological positions preoccupied with prescribed racial codes. I argue that *Harlem Duet* emphasizes the potential of disidentificatory subject positions as a bringing together of positions.[17]

In challenging dichotomous political responses to patriarchal and racial norms, *Gertrude and Ophelia* and *Harlem Duet* gesture toward the potential of the third position – that of disidentification, or the strategy of simultaneously identifying with and against a dominant ideology in order to change it from within.

The Citational Doubleness or the "Am" and "Am Not" of Political Adaptation

The paradox of a citational history that frames and constrains sites of self-naming and protests defines political adaptation and its performance of disidentification. Butler emphasizes the precarious state of identities based on performance and visible cues by pointing to the provisionality of identity as merely a "stylized repetition of acts through time" ("Performative Acts" 2). Similarly, Clarke's and Sears's plays demonstrate how prescribed performances of gender and race, whether through self-naming, actions, or appearance, rely on culturally accepted identificatory labels and codes of behaviour that have been repeated through time. Although these labels and codes can be used as empowering identificatory tools for self-naming, they can also carry a citational history that precedes the speaker and the speaker's identity. In this way, identificatory statements at once announce and denounce the speaker's autonomy. The historicity of Othello's "I am not my skin" statement (*Harlem Duet* 356) – in particular, the echo of Iago's "I am not what I am" (*Othello* 1.1.69) – provides a model for the paradox of self-defining utterances because the declaration simultaneously demonstrates Othello's agency and relies on Iago's earlier usage.

Building on the structural doubleness – working with and against – that characterizes political adaptations and disidentificatory performances, Clarke's and Sears's plays complicate the categories of failed or successful speech acts in their performances of disidentification. J.L. Austin works from the premise that performative utterances succeed in creating a bond between the speaker and listener, and chooses to ignore "non-serious" or dramatic utterances, whereas Butler works from almost the reverse premise that all speech acts fail and that all utterances, and by extension all identities, are performative or "non-serious." *Gertrude and Ophelia* and *Harlem Duet* contribute to this theoretical debate by exemplifying the potential interplay of success and failure in a single speech act. Butler gestures towards the mix of success and failure in performances of identity when she describes disidentification as "misrecognition" and as an "uneasy sense of standing under a sign to which one does and does not belong" (*Bodies* 219). Despite Butler's insistence on the failure of all performances, this doubleness ("one does and does not belong") signals the implicit success in "misrecognition" that includes a belonging even if it is only a counterpart to an un-belonging. In *Harlem Duet*, for instance, Othello's argumentative "I am not my skin. My skin is not me" speech succeeds in his mind but fails in the minds of Billie and the audience. Butler concedes to another element of success when she explains that "The authors of gender [or race as the case may be] become entranced by their own fictions" ("Performative Acts" 3), which helps to explain the success of Othello's counteridentification in his own mind. In *Gertrude and Ophelia* and *Harlem Duet*, it is the simultaneous success and the failure of identificatory performances that destabilizes accepted performances of gender and race, thereby revealing the provisionality of identificatory performances.

Gertrude and Ophelia and *Harlem Duet* perform what Austin calls failed or infelicitous speech acts, and these failures demonstrate the precariousness of self-declarative utterances in both plays. Austin explores the "infelicities" of performative utterances and classifies "types of cases in which something goes wrong and the act – marrying, betting, bequeathing, christening, or what not – is therefore at least to some extent a failure: […] And for this reason we call the doctrine of the things that can be and go wrong on the occasion of such utterances, the doctrine of the Infelicities" (14). Among these infelicities, Austin categorizes "Abuses" wherein the act is carried out but void. These abuses suggest an internal problem, wherein, for example, the speaker is "misleading" and "probably deceitful" (11). The second main category of infelicities is "Misfires," which denotes an external problem with the act itself. Austin explains that "when the utterance is a misfire, the procedure which we purport to invoke is disallowed or is botched: and our act … is void" (16). Austin, however, dismisses theatrical performances as unserious utterances; he claims that all ritualistic speech acts on stage, such as a nuptial scene, are by extension misfires because the invoked procedure is "disallowed." To follow Austin's logic, then, all the words spoken on stage would be failed speech acts because the audience knows that they are merely fictional and because the related governing agencies do not recognize them as official acts.

Before examining the infelicities of Iago's and Othello's "I am not" statements, I want to add a qualification to my integration of performative utterances and identification theory in relation to *Gertrude and Ophelia* and *Harlem Duet*: I disagree with Austin and contend that performative utterances can succeed within the diegetic worlds that the two plays represent. The play's world, after all, is real to the characters that inhabit it. The audience's suspension of disbelief further complicates the structural premise that all theatrical utterances are misfires – the audience members as well as the characters believe the performed speech acts within the context of these plays. When watching a realistic representation on stage, an audience collectively accepts the performative utterances and actions as real. Furthermore, the characters intend their speech acts to succeed within the play's diegetic realm so they do not deliberately perform abuses. What I'm suggesting is that speech acts and performed rituals can be successful within the diegetic world of the play – Billie, for instance, accepts Othello's pronouncement of their marriage as null and void – which further nuances Austin's contention that all theatrical speech acts fail.

This nuanced understanding of the audience's effect on the success of a speech act reveals a significant difference between Othello and Iago's "I am not" utterances: while Iago's "I am not what I am" signals an intentional abuse, Othello's "I am not my skin. My skin is not me" misfires because there are problems with the structure of the utterance itself. This difference is key to Sears's political commentary on Othello's performance of race and self-identification as American. Iago characterizes his past and future performances of a trustworthy counsellor as intentionally infelicitous, but in doing so, he exerts agency over the infelicity of his speech acts. Othello's infelicitous speech act, by contrast, is unintentional. The context of Othello's performative utterance and the presence of his Black body undermine his attempt to identify with white culture. Othello's dismissal of the history of racism and his racialized skin also misfires because there is no accepted linguistic speech act by which he can successfully re-identify his race. Unlike Iago's conscious infelicities, Othello has little control over the failure of his speech act. Othello's speech act arguably succeeds as an ideological argument (that skin should not function as a marker for racial identity) and as an expression of self-conception (he does not connect with Africa or his Black ancestry). But the context and structure of the speech act – Othello's Black body and Billie as the inset audience – undermine the legitimacy and success of his "I am" declarations. While Othello's self-defining speech act may succeed to his own mind and on a conceptual level, the context of the speech renders it a failure to both the onstage audience and the real spectators.

Billie, the scene's onstage audience, contributes to the failure of Othello's self-identificatory speech acts by functioning as a model audience that does not believe Othello's self-identifications as "American." For Billie, America is not, as Othello says, "beyond this race shit bullshit now" (73). As the addressee of his monologue, her belief in the prevalence of race as a cue to one's identity structures his self-defining utterances. In *Giving an Account of Oneself*, Butler explores the structuring role of the addressee in a self-narrative: "I am my relation to you" (81). In other words, the addressee and the social context constitute the self. As Butler says, "the 'I' that I am is nothing without this 'you,' and cannot even begin to refer to itself outside the relation to the other by which its capacity for self-reference emerges" (82). In *Harlem Duet*, Othello's self-reference, for instance, emerges as a response to Billie's indictments of his racism. Her political beliefs thus instigate his speech, and her role as the "addressee" helps to constitute his monologue's content. Billie's role as the "you" to Othello's "I" binds the two figures in a mutually constitutive relationship. While Butler describes the invisible structure of self-narration, Billie manifests this structure with her physical presence onstage. She gives an embodied presence to the interlocutor that Butler theorizes as the constitutor of all self-narrations. In dramatizing Ophelia's, Othello's, and Billie's failed self-identifications, *Gertrude and Ophelia* and *Harlem Duet* place the spotlight on the audience as an implied and constitutive "you" who must take a key role in the characters' identificatory processes as well as in the political adaptation's projects of changing the way we perform canonical characters.[18]

Austin's categories of locutionary, illocutionary, and perlocutionary acts help to further distinguish Iago's and Othello's "I am not" declarations: a locutionary act is the actual utterance and its ostensible, linguistic, or semantic meanings; an illocutionary act is the intended meaning or the force of the utterance; and a perlocutionary act is the psychological or social effect of the utterance (Austin 102). The illocutionary and perlocutionary effects of Iago's "I am not what I am" support one another: Iago confesses his mischievous posturing as trustworthy confidante, which supports the audience's perception of Iago as a villain. The perlocutionary effect of Othello's "I am not my skin," however, contradicts the illocutionary intention. Billie "*sits on the floor by the bed watching him from the bedroom*" (355) and remains unconvinced by Othello's argument that America has moved beyond "this race shit bullshit now" (356). For Billie, Othello's "I am not my skin" statement and preference of white women only reaffirm the significance of skin colour as a repeated cultural marker of race and identity.

In fact, Othello's rejection of his racialized skin aligns him with the canonical Moor of Shakespeare's play – who is celebrated as "far more fair than black" in both *Harlem Duet* (99) and *Othello* (1.3.315) – and with what Billie describes as the "coitus Denegrification" (55) of popular figures such as Michael Jackson. The opening scene of *Harlem Duet*'s second act, for example, begins with audio clips from "Michael Jackson and Lisa Marie Presley's interview on ABC's 'Dateline'" (79), which remind the audience of Jackson's contentious inter-racial marriage and physical self-modifications.[19] Michael Jackson sought to "White wash his life" (353) by marrying Lisa Marie Presley, and he also underwent drastic reconstructive surgery to alter his face and adopt white features, such as a pinched nose, a small cleft chin, and high cheekbones. The interview is doubly applicable to *Harlem Duet*'s racial issues because Lisa Marie is the daughter of Elvis Presley, who appropriated Black music for the white rock scene. As a couple, Michael Jackson and Lisa Marie Presley represent a Black man's voluntary self-whitening as well as the dominant culture's appropriation of Black culture. The allusions to Michael Jackson present Othello's "I am not my skin" declaration as merely another failed rejection of racialized Black skin. With Michael Jackson's death in 2009 the sound clips about his marriage and surgeries take on a new meaning. Jackson and HIM/HE are now even more intertwined as all three of these entities die despite their best attempts at "coitus denegrification" (66).

As Emmanuel Levinas says, "The corporeality of one's own body signifies, as sensibility itself, a knot or denouement of being ... a knot that cannot be undone" (77). Despite his attempts to replace skin with literature and television as new markers of a cultural identity, Othello cannot undo the racial significance of his own skin. His body is an identificatory "knot" that cannot be undone with "I am not." In this way, Othello has no control over the social effect (or perlocutionary consequences) of his soliloquy. Instead, the scene's location, his Black body, the citational history of this declaration (in the two subplots and in Shakespeare's *Othello*), Billie's role as addressee, and his logical fallacies all render his statement "void." Othello fails to convince his inset audience and audience proper that "My skin is not me." As Billie says, Othello suffers from "Corporeal malediction" and "A crumbled racial epidermal schema" (66). Othello's failed attempts at counteridentification coupled with Billie's problematic identification with Blackness only serve to reinforce the potential of disidentification – after all, the play as a whole is a successful performance of disidentification with white culture and its Bard.

Gertrude and Ophelia and *Harlem Duet* ultimately gesture towards the radical potential of failed performances of identity. Jacques Derrida critiques Austin's opposition of "success/failure" as "insufficient and extremely secondary," explaining "it presupposes a general and systematic elaboration of the structure of locution that would avoid an endless alternation of essence and accident [or essential and accidental]" (15–16). According to Derrida, Austin focuses on the infelicity of the speech act's context and fails to examine the conventionality of the locutionary structure itself, namely its iterability or the inherent repeatability of the performative utterance. In reaction to Austin's dismissal of theatrical performances as "hollow," "void," and "parasitic" (22), Derrida suggests:

> what Austin excludes as anomaly, exception, "non-serious," citation (on stage, in a poem, or a soliloquy) is the determined modification of a general citationality – or rather, a general iterability – without which there would not even be a "successful" performative? So that – a paradoxical but unavoidable conclusion – a successful performative is necessarily an "impure" performative (17).

While Butler argues that all performances fail, Derrida similarly asserts that an implicit citationality renders all speech acts "impure," thereby destabilizing Austin's binaries of pure/impure, serious/non-serious, or successful/unsuccessful speech acts. Derrida objects to Austin's categorizations of successful and failed performative utterances because all speech acts are inevitably citations of an earlier act, but I contend that this does not necessarily render Austin's categories of infelicity meaningless.

Connecting speech-act theory with disidentification theory recuperates failed performance as a potential strategy of resistance and disidentification. Derrida convincingly renders the locutionary structure "impure" and innately derivative of pre-existing linguistic codes, but this does not undermine the relevance of a speech act's success or failure in relation to its context or audience. For instance, Iago's "I am not what I am" utterance successfully colours all his past and future declarations as intentional lies, or in Austin's terms, as abuses: it is a perlocutionary success. Furthermore, in Clarke's and Sears's plays, failed performances are not "void" but instead enact disidentification and transform the sources by productively calling attention to the limits of the locutionary structures and codes for self-identification. In *Gertrude and Ophelia* and *Harlem Duet*, the failure of the speech acts and identity performance reveals the code of normative citizenship to be quite precarious indeed. While Derrida emphasizes the citationality and iterability of all linguistic acts, I suggest that the failed performances in these two plays expose this citationality with overbearing Shakespearean intertexts and thereby de-naturalize the performer's identity constructions.

Adaptations of canonical works announce their citational relationship to a mainstream narrative but political adaptation points to this relationship only to try to renounce it. Political adaptation, therefore, is the generic equivalent of the characters' overtly iterable performative utterances: Clarke's and Sears's plays unavoidably cite a canonical narrative despite their best efforts to destabilize the original; but, in turn, *Gertrude and Ophelia* and *Harlem*

Duet could not destabilize the source without citation, and the endless cycle of iterability brings this circularity out to light.

Promoting Political Adaptation as Disidentification

While Clarke's Playwright and Sears's Billie seek to invert dominant gender and racial structures, the plays themselves engage in a more nuanced negotiation with Shakespeare's work. As a survival strategy as well as a theoretical approach, Muñoz explains that disidentification "resists an unproductive turn toward good dog/bad dog criticism and instead leads to an identification that is both mediated and immediate" (9). To apply disidentification to *Gertrude and Ophelia* and *Harlem Duet*'s adaptation process, Clarke and Sears resist their protagonists' "good dog/bad dog criticism" in order to disidentify with their overbearing canonical forbearers. After all, Clarke includes Hamlet in the play proper and introduces *Rosencrantz and Guildenstern Are Dead* as an intertext by mentioning Stoppard and his work. In dramatizing Playwright's failed counteridentification with Shakespeare's original *Hamlet* and Gertrude's failed identification with patriarchal expectations, Clarke simultaneously rejects and embraces Shakespeare's play, thereby disidentifying with the source. *Harlem Duet* also reveals political adaptation's inherent performance of disidentification with its source material. Although it is set in present-day Harlem, the narrative actions of *Harlem Duet* precede the action of Shakespeare's *Othello*. *Harlem Duet* is thus simultaneously descendant from and antecedent to Shakespeare's *Othello*, which effectively displaces the criticisms of parasitism that plague adaptations. In this way, *Gertrude and Ophelia* and *Harlem Duet*'s promotion of political adaptation as disidentification avoids the common traps of adaptation proper.

In plays that must pay homage to the very tradition they reject, it is fitting that the characters also struggle with insufficient, and often oppositional, strategies for negotiating gender and racial demands. *Gertrude and Ophelia*'s frame narrative places Playwright's counteridentification and Actor's identification with patriarchal theatre traditions in dialogue with each other as they fight about the importance of Hamlet and the other male characters. Similarly, in *Harlem Duet*, Billie and Othello's arguments can be pared down to a debate over whether to counteridentify or identify with white culture. The plays' dramatization of archetypal figures of identification and counteridentification demonstrate the failure of these strategies and the potential of disidentification.

Harlem Duet warns against identification with Shakespeare and faithful retellings of *Othello*. Sears explains that "using three time periods was very important" because "it gave the depth that I wanted. It supported many layers of the play, of the language, and of the contradictions around race" (Sears and Sealy-Smith, "Nike" 25). In each time period, Othello leaves Billie for a white woman because of prescribed codes of white superiority, and this trans-historical repetition heightens the tragedy of Othello's abandonment of Billie. Kidnie expresses the audience's reaction: the "instant recognition of the actors' bodies in performance – the realization that the same two actors portray Billie and Othello in all three settings – creates the sense that we are witnessing a single story, stretched across time" ("There's Magic" 33). Yet it is not merely a single story "stretched," but a single narrative pluralized; and the tragedy does not just come from the murder of Othello in the subplots or from Billie's breakdown but from the repetition of the same story over and over again. The sound clips that open each scene reinforce the overarching narrative of repetition: the same "*cacophony of strings*" plays over and over again in act 2 scenes 4, 5, 6, and 7, which quickly "*becomes a grating repetition*" (361). As well as adding dramatic tension, the three parallel storylines and sound clips enact stasis.

By charting the same racial conflicts from the Elizabethan era to the present, *Harlem Duet* dramatizes the tragedy of repetition. As Fischlin says, the "three similar storylines from different historical periods emphasize the traps of historical amnesia and repetition, all repeating the basic motif of a Black man leaving a Black woman for a white woman" ("Nation and/as Adaptation" 318). Nuancing Fischlin's interpretation, I argue that the play does not critique repetition but repetition without difference. It is repetition with political variation, after all, that enables Sears to work simultaneously with and against the dominant narratives of racial marginalization. Repetition with political difference, then, acts as a corrective to the tragedy of stasis. In using adaptation as a vehicle for change and in dramatizing the damaging potential of mere repetition or reversal, Clarke and Sears demonstrate the counter-discursive power of political adaptation as disidentification.

"I am" declarations and dramatic adaptations have an implicit citationality because they garner meaning from earlier performances, but it is on the basis of this citationality that the political work takes place. The failure of Othello's "I am not my skin" suggests the precariousness of normative identities, and the inability of Gertrude and Ophelia to fully conform to female stereotypes highlights the performativity of gender roles. Iterations of self-identification are either undermined by their narrative context (as is the case with Othello's self-defining soliloquy) or fail to be completed (as is the case with Ophelia who cannot define a "me"). The characters' failure to successfully identify or counteridentify with normative structures of gender or racial identities performs disidentification, just as the playwrights' failure to fully identify with or against their source texts enacts political adaptation. Approaching failed performances of normative identity and narrative fidelity as disidentification not only challenges popular denouncements of adaptations as derivative, but also foregrounds the precariousness of the dominant identificatory structures that the plays fail and refuse to uphold.

Gertrude and Ophelia and *Harlem Duet* emphasize the performativity of identity, while calling attention to the flimsiness of these very performances. The self-negation "I am not what I am" applies to the main characters' identities because they are dependent on the very scripted performances of gender and race that they seek to reject. It is this paradoxical doubleness – the "am" and "am not" – that defines the central characters in these two plays as well as the political adaptations' relationship to their sources. *Gertrude and Ophelia* and *Harlem Duet* at once perform and promote adaptation as an artistic act of disidentification, as a personal act of survival.

Clarke's and Sears's plays change our relationship to gender and race in *Hamlet* and *Othello*, respectively. After viewing Clarke's adaptation, Hamlet is a rapist, King Hamlet is no longer the father, Gertrude is an empathetic mother figure, and Ophelia is the victim of betrayal. Clarke recasts the male or paternal figures as antagonists and the female or maternal figures as complex protagonists. These changes to the characters and plot invite the audience to align with Ophelia and Gertrude rather than with Hamlet and his father. In short, *Gertrude and Ophelia* reframes *Hamlet* as a play about gendered power dynamics and maternity. Comparatively, *Harlem Duet* presents *Othello* as a play about racism. *Harlem Duet*'s three timelines and multiple intertexts show how the *Othello* narrative repeats itself in history and popular culture with interracial marriages that end in violence. *Harlem Duet*, then, frames *Othello* as a racially driven play about miscegenation. Because of work like *Harlem Duet* and the type of critique Sears makes, Canadian theatres can no longer ethically produce *Othello* without foregrounding issues of racial discrimination. Walterdale Theatre in Edmonton, Alberta, for instance, cancelled its production of *Othello* in 2017 due to public outcry after it cast a white female actor in the titular role. The production team received threats because of its gender-focused approach to *Othello* that overlooked the significance of race (Snowdon). This cancellation demonstrates how the production and viewing of *Othello* has changed since Olivier wore blackface as the famous Moor in 1965. Political adaptations transform the way we approach canonical source material and in doing so they are changing the way we perform gender and race, among other identity issues.

Building on this consideration of how political adaptations transform the source material, the following chapter concentrates on two feminist adaptations that feature choruses of onstage spectators – Margaret Atwood's *The Penelopiad* and Erin Shields's *If We Were Birds* – in order to further investigate the effect political adaptations have on the real audience and on how source materials are remembered or survive on mainstages. Atwood's and Shields's plays utilize the immediacy of theatre performance to call out to the real audience and demand that we change the way we approach the representation and treatment of women in ancient and contemporary military battles. While Sears's and Clarke's feminist plays transform the enduring male script, Atwood's and Shields's productions showcase the impact of political adaptations on their spectators.

3 Popular Yet Political Audiences in *The Penelopiad* and *If We Were Birds*

An onstage chorus of murdered women call for action as they shout, "And now we call / to you to you" (82) in the final moments of Margaret Atwood's *Penelopiad: The Play* (2007).[1] Erin Shields's *If We Were Birds* (2008) similarly ends with a plea for revenge as "you" echoes violently throughout the theatre: "You you you you / you you you you / YOU YOU YOU YOU" (76). These plays' onstage choruses of disenfranchised women address the audience and model strategies for how the offstage "you" can effect positive political change. Premiering within one year of each other at mainstream theatres, Atwood's and Shields's plays offer feminist adaptations of Homer's *The Odyssey* and Ovid's "Tereus, Procne, and Philomela" from the female characters' perspectives.[2] These plays illuminate political adaptations' performance of disidentification because they retell and thereby potentially reinscribe the very source material they seek to undermine. Building on the arguments from the introduction and previous chapters that political adaptations perform what Michel Pêcheux and José Esteban Muñoz term disidentification – by at once identifying with and against a canonical narrative – this chapter focuses on spectatorship and considers how plays foster the audience's disidentificatory relationship to the source material. Political adaptations address a specific "you," or audience, that at once aligns with and against the canonical source narrative, thereby disidentifying with the sources' normative ideologies. In this way, the spectators form a specific type of public – a dispublic – that disidentifies with and transforms dominant narratives. A dispublic participates in normative culture but challenges facets of its popular ideologies from within; the concept of a dispublic, as a result, applies to audiences beyond political adaptation and accounts for the increasingly political nature of popular performances today. The conclusions of *The Penelopiad* and *If We Were Birds* capture their ultimate political message: the plays confront the audience as a dispublic with potential to incite real-world change.[3]

Adaptation is a popular method of storytelling, but it is also a leading strategy of political theatre with plays such as Timberlake Wertenbaker's *The Love of the Nightingale* (1988). Wertenbaker's play offers what Nursen Gömceli describes as a "radical feminist" adaptation of a Greek myth, and premiered at the Royal Shakespeare Company's The Other Place in Stratford-upon-Avon (77).[4] Ellen McLaughlin's *Iphigenia and Other Daughters* (1995) presents a feminist adaptation of Greek mythology (the *Oresteia* legends) that addresses "the margins of the epic" but finds its home on the mainstage – it premiered at New York City's Classic Stage Company (14).[5] Mary Zimmerman's *Metamorphoses* (1996) reformulates Ovid's eponymous work; in 2002, her adaptation, and its feminist aesthetic, was performed on Broadway to critical acclaim.[6] These popular feminist productions of the late 1980s and 1990s reflect Janet Brown's assertions that during this time performance began to be accepted "as a political gesture, not merely a psychological or spiritual one" because "all performance … is public and therefore political in nature, impacting the larger society" (157). Mainstage adaptations of canonical narratives in plays by Atwood, McLaughlin, Shields, Wertenbaker, Zimmerman and others are simultaneously popular and political; and these are only examples of feminist adaptations of Greek myths. While these plays demonstrate the political nature of mainstream performance, I examine the type of spectator they address and argue that political adaptation gathers a dispublic.

Mainstream theatre often stages political art but the type of spectator it establishes invites definition.[7] Jürgen Habermas and Michael Warner offer possible approaches to theatre audiences, but their theories tend to bifurcate groups of viewers as either normative publics or radical counterpublics, respectively.[8] More and more mainstream theatre audiences occupy the space between these two types of publics as they attend performances that at once advertise to middle- or upper-class audiences as well as perform political intervention. Theatres are gathering and constructing an alternative public – a dispublic – that participates in mainstream culture and can thereby transform it from within. Habermas's public and Warner's counterpublic are too stratified, and, as a result, do not readily apply to many contemporary audiences who are at once part of normative middle-class culture and yet share politically radical ideologies. The dispublic, then, is at once popular and political

– a spectatorship that calls for a classification of a third type of audience. Popular yet political works, such as Atwood's and Shields's plays, necessitate a new model of spectatorship and define the offstage "you" as a dispublic.

In classifying a dispublic, I use the prefix "dis-" to engage Pêcheux's and Muñoz's theories of disidentification wherein a subject at once identifies with and against a dominant ideology. A dispublic performs disidentification by simultaneously participating in and transforming the popular cultural imaginary. As illustrated in the previous chapters, Pêcheux and Muñoz theorize three identificatory positions: identification (participating within the dominant culture), counteridentification (functioning outside and against dominant culture), and disidentification (working with, on, and against dominant culture). I see Pêcheux's tripartite concepts of identification, counteridentification, and disidentification as the identificatory positions of a public, counterpublic, and dispublic, respectively.

Like the dramatic form of political adaptation, the dispublic is a form of spectatorship that at once identifies with and against a dominant narrative, ideology, or value, thereby participating in the dominant public sphere by transforming it from within. Using Atwood's and Shields's plays as case studies, I begin the chapter by examining the audience dynamics of dispublics in relation to Habermas's and Warner's theories of publics and counterpublics, respectively. I then contextualize the performance history of each case study in order to establish the significance of the onstage choruses as model radical spectators. The next section analyzes how these choruses use direct address in order to constitute the audience as a politically conscious dispublic: in addressing a dispublic as an engaged "you," Atwood and Shields help to advance their political goals of effecting change on the page, stage, and beyond. Taking a materialist approach, I further develop my theory of the dispublic by demonstrating how the plays' production venues, advertising, and theatre reviews target a university-educated, middle-class audience with interest in political or intellectually engaging theatre.[9] The final section considers how an audience that is part of a socially conscious, normative public can effect positive political change. Ultimately, the dispublic not only defines the audience of political adaptations it also helps define the predominant audience in twenty-first-century mid-size mainstream theatre.

Theorizing Publics, Counterpublics, and Dispublics

Atwood's *The Penelopiad* and Shields's *If We Were Birds* model a type of theatre spectatorship that bridges publics and counterpublics because they dramatize onstage radical audiences but gather offstage viewers in mainstream, well-attended, socially sanctioned theatres. As political adaptations, *The Penelopiad* and *If We Were Birds* perform disidentification with their source material, which reinforces the audience's disidentificatory relationship with the canonical narratives that normalize rape. *The Penelopiad* re-envisions Trojan War material, such as Homer's *The Odyssey*, from the perspective of Penelope and her twelve most-trusted handmaidens.[10] Penelope narrates the play from Hades and reflects on the years she spent waiting for her husband, Odysseus, to return from Troy as male suitors flocked to her side and stormed her home. Although Homer gives short shrift to the handmaidens in his version, Atwood develops the characters by dramatizing how they help Penelope delay the suitors' marriage proposals. Despite the handmaiden's key role in Penelope's survival during Odysseus's absence, he suspects them of conspiring with the suitors and orders their deaths upon his return; Penelope does nothing to save them. Atwood's play, then, shifts the focus from the Trojan War to the homestead and from male-driven battles to female betrayal.

If We Were Birds, in turn, is Shields's adaptation of Ovid's Tereus, Procne, and Philomela myth from *Metamorphoses*, wherein Tereus rapes and then mutilates Philomela (the sister of his wife Procne) by cutting out her tongue so that she cannot accuse him. To ensure his own safety, Tereus hides Philomela and tells her family that she has died. Philomela, however, escapes and the two sisters reunite to enact gruesome revenge on Tereus: they kill Itys (Procne and Tereus's son) and serve the boy's remains to Tereus. Shields updates the narrative with real-life reports from twentieth-century survivors that demonstrate the continuing use of rape as a weapon of war. The play ends, as Ovid's myth does, with revenge and murder as the gods turn the three titular characters into birds.

Atwood's *The Penelopiad* and Shields's *If We Were Birds* update the Greek myths by introducing a female chorus; these groups of women invert the conventional all-male Greek chorus and speak back to the source texts' fetishization of rape and violence. Atwood's twelve handmaidens form the chorus to demand justice for their undeserved hangings and model a radical, collaborative heterogeneous group (see figure 3.1). Similarly, Shields fuses an ancient

Figure 3.1 Megan Follows (Penelope) and the all-female chorus Maev Beaty, Christine Brubaker, Raven Dauda, Sarah Dodd, Monica Dottor, Kelli Fox, Cara Gee, Pat Hamilton, Tara Rosling, Pamela Sinha, Sophia Walker, and Bahia Watson in Nightwood Theatre's 2012 production of *The Penelopiad*.

Greek tragedy with contemporary war reports as a chorus of multi-generational and cross-cultural women challenge the pervasive use of rape as a tool of military conquest. Through these choruses, *The Penelopiad* and *If We Were Birds* instruct popular audiences on how to act as a dispublic and speak out for marginalized voices.

Dispublics exhibit both the security of Habermas's public and the values of Warner's counterpublic. Habermas concentrates on bourgeois literary societies, or publics, that create normative attitudes, whereas Warner takes interest in subaltern, counter-cultural groups and their role as reactionary counterpublics. The public is the "dominant" group who "take their discourse pragmatics and their lifeworlds for granted, misrecognizing the indefinite scope of their … universality or normalcy" (Warner 122). Habermas, however, acknowledges the potential of publics to counter dominant ideologies and sees the public as both a hegemonic force and an engine of reform. Counterpublics speak to the ability of publics to act as vehicles for change, they "are, by definition, formed by their conflict with the norms," and they aim at transforming these norms through an alternative discourse that is received by the dominant public with hostility (Warner 63). While Habermas and Warner define the characteristics and social formations of literary publics throughout history, they neglect theatre spectators who also gather as a public in a set time and space that can act as a "carrier of public opinion" (Habermas 2). Theatre, as Hannah Arendt reminds us, continues to be a driving force that makes publics and affects political change.[11]

Just as publics readily apply to theatre audiences, Warner's theory of counterpublics is especially applicable to political drama that speaks from and for the margins. Warner himself classifies performance as the preferred mode for expressing the politics of counterpublics or minority cultures (123). According to Warner, counterpublics are groups that oppose a dominant public or discourse; aim to transform and not merely replicate the dominant group or discourse; use alternative idioms or forms, such as performance, to effect change; and are looked upon with hostility or distrust by the dominant public (119). Atwood's and Shields's onstage strategies of resistance illustrate these four characteristics. *The Penelopiad*'s and *If We Were Birds*' choruses oppose patriarchal war heroes through their actions as well as their discursive modes; in both plays the choruses engage in cacophonous, multivocal narrations to subvert Homer and Ovid's seemingly objective, univocal narratives. The choruses also reject epic poetry by using profanity and mock-epic laments. Demonstrating the last element of counterpublics, the choruses and their discursive forms are dismissed with violent opposition as the male characters label them "whores" and "the spoils of war" (*The Penelopiad* 77, *If We Were Birds* 17). In short, the choruses are counterpublics.

Although Atwood's and Shields's audiences may align politically with the choruses' fight against the systemic silencing of rape victims, they do not fulfill Warner's criteria of a counterpublic or face social ostracism. In fact, in some respects Atwood's and Shields's audiences resemble a public because they are a self-organized group of strangers with socio-economic access to a mainstream production. The productions of *The Penelopiad* and *If We Were Birds* were advertised with large citywide billboards and garnered international renown. Atwood's play, in particular, was well funded, well attended, and well received. The Royal Shakespeare Company in association with Canada's National Arts Centre first performed *The Penelopiad* at England's Swan Theatre, in Stratford-upon-Avon, on 27 July 2007.[12] Since then, Toronto's Nightwood Theatre produced a directors' showcase of *The Penelopiad* in 2009 that featured ten different directors who were each responsible for a specific section of the play.[13] The play was also produced by Alberta Theatre Projects in 2010. Vancouver's Arts Club Theatre Company mounted the play at the Stanley Industrial Alliance Stage in 2011, and most recently, Nightwood staged a production at Toronto's Buddies in Bad Times Theatre directed by Kelly Thornton and starring Megan Follows (known for her iconic portrayal of Anne of Green Gables) as Penelope in 2012 and 2013 (see figure 3.2). *The Penelopiad* has been produced across Canada to wide appeal.

Atwood's and Shields's audiences meet the contexts of a public but align with the counterpublic's political message and goal of inciting change. In this way, they form a dispublic, which I define as a combination of public and counterpublic elements with its own unique characteristics: they participate in the dominant public; they gather in a safe, socially sanctioned space; they oppose a dominant ideology, structure, or discourse (either prior to the viewing experience of as a result of it); and they participate in the transformation of the dominant group or discourse. The dispublic's participation in the public sphere is key to their political work because it enables them to transform dominant ideologies from within the dominant public. In *The Penelopiad* and *If We Were Birds*, the choruses align themselves with the audience to help ensure that the spectators oppose a patriarchal and violence-driven perspective and advocate the stories of female victims and survivors.

The dramatization of the plays' choruses as onstage counterpublics complicates the real audiences' status as a public. As Jerzy Grotowski, Richard Schechner, Susan Bennett, and others argue, the actor and spectator have a mutually constitutive relationship. In questioning whether theatre can exist without an audience, Grotowski concludes, "At least one spectator is needed to make it a performance" (32). Similarly, for Richard Schechner, performance must include a viewer and an intentional action intended to be viewed (*Performance Studies* 28). The audience and performance, according to Bennett, are "involved in a reciprocal relationship which can change the quality and success of a performance" (21). In short, performance depends on spectatorship as much as the spectator depends on a performer. *The Penelopiad* and *If We Were Birds* capitalize on the actor and spectator's reciprocal embrace by using the choruses to model a politically active spectatorship. My concept of the dispublic defines this specific type of audience who are at once part of the dominant public and yet critical of its inherited narratives and values.

Performance Contexts

The Penelopiad and *If We Were Birds* are ideal case studies for the dynamics of a dispublic because they feature onstage audiences, or choruses, that model a radical spectatorship and that fight to change dominant myths by speaking out. The choruses, then, elucidate the plays' political messages and formation of dispublics. Despite the international popularity of Atwood studies, the novella version of *The Penelopiad* and Penelope have garnered much more attention than the play and its staging of a radical chorus; similarly, the critical acclaim of *If We Were Birds* has not led to scholarly attention. Sarah Appleton and Sudha Shastri focus on the novella version of Atwood's *The Penelopiad* and its feminist revisions to *The Odyssey*, but both critics overlook the chorus. Similarly, Mihoko Suzuki, Hilde Staels, and Earl G. Ingersoll approach Atwood's prose-fiction version as literary satire, as parody, and as a "novella," respectively, neglecting the role of the chorus. These articles provide valuable insights into the novella's literary form, but they have little application to Atwood's dramatic adaptation or to the chorus.

The dramatic version of *The Penelopiad* is especially important to consider because it changes the significance of Atwood's chorus. The audience's relationship to the chorus is different when we are together in a theatre house rather than isolated as individual readers. While Penelope, with her first-person narrative perspective, offers a more identifiable figure for the solitary reader, the chorus as both a group and an onstage audience better mirrors the collective theatre audience. With the stage version, both chorus and audience are joined in a shared space and time as we all watch the main action of the play. The twelve Maids form the chorus and also use their bodies to create stage props on an impressive scale, including a ship that Odysseus uses to sail to Troy (as shown in figure 3.2). In this way, the Maids physically dominate the stage in their sheer number and are essential to most scenes either as speakers or as embodied props. In performance, the audience's role as a collective group and the chorus's blocking encourage the audience's identification with the chorus and their collective narrative. The chorus's alignment with the audience is a key distinction between the two versions because the

Figure 3.2 Together, Megan Follows (Penelope) and Maev Beaty, Christine Brubaker, Raven Dauda, Sarah Dodd, Monica Dottor, Cara Gee, Pat Hamilton, Pamela Sinha, Sophia Walker, and Bahia Watson (the chorus) form a ship as Kelli Fox (Odysseus) sets sail alongside Tara Rosling (a Naiad) in Nightwood Theatre's 2012 production of *The Penelopiad.*

chorus is much more radical than Penelope in their calls for justice and action; the play version, as a result, best illustrates the formation of a dispublic. While critics such as Appleton and Shastri tend to focus on how Atwood changed Homer's *The Odyssey*, I argue that it is Atwood's concentration on the chorus that has the most impact upon an audience's relationship to the original Greek myth and, more importantly, that transforms what it means to be part of a collective or audience.

While Atwood's and Shields's works have garnered international attention and productions, the Toronto productions of *The Penelopiad* by Nightwood Theatre in 2012, and of *If We Were Birds* at Tarragon Theatre in 2010, offer an ideal lens with which to examine the dynamics of dispublics because many Canadian theatres promote political mandates while generating large audiences in mainstream venues.[14] Nightwood Theatre, for instance, produced *The Penelopiad* and is dedicated to supporting works by women. Many Toronto theatres (including Tarragon and Nightwood) began as smaller alternate venues with political mandates, but they came to resemble mid-range mainstream theatres with subscription seasons and audience surveys.[15] In his material-historicist analysis of Toronto theatres since 1967, Michael McKinnie explains that "Toronto Workshop Productions, the small not-for-profit theatre company that was the only consistent alternative to 'high culture' operations like Crest theatre in Toronto," in 1970 "moved into a 300-seat theatre space downtown, having outgrown its 100-seat basement in the old city's working-class west end" (6). Ric Knowles asserts that although there is a persistent "hegemony of whiteness on the city's stages" in twenty-first-century Toronto, an emerging intercultural performance scene "reflects the cultural differences that are visible and audible on the city's streets and streetcars" ("Multicultural Text" 74). The Toronto productions of *The Penelopiad* and *If We Were Birds* take place in this larger context of mid-range mainstream theatres and the prevalence of "whiteness on the city stages" as they aim to promote political activism and diverse identities through cross-cultural, intergenerational female choruses with individualized experiences of sexual violence (see Shields's diverse Chorus in figure 3.3). While these two plays model a distinct form of spectatorship in mid-range mainstream Toronto theatres, this chapter serves as an invitation to the study of dispublics more broadly as a form of popular spectatorship that engages in political change in different plays, theatres, and cities.

Atwood's and Shields's plays not only aim to change the way we think about two Greek heroines, Penelope and Philomela, they encourage a structural change in the way stories are told, retold, and remembered: the plays fight for a plurality of perspectives. In her discussion of immersive and experiential theatre, Jen Harvie explains what is at stake when the contemporary performances actively engage audiences:

> We need to learn from and about each other, to be able to rely on and support each other and to negotiate our similarities and differences if not always, if ever, to resolve them. We need some 'fellow feeling', some social sympathy, to check unreserved self-interest. We also need social engagement to sustain democracy, people's shared exercise of power. (2)

Harvie's eloquent discussion of immersive theatre (which offers another possible application of the dispublic) articulates the goals of *The Penelopiad* and *If We Were Birds* as well as the pulse of theatre that seeks a positive recognition

Figure 3.3 Shannon Perrault, Karen Robinson, Daniela Lama, Stephanie Jung, and Barbara Gordon (the Chorus) take bird-like postures as Tara Rosling (Philomela) lies on the ground in Tarragon Theatre's 2010 production of *If We Were Birds*.

of differences. Atwood's and Shields's plays share this goal of promoting "social sympathy" and do it by gathering a dispublic, that is, a socially conscious, mainstream audience.

A Reciprocal Embrace: The Onstage "We" and Offstage "You"

Like publics and counterpublics, dispublics are formed through address. As Warner explains, "all discourse or performance addressed to a public must characterize the world in which it attempts to circulate and it must attempt to realize that world through address" (114). In addressing and thereby constituting the offstage "you" as a dispublic, *The Penelopiad* and *If We Were Birds* use distinct narrative methods and poetics to model a counter-discourse that privileges the disenfranchised choric collective over the affluent central protagonists.[16] Immediately establishing a politically active collective, Atwood's opening two scenes contrast the inarticulateness of the lone "I" with the powerful narrations of the choric "we." The Nightwood production (in 2012) had audiences walk on a metal grate bridge in order to get to the auditorium seating and descend below ground level – a fitting entrance that helped immerse audiences in the fictional underworld. In the opening scene, fog floods the theatre as the back wall of the stage opens and Penelope emerges; the fog and dim lighting give the sense of a dusty stage, helping to suggest that Penelope is a figure too often forgotten. The ghost of Penelope stands alone onstage in a state of "bonelessness, liplessness, breastlessness" – a self-reflexive description that establishes the theatre's power to embody even the disembodied (3). She is unable to "scream" or correct her own myth: "Don't follow my example, I want to scream in your ears – yes, yours! But when I try to scream, I sound like an owl" (4). The Maids, by contrast, "*interrupt Penelope*" (4) with a narrative empowered by the "we." While "*jumping ropes, or doing other rope tricks*," the Maids proclaim:

> We are the maids
> The ones you killed
> The ones you failed
> We danced in air
> Our bare feet twitched
> It was not fair
> With every goddess, queen and bitch
> From there to here
> You scratched your itch. (4)

The Maids' song immediately and effectively resists the same legend that Penelope longs to correct. As "the ones you killed" and "failed," the chorus of women at once addresses Odysseus, who "scratched [his] itch" with "every goddess, queen and bitch," Penelope, who failed to stop the murder of her favourite Maids, and the audience, who have been complicit in the transmission of the myth. The Maids symbolically interrupt Penelope's faltering narrative of forced female silence to powerfully define themselves ("we are"), accuse the epic hero of murder ("the ones you killed"), transform instruments of punishment into vehicles of pleasure (the jumping ropes are also used as their noose), and undermine the high poeticism of *The Odyssey* with profanity ("bitch"). In short, the choric "we" model a radical collective's strategies for effecting change by harnessing their actions, words, and discursive form to redefine Odysseus as a callous philandering murderer.

The Maids' opening speech targets the audience through their address to a general "you:" the Maids are "The ones you killed / The ones you failed" (4). When delivering these lines in the 2012 Nightwood production, the Maids encircled Penelope but also looked out into the audience. In a stirring review of Alberta Theatre Project's 2010 production of *The Penelopiad*, Tina Lambert similarly notes how "at the start of the show, ATP's thrust stage, configured to amplify the exchange between audience and actor" (673). With this choreography and their use of the general subject "you," the chorus implicated the audience in the historical marginalization of the Maids to a mere footnote. This opening speech, then, targeted the audience's culpability and potential both as part of the problem and also as part of the solution. In both plays, a direct address to the audience is key to implicating and activating a dispublic as agents in political intervention.

Shields's play similarly begins with Philomela fighting to narrate her own version of Ovid's myth. With a newly attached tongue and bird songs, Philomela must narrate her own story: "I think they've sewn it back so I can sing through the night, so I can mourn my fate with a sweet song" (3). Philomela, however, finds her own voice only with the help of the chorus. There is a marked transition from Philomela's fear-ridden "I" to an empowered "we" after the chorus directs her to "speak":

> PHILOMELA: Not much has changed, now that I'm a bird.
> Especially the size of my fear:
> Large enough to get caught in the throat but not enough to die.
> CHORUS: Speak it, speak it, / speak it, speak it –
> PHILOMELA: We were born for fear because the gods made us weak,
> but when we were girls we could run as fast,
> jump as high, yell as loud as the boys,
> so you can see why we forgot to shake. (4)

The command "speak it" functions as a refrain throughout this scene, which at once encourages Philomela to narrate her own version of Ovid's myth and to say "we," or what I read as the true "it" or goal of the scene, because the

Figure 3.4 Philippa Domville (Procne) holds Tara Rosling (Philomela) surrounded by Shannon Perrault, Karen Robinson, Barbara Gordon, and Daniela Lama (the Chorus) in Tarragon Theatre's 2010 production of *If We Were Birds*.

coming together of all the women – the chorus, Procne, and Philomela – transforms Philomela from a cowering bird (see figure 3.4) to a commanding woman. The chorus is the agent of change offering a model of narrative adaptation as political protest for the audience.

In *If We Were Birds* the narrativizing collective empowers Philomela, draws Procne onto the stage, and brings together all of the play's female characters, which models the audience's potential strength as a unified dispublic. Neither Philomela's bloodied tongue nor Procne's entrance comprise the main action of the first scene; rather, the crux of the action is the women's coming together as a fearless "we":

> CHORUS: Speak it, speak it, speak it / speak it –
> PHILOMELA: Before the fear.
> CHORUS: Yes?
> PHILOMELA: Oh, before the fear we …
> CHORUS: Yes?
> PHILOMELA: We moved in such different ways.
> When we were children, Procne and I,

> [… PROCNE enters …]
> BOTH [PROCNE and PHILOMELA]: We were not frightened of darkness then;
> PROCNE: We were not nervous with lightening bugs or spiders.
> […]
> CHORUS, PHILOMELA, PROCNE: We were not frightened of darkness then. (4–5)

Further demonstrating the power of the "we," the line "*We* were children, Procne and I" (emphasis added) functions as a type of incantation that brings Procne onto the stage. Procne and Philomela are the first to harmonize with their shared line: "We were not frightened of darkness then" (5). The chorus then joins the two women as they all triumphantly repeat "We were not frightened of darkness then" (5). Philomela's story picks up more and more voices as the women gradually coalesce in an audible way. It is not an immediate unity, but a coming together that is expressed through the interweaving of voices. As with *The Penelopiad*, the opening scene of *If We Were Birds* builds up to the empowering force of a choric "we." These choruses, however, do much more than establish the power of collective narration as the plays progress – they model the political potential of an audience.

In addressing the audience as a politicized "you" and "we," the choruses help to change the way the spectators conceive themselves as a group. In a cry for justice, *The Penelopiad*'s Maids

> invoke the law of blood guilt!
> We call upon the Angry Ones!
> O Angry Ones, O Furies, you are our last hope!
> We implore you to inflict punishment and exact vengeance on our behalf!
> Be our defenders, we who had none in life! (78)

The Maids deliver this invocation out to the audience, momentarily casting the real spectators as Furies who must enact revenge on behalf of the Maids. By invoking the audience's help, the Maids garner support and align themselves with the viewers. Although "Spectatorship is a state constituted in the moment of performance," Alan Filewod is quick to remind us that spectatorship is at once "conditioned by subjectivity and by address" (*Committing*

Theatre 20). The audience's subjectivity – which I interpret as their participation in the dominant public – needs to be considered alongside the chorus's radical address. Unlike the chorus, the real audience does not partake in an alternative discourse nor does it receive hostility from a dominant public; it is not, as a result, a counterpublic. In this way, Atwood encourages the audience to act on the part of the choric collective and unite as a dispublic that refutes existing notions of Odysseus's heroism. Atwood works to transform the spectators into a united and political dispublic: Atwood invites the audience to share in the chorus' viewpoint and assessment of their callous slaughter, but we do not receive the same social ostracism.

Just as Atwood's use of "you" implicates the audience, so too does Shields's repetition of "we": these inclusive addresses involve the spectators in the onstage action and forge a collective that extends beyond the stage and into the auditorium. As Warner reminds us, a public "exists only by virtue of address" and these onstage counterpublics address the audience as sympathetic allies, transforming the offstage audience into a dispublic (87).

Theatre Dispublics: A "Me" and "We" Experience

A theatre production of a political adaptation creates a specific type of viewing public that is heterogeneous yet unified, individualized yet collaborative. A participant in a reading public is at once a personal "me" and an impersonal part of a collective "we": "'the text addresses me' and 'It addresses no one in particular,' is a ground condition of intelligibility for public language" (Warner 161). Comparatively, the theatre audience experiences this same paradox: the play addresses its audience members simultaneously as a "me" and a "no one," and, as a result, the audience participates as an "I" and a "we." Although the actors can physically see their viewing public, the actors, directors, and theatre designers still conceive of the audience as an unknown collective group that constantly changes; the theatre performance addresses the theatre public as a "no one" much like a text's author who cannot foresee the reader. The theatre audience emulates the reading public's experience, as theorized by Warner, because "we know that it [the public speech or performance] was addressed not exactly to us but to the stranger we were until the moment we happened to be addressed by it" (76). In this paradox of audience reception – where the theatre production, like a text, addresses a "me" and a "no one" –

each theatre member interacts with the performance as both a personal individual and an impersonal collective. The experience is *personal*, given his/her unique point of view in the theatre space and private emotive or thinking perspective, and *impersonal* because the singular audience member also partakes in the collective by applauding with the crowd and reacting with the rest of the group. The playgoer, therefore, has a double experience: responding both as a private "me" and as a public "we."

This two-fold experience is important because there is lived dissention or difference among the "we." The personal experience of each "me" prevents or at least complicates and qualifies a homogenous group experience. The individual members not only have different relations and responses to the public discourse but also recognize their own difference or "me-ness." In participating in a public as a "me" and a "we," the individual members become conscious of the parameters that define their public: "as participants in the mass subject, we are the 'we' that can describe our particular affiliations of class, gender, sexual orientation, race, or subculture" (171). The theatre audiences' paradoxical experience as a "me" and "we" creates a self-reflexive and heterogeneous audience that is aware of their participation in a popular yet politicized "we" or dispublic.

Political Adaptations' Counter-Discursive Strategies

In gathering and addressing a dispublic, the plays promote counter-discursive strategies and the political potential of performance-based modes as powerful vehicles for adapting inherited mythologies and for transforming prescribed identities. Political adaptations often use the discursive form itself as a method for challenging the source material (as outlined in the first chapter's list of political adaptation strategies). This technique is quite fitting for a dramatic mode that performs disidentification with a dominant narrative because, as Warner explains, a public or group is defined in part by its discursive form. Warner sees the dominant public's discursive form as primarily text and reading-based; counterpublics, by comparison, are often performance-based and "one that in other contexts would be regarded with hostility or with a sense of indecorousness" (119). The choruses are "'counter' to the extent that they try to supply different ways of imagining" the dominant Greek myths and different ways of telling these stories (Warner 121).

The Penelopiad's and *If We Were Birds*' choruses pit themselves against a text-based diegetic mode and relish the performance-based mimetic mode of theatre. Warner directly associates textuality, reading, and rational-critical discourse with dominant publics, and the more embodied medium of performance with counterpublics: the verbs for public agency "are verbs for private readings," such as "scrutinize, ask, reject, opine, decide, judge, and so on," whereas counterpublics do not privilege "rational-critical reflection as the self-image of humanity" and instead "depend more heavily on performance spaces than on print" (123). Speaking to the distinctions between print and performance, critics like Hutcheon often contrast print as a "telling" mode with performance as a "showing mode" (*Theory* 38). Reaffirming definitions of performance as a showing mode, Richard Schechner defines theatre performances in relation to "explaining, showing, doing" (*Performance Studies* 22). Working with these established definitions of literary and dramatic form, Warner goes on to suggest that reading is the mode by which publics form and establish dominion: "the attribution of agency to publics works in most cases because of the direct transposition from private reading acts to the sovereignty of opinion" (123).

While Warner's parallel binaries of text/performance and publics/ counterpublics have been critiqued as reductive – after all performance, just like texts, can reaffirm the dominant public – his definition of performance as a bodily medium for a subaltern discourse is constructive: it helps to explain theatre's potential for staging political drama, performing onstage counterpublics, and gathering offstage dispublics. But, if the "verbs for public agency are verbs for private readings," then what are the verbs for counterpublic agency? These verbs, if we are to extend Warner's theories, are performance-based ones, such as "to show," "to do," and "to embody." Unlike print-based rational-critical verbs, such as "scrutinize, ask, reject, opine," Atwood's and Shields's plays align their inset viewers (chorus members) with verbs connected to the body and performance like "show," "do," "act." It is with these markedly performance-based verbs that both plays begin.

The Penelopiad's and *If We Were Birds*' opening scenes dramatize the loss of the rational-critical "telling" mode of linear narration: Penelope is an inarticulate ghost trapped in Hades, while Philomela first appears as a fowl with a bloodied tongue. The opening scenes to Atwood's and Shields's plays, with their references to absented stories and lost words, bring attention to the past failures of "telling" modes; but, as Penelope's and Philomela's physical bodies communicate from beyond, these initial scenes also demonstrate the restorative potential of theatre as a "showing" medium and the importance of sharing their stories. In this way, the plays privilege the medium of theatre or performance as an alternative artistic mode that has the ability to at once "show" and "tell" with bodies on the stage.

The Penelopiad and *If We Were Birds* resist the dominant form (text) and discursive style (epic) of their source texts by presenting an alternative narrative methodology: collective narration, bird sounds, and low literary or parodic forms (mock-lament, jump rope rhymes). In *If We Were Birds*, for example, the chorus members' lines alternate, overlap, and occasionally interrupt one another, creating a brocade of narratives. Exemplifying what Warner would call an "alternative idiom," Atwood's twelve Maids and Shields's disenfranchised chorus speak as cacophonous collectives and, ultimately, with non-human voices and bird sounds. In both plays, the choruses of servant women appear before the audience as the embodiment of female collectivity and their narrative forms reinforce this collaboration.

The Penelopiad features bird sounds as a way of calling out against the official version through a markedly non-rational (and non-human) discourse. Homer includes only a few lines to mark the death of the handmaids, describing them as doves with impure souls:

> Thus speaking, on the circling wall [the Prince] strung
> A ship's tough cable, from a column hung;
> Near the high top he strain'd it strongly round,
> Whence no contending foot could reach the ground.
> Their heads above, connected in a row,
> They beat the air with quiv'ring feet below:
> Thus on some tree hung struggling in the snare,
> The doves or thrushes flap their wings in air.
> Soon fled the soul impure, and left behind
> The empty corse to waver with the wind. (499–508)

Homer uses bird imagery to capture the deaths of the Maids as they "flap their wings" in futility and their "empty corse" is left to merely "waver with the wind." Atwood uses this imagery as an overarching topos for Penelope (Duckie, owl) and the Maids (doves, geese). Atwood harnesses Homer's de-humanization of the Maids by dramatizing their transformation into birds as a site from which to call for an uprising and to curse Odysseus and Penelope:

> and now *we* follow
> you, *we* find you
> now, *we* call
> to you to you
> too wit too woo
> too wit too woo
> too woo (82; emphasis added)

The Maids' words transform into bird sounds: "to you" and "too woo" audibly mix as the similarities of their sounds makes them almost interchangeable. In this way, one of the overarching narratives in both plays is the transformation from a word-based and logical discursive mode into a performative discursive form founded on embodied metamorphosis. In short, the plays employ the political adaptation strategy of subverting not only a dominant ideology but also its linguistic and rational discursive form in order to call out to "you" the audience to carry on their transformation of the myth.[17]

Both plays model group collaboration and the social formation of a "we" through the dominant weaving metaphors, which signify the strength of a collective (or the audience) as a braid of individual strands. This weaving functions as another action-based supplement for the more traditional diegetic mode. In *The Penelopiad* as in *The Odyssey*, the weaving and unweaving of a burial shroud helps delay Penelope's decision because she must choose one of the suitors to marry when the shroud is complete. Classics scholars typically interpret the weaving trick as a symbol of storytelling (Clayton) and of Penelope's "constancy and cleverness" (Katz 5). Barbara Clayton convincingly argues that "Penelope's web text is an intricate self-reflexive gesture in which we can read both narrative reversal (stories that 'undo' one another) and narrative return (to a retelling of the *Odyssey*), in what amounts to a final poetic mimesis of Penelope's unweaving" (52). Clayton's emphasis on self-reflexive storytelling reveals *The Odyssey*'s many inset reinterpretations of its own narratives. "The story of Penelope's web trick," Clayton points out, is "repeated almost verbatim by three different narrators": Antinous, Penelope, and the shade of Amphimedon (23). *The Penelopiad* reinforces Clayton's reading by using weaving as a metaphor for storytelling and Penelope's agency: as Atwood's Penelope puns, "I'll spin a thread of my own" (5). Atwood's Penelope, then, simultaneously resists the many different scholarly interpretations of her character as well as the many different narrations of her actions within *The Odyssey* itself.

Weaving, however, accrues another significance in Atwood's version – that of female interconnectedness. The first time that Penelope participates as a member of the Maids' collective "we" occurs when they (un)weave the shroud together:

> For more than three years *we* picked away at my weaving at the dead of night. And though *we* were permanently exhausted, these nights had a touch of festivity amongst them. They were such pleasant girls, full of energy; a little loud and giggly sometimes, as all maids are in youth, but it cheered me up to hear them chattering away, and to listen to their singing. They had such lovely voices, all of them. *We* told stories as *we* worked away at our task of destruction; *we* shared riddles; *we* made jokes. *We* became like sisters. (54; emphasis added)

The repetition of "we" accompanied by the descriptions of "weaving" phonetically merge so that we-aving also becomes an index of the "we." The accompanying weaving actions and group choreography reinforce the "interwinding" (51) of the Maids and Penelope: the Maids themselves form the loom by holding a rope and performing a "*twining dance, as Penelope weaves*" before her audience of suitors (50). Through the weaving of the shroud, Penelope and the Maids "form a [social] fabric" (51) – a secret group. Penelope survives and maintains her household by forming this powerful "we" – yet another dramatization of the power of a collective for the offstage audience.

The braiding of ropes, however, also foretells the eventual hanging of the twelve Maids and the subsequent fraying of the collective.[18] In the Nightwood productions (2009 and 2012), the directors used the same ropes for the unweaving and the Maids' hanging. In the 2009 production, the Maids are hung on individual strands, symbolizing the unraveling of their past secret bonds.[19] In the 2012 production, Telemachus used a single rope to successively hang each Maid, which emphasized the unifying act of their collective death. Penelope's breaking apart from the group and dissolution of the collective "we" becomes the central tragedy in the play. In Nightwood's 2012 production,

Figure 3.5 Megan Follows (Penelope) in Nightwood Theatre's 2012 production of *The Penelopiad*.

Penelope found herself alone encircled by the ropes that hanged her beloved Maids (see figure 3.5). In this way, the play instructs the real viewers on the importance of maintaining their formation of a collective or dispublic even after the production has ended.

In *If We Were Birds*, as in *The Penelopiad*, weaving functions as a controlling metaphor that signals the importance of a group's (and the audience's) interconnection. Philomela weaves her tale into a tapestry, but must rely on a servant woman to help deliver the story to Procne. As "*Procne and the servant stretch out the tapestry*," it retells the gory violence of Philomela's rape and mutilation through movement: "*Lighting shift: the sheet is lit from behind. Movement Piece: Silhouetted tableaux of the rape and dismemberment are projected onto the tapestry.* PROCNE *understands every image*" (65). Philomela narrates her traumatic rape through a group act that involves chorus members (servants) and Procne. In this instance, the discursive mode of the female collective is again action-based and performative, instead of reading-based and literary, in its use of movement.

The set design of *If We Were Birds* further reinforced the significance of the collective weaving and tapestry as overarching metaphors. At the Tarragon production, red strips of fabric were interlaced to form the backdrop, which recalled the image of a woven tapestry and, as lights moved over the stage, of weaving. With the backdrop and the re-enactment of rape behind the fabric, the tapestry became a narrating device itself, but one that involved multiple authors (servant, Philomela, the chorus) and actions instead of words. With the addition of feathers, the play's woven backdrop transformed into a nest that signaled the characters' shared fate – Philomela, Procne, Tereus, and the chorus are all birds by the play's end. Shields poeticizes birds and weaving as symbols of an alternative discursive mode, one that is collective, performance based, and counter-hegemonic.

In productions of the two plays, the set design, choreography, and props underscored the interweaving of individuals into a collective. Atwood and Shields perform a poetics of the choral "we" and this "we" is heterogeneous yet united, non-lingual, and performance-based. Atwood's and Shields's on-stage choruses model the potential of an off-stage audience to change shared interpretations of Greek mythologies and combat the marginalization of female figures through the use of performance as a counter-discursive form.

Half Political, Half Popular: Dispublic Demographics

The use of audiences in *The Penelopiad* and *If We Were Birds* illustrates the criteria of a dispublic by participating in the dominant public, gathering in mid-size mainstream theatres, challenging a dominant ideology, and transforming a dominant cultural imaginary. The theatres promoted *The Penelopiad* and *If We Were Birds* as feminist adaptations of Greek myths, but a closer inspection of the advertisements speaks to the two-sided characteristics of the dispublic. Billboards and advertisements across Toronto heralded *The Penelopiad* as "half-Dorothy Parker, half-Desperate Housewives." The advertisement's bisection of Atwood's play as half political satire (Parker) and half popular culture (Desperate Housewives) speaks to the split characteristics of the audience itself who participates in elements of the counterpublic and public, respectively. The advertisement also aligns the play's key figures with popular and political culture: Penelope is the passive yet comedic desperate housewife who fails to help her female collective, whereas the Maids are the biting political satirists that incite critical reflection. If audience members missed these advertisements, Thornton's director's message in the 2012 playbill of *The Penelopiad* announced that "Atwood steps out from behind the tall shadow of patriarchal myth-making to 'spin a thread of her own'" because "in history, in myth, in culture, the truth of women's lives was at best reduced to two-dimensional portraits of trustworthy wives and at worst ignored altogether" (3). Reviewers, in turn, were quick to present the play as a "feminist version of the great myth" of Odysseus (Nestruck "Fine female cast"). The reviewers of *If We Were Birds* similarly framed Shields's play as a "feminist" (Citron) work that "centres around female issues" (Ouzounian). In *The Globe and Mail*, Kelly Nestruck's review explains that Shields takes a feminist perspective by "channel[ing] her rage at the brutality inflicted on women in wars over the past century" but Nestruck is quick to assure readers that Shields avoids the trap of "dehumanizing the male perpetrators," which "is what is impressive." In this way, the media presents *The Penelopiad* and *If We Were Birds* as plays with palatable politics. The plays' advertisements, playbills, and reviews not only invite an audience to witness overtly feminist adaptations but also define a spectator that is a politically conscious participant of popular culture: "half-Dorothy Parker, half-Desperate Housewives."

Atwood's and Shields's audiences share a privileged set of criteria (class, education, geographical location) and they gather in national or mid-size theatres while the plays work to unite them in opposition to the popular dissemination of myths that celebrate masculine violence, wifely duty, and rape. *The Penelopiad*'s and *If We Were Birds*' audiences have been generally middle to upper-class individuals attending a production at a mainstream venue, such as Ottawa's National Arts Centre or NAC (*The Penelopiad*), Stratford-upon-Avon's Swan Theatre (*The Penelopiad*) as well as Toronto's Nightwood Theatre (*The Penelopiad*) and Tarragon Theatre (*If We Were Birds*).[20] Nightwood Theatre has the smallest theatre space of the theatres listed and is dedicated to "women artists from diverse backgrounds" (Nightwood, "Sponsor a Performance" 4). Nightwood, as a result, may seem to be on the fringe of the other theatres such as NAC, but audience demographics indicate that Nightwood attracts mostly "affluent" and "educated" viewers "aged 30–65" ("Sponsor" 5; see table 3.1). As the tables below illustrate, 79 per cent of the audience are university-educated, 70 per cent have a household income of over $60,000,

Table 3.1

The audience demographics of Nightwood Theatre in 2016

Nightwood's patrons are part of a community of theatre-goers that were found by the most recent Toronto Alliance for the Performing Arts' Audience Report to be:

Educated

Highest level of education completed	%
High school	3
Some college	3
Completed college	7
Some university	7
Undergrad degree	33
Post-grad/professional	46

Affluent

Household income	%
<$40,000	17
$40,000-<60,000	13
$60,000-<80,000	14
$80,000-<100,000	14
$100,000-<150,000	20
$150,000-<200,000	12
$200,000+	12

Loyal

	Age					
	18-24	25-34	35-44	45-54	55-64	65+
% of audience	4	15	14	20	26	22

Times attended per year	18-24 & 25-34	35-44	45-54	55-64	65+
1	3%	2%	2%	1%	1%
2-3	13%	14%	10%	6%	5%
4-5	11%	15%	16%	12%	11%
6-10	20%	24%	26%	30%	25%
>10	52%	44%	46%	51%	57%

Table 3.1 (continued)
The audience demographics of Nightwood Theatre in 2016

Employment	%
Full-Time	43
Part-Time	11
Retired	26
Self-Employed	20
Full-Time Student	4

Median household income = $88,000
Median age = 53
Female = 66%
Male = 34%

Source: Nightwood Theatre, "Sponsor" 5.

and over 68 per cent of members at every age group attend six or more Nightwood productions a year. While the director of communications for Nightwood explained that *The Penelopiad* was markedly one of the theatre's more popular productions, the theatre's general audience is a middle- to upper-class, university-educated public (table 3.1).

"Theatre in Toronto," as McKinnie suggests, "has become affiliated with sentiments of urban affluence" because it represents something more than economic capital: theatre "has come to be seen in Toronto as a way to achieve" the "ideals of public benefit" and "well-being" (11). More than a symbol of urban affluence, Tarragon Theatre and Nightwood Theatre gather affluent audiences with politically or intellectually driven motivations. Nightwood Theatre's audience demographics are consistent with other mid-level Toronto theatres. Tarragon Theatre, which produced *If We Were Birds*, similarly reports a middle class urban audience; through personal correspondence, the Tarragon Theatre Director of Communications in 2016, Lauren Vandervoort, confirmed that "50% have an annual household income of $100k or more" and "over 50% of the audience live in downtown Toronto, with another 30% in the GTA." A 2010 "Audience Engagement" survey was emailed to over 30,000 contacts who attend "Toronto's mid-size and small music, theatre, opera, and dance companies"; of those recipients, 3,662 completed the survey and answered a number of questions (Creative Trust 5).[21] According to the survey, theatre audiences from eight mid-size Toronto theatres report the following statistics: forty-eight years is their average age; 61 per cent are married or partnered; 57 per cent work full time; 72 per cent identify as female (Creative Trust 6–8). These audience demographics indicate that even "small" and "mid-size" theatres attract a mainstream urban audience. As one respondent says, the theatres and their performances express "dominant and middle class culture" (Creative Trust 17).

Overtly inviting an audience drawn to popular theatre, reviews of Nightwood's *The Penelopiad* touted the production as a canonical piece of theatre that appeals to the masses or to "anyone who wants to see just how great a piece of Canadian theatre can be" (Ouzounian, "The Penelopiad"). As Nightwood's director of communications, Taylor Trowbridge, explained in private correspondence, the productions' advertising campaign capitalized on Atwood's wide appeal by extending the regular advertisements in *Now* and *The Globe and Mail* to also include billboards in the Toronto Transit Commission (TTC) subway system and booths at book fairs (Taylor Trowbridge and Kailin Wright, pers. comm.). While selectively placed ads in the arts section of newspapers appealed to a specialized viewership, the subway posters targeted a larger and more general audience. Nightwood Theatre advertised to a general urban public, but the category of a dominant or mainstream public does not account for the political activism that the play can potentially incite. After all, the same review that promises *The Penelopiad* will appeal to "anyone" also frames the production as a political and "pitiless indictment of the horrors that men bring onto women" (Ouzounian, "The Penelopiad").

Nightwood Theatre and Tarragon Theatre's productions of *The Penelopiad* and *If We Were Birds* offered political messages that appealed to Toronto audiences' reported desire for "intellectual engagement" while the markedly feminist perspectives suited the predominantly female audience demographics. In Toronto, attendees of mid-level theatres such as Tarragon, Nightwood, and Buddies in Bad Times (which rented theatre space to Nightwood for *The Penelopiad* production), reported intellectual engagement as their primary reason for attending theatre.[22] Audiences were asked to "choose the three most important reasons why you attend dance / music / opera / theatre" (Creative Trust 15). Out of the four arts categories, the theatre audience members were the only ones that ranked "To engage intellectually with the art" as the top reason for attending a performance: the majority (53 per cent) of the theatre respondents cited intellectual engagement as the number one reason they attend the

Table 3.2 (below and opposite page)
Creative Trust's *The Audience Engagement Survey Report* of Toronto's midsize mainstage theatre audiences in 2010

People go to dance/music/opera/theatre performances for many reasons. From the list that follows, please choose the three most important reasons why you attend dance/music/opera/theatre.

- Being inspired or uplifted is a very popular motivation in all disciplines (but not *the most popular* in all).
- The three most commonly chosen motivations differ between the disciplines.
- Dance: 1) being inspired or uplifted; 2) discovering new choreographers and companies; 3) engaging intellectually with the art.
- Music: 1) being inspired or uplifted; 2) hearing great works by the masters; 3) discovering new composers and pieces.
- Opera: 1) discovering new operas that you've never heard or seen before; 2) being inspired or uplifted; 3) hearing and seeing great works by the masters. (Note: The opera results should be viewed with regard to the fact that the only opera company participating was Tapestry New Opera, which specializes in the creation, development and performance of new works.)
- Theatre: 1) engaging intellectually with the art; 2) being inspired or uplifted; 3) discovering new plays and playwrights.

theatre (Creative Trust 15; see table 3.2). Atwood's and Shields's feminist retellings of canonical Greek myths, then, cater to the female-driven audience and their requests for "intellectual" stimulation and for "new" perspectives.

Theatre reviews can reinforce what is reflected in the findings of the audience surveys by identifying the audiences' interests in new, intellectual, and political plays that have wide appeal. In response to the early performances of *If We Were Birds*, the reviewers clearly anticipated an experimental yet cautious audience by taking care to warn of the play's visceral impact and by assuming that the audience will be shocked by the honest portrayal of rape and violence. Jon Kaplan opens his "Preview" discussion of *If We Were Birds* by likening the viewing experience to being "punched in the gut" and Nestruck

	Dance %	Music %	Opera %	Theatre %	Total %
To be inspired or uplifted	58	60	48	47	51
To engage intellectually with the art	41	29	36	53	45
To discover new plays and playwrights/choreographers and companies/composers and pieces/operas that you've never heard or seen before	42	30	50	38	37
To hear and see great works by the masters	24	54	47	23	30
To relax and have fun	16	23	19	32	27
To have an intense emotional experience	24	25	32	27	26
To spend quality time with family or friends	12	14	12	27	21
To become a better appreciator of dance/music/opera/theatre	28	23	21	13	18
To expose others to the arts	13	4	5	14	12
To learn about cultures other than my own	17	10	4	9	11
To celebrate or observe my own cultural heritage	9	5	2	8	7
To feel calmed, at peace, serene	3	16	5	2	5

Source: Creative Trust, *The Audience Engagement Survey Report* 15.

similarly begins his review by stating that Shields writes this play with her "stomach strongly girded." In warning of the play's impact, these reviews cast the audience as "adventurous theatregoers unafraid of confronting the most unwanted of truths – that inhumanity is only human" (Nestruck, "If We Were Birds"). *Now* reviewer Glenn Sumi sets up the play and its audience as daring, asserting that "Anyone doubting the relevance and primal pull of myth needs to see *If We Were Birds*. Scratch that. Anyone interested in powerful theatre should see it." These reviews establish that the play is shocking and that its audience must be open to theatre outside of their comfort zone. Robert Crew ends his review in *The Star* by enticing readers with the following: "Comfortable? No. Heavy-handed? Yes, at times, but there are moments here that sear the memory." These reviews solicit audiences that are open to feminist politics and gut-wrenching scenes of violence – a mainstream audience that is politically "adventurous" (Nestruck, "If We Were Birds").

Many audience members may already share the plays' feminist politics and assessment of the Greek myths prior to the viewing experience; a public, as Warner explains, "appears to be open to indefinite strangers but in fact selects participants by criteria of shared social space (though not necessarily territorial space), habitus, topical concerns, intergeneric references, and circulating intelligible forms (including idiolects or speech genres)" (106). To put this in relation to theatre, the dramatic performances of Atwood's and Shields's plays gather a group of strangers, but at the same time, these strangers share the same set of criteria as dictated by the event: they are participating in the circulation of feminist politics, they share the same language (English), they are willing and able to pay to attend the theatre, and they are all gathered, however momentarily, in the same geographical location particular to the theatre house. This is to say that theatres are ideologically informed institutions with a set of politics and values that frame the act of viewing. The political mandates of theatres imbue the playhouse itself with a political resonance so that the audience members are gathered with the presupposition, however nominal, of attending a production influenced by particular issues. While Nightwood theatre has a markedly feminist theatre mandate that aims to foster plays by and about women, adding to the political resonance this 2012 production was held at Buddies in Bad Times Theatre, which is committed to queer theatre. In contrast, Atwood's play was one of Nightwood theatre's more mainstream and popular productions of 2012 – a season that also featured the premiere of new, lesser-known plays such as Rose Cullis's *The Happy Woman* and the annual Groundswell Festival of original works. Tarragon Theatre similarly draws a middle-class and middle-aged audience; as explained above, however, the advertisements and reviews for *If We Were Birds* were explicit in their labelling of Shields's play as feminist and political.[23] These theatres, then, gather and foster audiences with interests in political drama either prior to the theatrical event or as a result of it. In other words, *The Penelopiad*'s and *If We Were Birds*' theatre performances seem to address strangers but actually reinforce a dispublic with shared socio-economic criteria and political interests.

Atwood's and Shields's audiences necessitate the classification of a dispublic by functioning within the discourse of the dominant public while also resisting its normative ideologies. Although spectators of both plays may have a previous knowledge of Homer and Ovid's Greek myths (even if it is merely from other contemporary adaptations or the playbills themselves), the playwrights demand a reconsideration of these myths, as we know them.[24] I argue that the plays' doubled message – as works that resist the popularity of the very Greek myths they are dramatizing – defines the essential doubleness of a dispublic.

The Penelopiad and *If We Were Birds* identify with, and against, the Greek source narratives, while the spectators, in turn, are prompted to share the plays' disidentificatory relationship to the original. As plays that not only retell but also arguably capitalize on the Greek myths and the canonicity of these sources, *The Penelopiad* and *If We Were Birds* function within the sphere of the dominant public imaginary. These political adaptations may dramatize inset counterpublics, but the plays as a whole will never form real counterpublics. Instead, they occupy the sphere of the dispublic, forming audiences that participate in dominant society while working on and against its popular mythologies. The two plays demonstrate theatre's potential to form a resistive audience both onstage and off.

Dispublics: Potential for Political Change

Arendt's description of theatre as "political art par excellence" warrants consideration when dispublics gather today (188). The audiences that attend *The Penelopiad* and *If We Were Birds* are the vehicle through which Atwood and Shields alter Homer and Ovid's roles in the cultural imaginary. While the choruses parody, critique, and subvert the arguments and discursive forms of the original myths, their role as a "we" and their collective narration are their most powerful strategies for effecting change. The public, according to Habermas, is a propagating agent of the cultural imaginary because the public is a carrier of society's popular narratives and shared beliefs. Atwood and Shields call attention to their participation in a shared cultural imaginary and mythology through their political adaptation of popular Greek myths. While a counterpublic has measurable impact on public opinion, policy, or space, to name a few outcomes, a dispublic's impact on public opinion is at once immediate (in that they constitute the public) and gradual (they do not engage in riotous counterpublic measures but instead effect change from within). Atwood and Shields's dispublic enact immediate change by collectively imagining revised feminist versions of Greek myths that foreground disenfranchised women's perspectives in the theatre. At the end of *If We Were Birds*, Shields's Philomela simultaneously speaks of her personal trauma and the audience's memory of Shields's bloody play, explaining, "the memories are forever wedged in our thoughts. / There is no escape or release" (65). Atwood's *The Penelopiad* forms a palimpsest with Homer's *The Odyssey* and the many other versions of the Greek myth. Shields's play, in turn, layers itself with Ovid's *Metamorphoses*, altering the audience's earlier imaginings of the myth. If the early canonical versions of *The Odyssey* and *Metamorphoses* are part of the collective conscious of Western society, then Atwood and Shields's plays work to change the dominant imaginary. Frye describes the phenomena of the dominant or cultural imaginary as the "social imagination" (217) and explains that "literature is conscious mythology: as a society develops, its mythical stories become structural principles of storytelling, its mythical concepts, sun-gods and the like, become habits of metaphorical thought" (234) and these inherited stories are "conditioned in their attitudes by their predecessors, or by the cultural climate of their predecessors" (252). *The Penelopiad* promotes a counter-imaginary (or counter-discourse) that sees the Maids as pivotal characters and interprets Penelope as a flawed figure who is partially responsible for the handmaidens' deaths. *If We Were Birds*, by comparison, reframes Ovid's myth as a fetishization of female virginity and rape. By offering alternative political versions, *The Penelopiad* and *If We Were Birds* debunk the "originals" as the sole authoritative sources of the canonical myths and transform the role of myths in the public imaginary. In viewing the political adaptations, the audience participates in the transformation of the collective, public imaginary.

Speaking of the lasting effects of political adaptations, Julie Malnig asserts that McLaughlin's 1995 feminist revision of the *Oresteia* was "reclaiming the myth … for her generation" (32); Malnig goes on to explain that McLaughlin's adaptation "suggests that rewriting the myth may be imaginable but that we are not fully equipped to change it – just yet" (36). In 2006 and 2007, Atwood and Shields were equipped to change the myths' narratives, but the endings of their plays emphasize the fact that they need "you," the audience, to help them transform the myths in the collective imagination. The critical acclaim and rave reviews the plays received suggest that the audience is willing to participate in the playwrights' project of changing the way we think about myths that normalize sexual violence. *The Penelopiad* received many standing ovations in Canada "as if," Shannon Hengen suggests, "to show solidarity with its author." For Hengen, the play's performance on "large, prestigious national stages" moves Atwood's "rendering of Classical myth ... closer to the centre of her country's and perhaps the Anglophone world's cultural imagination" (49). The dispublic is the vehicle through which feminist adaptations become part of the dominant collective imagination. Because the collective imagination informs normative ideologies, these changes to our understandings of Greek myths will have far-reaching, though gradual, implications on the public's notions of heroism, female collectives, and sexual violence.

The dispublic's potential to affect positive political change also takes place through post-performance discourse about the plays and, for instance, the twentieth and twenty-first centuries' genocides as narrativized by Shields's chorus and their real-life stories of recent wars. After all, Nightwood and Tarragon Theatre audiences not only want "to engage intellectually" with a production, they also prefer to "vigorously" discuss the production after the performance (Creative Trust 26). After a show, 97 per cent of theatre audience respondents note a moderate to high-level interest in discussing the production (Creative Trust 26). Through these post-performance discussions, the plays' and their dispublics impact public opinion and the collective imaginary. Hengen highlights the importance of these post-performance reflections in relationship to *The Penelopiad*'s lessons on female collectivity: Atwood "is beckoning us to relive experientially and individually Penelope's neglect of her disadvantaged Maids and then as an audience to discern the instances and effects of similar neglect in our time" (49). The choruses, after all, directly call on the audience and their potential to "Be our defenders" (*The Penelopiad* 78).

Atwood's *The Penelopiad* further achieved positive real-world change through the creation of a female mentorship program and what Hengen describes as "an unusual connection ... between nine wealthy and influential Canadian women and the play's creative team" (52). Just as the play's chorus and staging establish a poetics of collaboration, the rehearsal and production process of *The Penelopiad* also enforced the collaborative potential of a "we." The productions of *The Penelopiad* involved "unprecedented" artistic partnership among Canadian and British actors, and between England's Royal

Shakespeare Company and Canada's National Arts Centre (Hengen 51). As Hengen says, "Somehow the telling of a Classical tale seems to have drawn artists, benefactors, and audience together uniquely. And, all of the actors, the writer, and the director are women, as are all of the benefactors" (52). Nightwood Theatre's 2012 playbill explains that each of the donors, now known as the Penelope Circle, helped to fund the National Arts Centre's production and also mentored "a young woman who she believes will have a profound impact on our society" (Thornton 3). Kate Hennig, an actor who played Eurycleia in the 2007 British and Canadian productions of *The Penelopiad*, writes of Penelope's Circle in her blog:

> These women constitute a circle of financial support for this project, specifically because of its focus on the creative achievements of Canadian women. Each of the women in the Penelope Circle has chosen a protégé to work with them on the philanthropy that they are giving to this project. How grateful can we be for people like this. And it is not some anonymous donation. Let me stress how much these amazing women have given us by being at the play, some of them four and five times, and really expressing our achievements with their voices and their response to our work. What a special opportunity it is to establish a real relationship with the patronesses of our art. (28 September 2007)[25]

Hennig appreciates Penelope's Circle not only for their role as behind-the-scenes patrons but also for "being at the play" as engaged audience members, underlining the significant contribution of spectators' "response to our work" (28 September 2007). Further illustrating the Penelope Circle's and cast's commitment to real social change, they participated in a panel discussion, "Leading by Example: Empowering the Next Generation of Canadian Women," at the governor general's residence, Rideau Hall, which, according to Hennig, was attended by "about 120 women altogether, including many recipients of the Order of Canada, and many high power [*sic*] executives from business, law, politics, and the Arts" (30 September 2007). *The Penelopiad*'s audience members, then, actively engaged in discussions about empowering women and brought together leaders in politics and art. The National Arts Centre's 2007–08 season program lists these donors by name because "their shared vision and belief in the power of women's leadership to effect positive social change is an inspiration to us all," which invites other audience members to participate as a dispublic in positive real-world change (9). The play's production, then, helped to activate and empower a dispublic made up of "socially conscious," "wealthy" women with "impact."

The twenty-first century continues to blur the line between the popular and the political, thereby making dispublics an especially relevant form of spectatorship. As Leah H. Miller asserts, "Our political world has become popularized, or our popular world has become politicized" (vii). The dispublic, as a result, is not limited to Atwood's and Shields's plays or to Canadian contexts and political adaptations. Atwood's and Shields's choruses are only two case studies of how political adaptations are engaging mainstream audiences in a dialogue that can change the way we think about inherited narratives and values. Given the pervasiveness of neoliberal politics and art with political messages, I argue that the dispublic is replacing the public as the new omnipresent audience.

One of the most effective ways for political adaptations to engage audiences is to recognize the viewers' role as political and popular participants, that is, to address them as a dispublic. In this way, political adaptations cultivate a dispublic by calling out to a pervasive "You you you you / you you you you / YOU YOU YOU YOU" (*If We Were Birds*, 76).

4 Beyond the Limits of Adaptation in *Princess Pocahontas and the Blue Spots* and *Almighty Voice and His Wife*

Political adaptations are entangled with their source material; this dramatic mode is ultimately a performance of disidentification that at once underlines and undermines the source. But what happens when the political adaptation only conveys the limits of the source? Can political adaptation critique source material without reinforcing its cultural relevance? The Kuna and Rappahannock playwright Monique Mojica's *Princess Pocahontas and the Blue Spots* (1990), and Daniel David Moses's (a Delaware and Tuscaroran from the Six Nations) *Almighty Voice and His Wife* (1991) adapt colonial myths of Pocahontas and Almighty Voice in order to cast the source materials as mere fictions of historical Indigenous figures. I argue that *Princess Pocahontas* and *Almighty Voice* move beyond the limits of political adaptation by replacing the source material with the authors' more authoritative versions of Pocahontas and Almighty Voice. Mojica's and Moses's plays, however, do not simply invert the hierarchy of source and adaptation; instead, the plays complicate my theory of political adaptation and show how adaptors can dismantle the persistent hierarchy that posits older art as better art by presenting stories as necessarily layered and transformative performances.

These two plays are not only political adaptations – they celebrate adaptation by presenting the self as revisable and adaptive. This renewed understanding of political adaptation and its potential extends to the historical title characters themselves as *Princess Pocahontas* and *Almighty Voice* foreground the performativity of history and legendary figures. In order to present a new understanding of the over-sexualized Pocahontas and criminalized Almighty Voice, Mojica and Moses offer distinct conceptions of identity. Mojica's Pocahontas is a combination of a storybook princess, a brave young woman, a sexualized squaw, a daughter, and a betrayer of her people, while Moses's Almighty Voice becomes more than the subject of Canada's largest manhunt when he appears as a husband, father, and warrior. Through these layers,

Mojica's and Moses's plays simultaneously challenge literary and identity hierarchies that celebrate an originating, singular source or core self, respectively – these hierarchies are all too often the root of cultural prejudice and even the validation of cultural genocide. In prompting the audience to appreciate narratives of *Pocahontas* and *Almighty Voice* from diverse and conflicting perspectives, Mojica and Moses invite us to read critically and question histories that celebrate colonists or demonize Indigenous peoples.[1] An analysis of the characters' transformations and performative utterances reveals how both plays promote political adaptation both as a theatrical mode for protest and also as a mode for understanding the self.

The previous chapters examined the limits and benefits of political adaptation's disidentification with (or simultaneous identification with and against) a source; this chapter focuses on political adaptation's transformation of the source material. While the first two chapters argue that political adaptation performs disidentification or a paradoxical embrace and rejection of inherited stories, chapter 3 considers the audience's resulting disidentification with source material and formation of a dispublic. Building on the ideas presented in chapter 3 and the impact of political adaptation on the audience, this chapter looks more closely at the impact of political adaptation on the sources. This chapter, then, further illustrates my definition of political adaptation as disidentification by emphasizing the transformative act of disidentification.

Princess Pocahontas and *Almighty Voice* change our understanding or approach to the source material while also challenging the dynamics of adaptation itself by replacing the source as the more authoritative version of the story. This is a radical effect because it changes adaptation's linear, hierarchical relationship to an earlier source. Mojica's and Moses's plays reveal political adaptation to be a layered, circular performance of multiple versions of historical figures. The plays invite a critical audience by encouraging them to question the valorization of a source as truth merely because it is earlier and documented. In challenging colonial text-based histories of Pocahontas and Almighty Voice, Mojica and Moses at once target the historicization of these specific figures and the value structures that inform our viewing experience of an adaptation. In *Princess Pocahontas* and *Almighty Voice*, adaptation is not a hierarchical art form that posits source above adaptation but rather a cyclical performance that layers diverse distinct viewpoints and versions.

Princess Pocahontas weaves together different narrative strands about the performativity of female Indigenous identity while re-telling the Pocahontas myth. Premiering in 1990 at Theatre Passe Muraille Backspace, the play's first production was directed by Muriel Miguel with Mojica and Alejandra Nuñez as the two actors who perform multiple roles. The play is a non-chronological account of Powhatan's daughter Matoaka (1596–1617) and how she became known as Princess Pocahontas. After being captured by the English, Pocahontas converted to Christianity, changed her name to Lady Rebecca, and married John Rolfe; she died not long after her trip to London in Gravesend. Mojica complicates the story of Pocahontas by introducing larger debates about the negative misrepresentation of Indigenous women in history, including performances of Malinche or Doña Marina – a Nahua woman who acted as an interpreter for Hernán Cortés during the Spanish conquest of the Aztec empire and who has also, as a result, been depicted as a traitor to her nation. The play ends with Contemporary Woman #1 and #2 calling on other women to join them in strength and solidarity as they navigate dominant understandings of feminism.

Almighty Voice and His Wife was first produced at the Great Canadian Theatre Company in 1991. Directed by Cat Cayuga, it featured Billy Merasty and Jani Lauzon as Almighty Voice and White Girl, respectively. In 2011, Native Earth mounted a production, starring Derek Garza as Almighty Voice and PJ Prudat as White Girl, and with Michael Greyeyes as the director. Like Mojica's *Princess Pocahontas*, Moses's play also reclaims a legendary Indigenous figure: Almighty Voice (or *Kisse-Manitou-Wayou* in Cree) was a Cree man who lived in Saskatchewan during the end of the nineteenth century. In order to feed himself and his community, Almighty Voice killed one of his father's cows. Colonial officials, however, believed that the cow – and all steers given to Indigenous peoples under the treaties – was the property of the Crown and subsequently arrested Almighty Voice for stealing property. He was incarcerated in the town of Duck Lake, which is where the second half of Moses's play takes place. There was construction outside of the jail and Almighty Voice overheard a jailer jest that they were building a scaffold for Almighty Voice's impending execution. Thinking the joke to be true, Almighty Voice fled prison and was chased by the mounted police. "A tasteless joke," as Jo-Ann Episkenew says, "set in motion one of the biggest manhunts in Canadian history" (156). His escape ended in a shootout with, as legend has it, over one hundred mounted police. Almighty Voice was killed. *Almighty Voice*'s two acts are radically different. The action of act one tells a tragic story of this hero figure that "*incorporates historic events and happens between the end of October 1895 and*

May of 1897" in Saskatchewan, while the second act jumps to a present-day comedic school presentation on Indigenous culture and "*occurs on the auditorium stage of the abandoned industrial school at Duck Lake*" (2). In act 2, Almighty Voice appears as his own Ghost and White Girl enacts the role of the white male Interlocutor: both characters wear whiteface. *Almighty Voice*, as Rob Appleford suggests, exposes the mainstream desire to possess Indigenous peoples through representation of the "real Indian," which further aligns with *Princess Pocahontas*'s political project, making them rich companion plays.

What distinguishes *Princess Pocahontas* and *Almighty Voice* from Optative Theatrical Laboratories' (OTL) *Sinking Neptune* and other political adaptations is that Mojica's and Moses's plays manage to adapt colonial myths without foregrounding the colonizer and reinscribing a colonial narrative. These two plays engage a number of strategies that political adaptors share – announcing source material, all-Indigenous casting, multiple role play – and they showcase the impact of self-declarations as a method for distinguishing Pocahontas and Almighty Voice from stereotypes of the all-too obliging or vanishing Indian (who is doomed to die in a modern world), respectively. The art of reclaiming one's narrative is a widespread form for resisting popular yet misleading conceptions of cultural identity. The stakes, however, are particularly high for these political adaptors because, as Paula Gunn Allen points out, the stereotype of the vanishing Indian has been used as an excuse for the cultural genocide of Indigenous people in Canada (*Sacred*).

Political adaptation is an especially pertinent form for these postcolonial responses to widely accepted national histories. Hutcheon, for instance, suggests that adaptation threatens to colonize the imagination by presenting one view of the source text, thereby forcing the audience to share in the singular imaginative response that effectively re-colonizes the viewer's initial imaginative reaction ("Performing Modernism"). Adaptation, as a form and as a theory, is thus already situated within the dynamics of colonial conquest but the overtly layered structure and performative mode of political adaptation preclude a singular perspective or, in Hutcheon's terms, a colonization of the imagination: put another way, the layered stories, performances, and characters in Mojica's and Moses's political adaptations refute the cultural hierarchy at the heart of colonial retellings of Pocahontas and Almighty Voice.

Although Mojica and Moses allude to a variety of narratives, I focus on the main legends about the titular historical figures. At the beginning of *Princess*

Pocahontas, Mojica herself lists some of the play's many intertexts, including Chrystos's *Not Vanishing*, Gloria Anzaldúa's *Borderlands/La Frontera*, and Allen's *The Sacred Hoop*.[2] In the first volume of *Staging Coyote's Dream*, Mojica and Ric Knowles describe *Princess Pocahontas* both as a critique of the colonial "Captain Whiteman" and also as a "rousing intertextual call for solidarity" (136).[3] Much like Mojica's *Princess Pocahontas*, Moses's *Almighty Voice* also draws on a number of sources in order to rework an often-told story of the dangerous "Indian." Almighty Voice has been the subject of many retellings, such as Pauline Johnson's poem "The Cattle Thief" (1900), Leonard Peterson's play *Almighty Voice* (1970), Rudy Wiebe's short story "Where Is the Voice Coming From?" (1974), the film *Alien Thunder* (also entitled *Dan Candy's Law*, directed by Claude Fournier and starring Donald Sutherland, 1974), and Pierre Berton's *The Wild Frontier: More Tales from the Remarkable Past* (1978), among others. Directly responding to these many versions and enactments of "*chanting*" Indians (Peterson 12), Moses's first act rewrites the myth, while the second act parodies a wide range of popular Indian commodifications and stereotypes such as a "cigar store" (30), "red man" (31), "Geronimo" (31), "Tonto" (31), the "Pontiac" car (32), and "the Vanishing Indian" (33). My analysis does not intend to overlook the dynamic range of source material, but rather to highlight how the political adaptations effectively challenge the source narratives of the respective titular figures.

"Indians," Allen explains, have been told that they "have to assimilate or perish" (*Sacred* 5), but political adaptation offers an alternative to assimilation and appropriation. In Mojica's and Moses's plays, adaptation, individual perseverance, and cultural survival are intrinsically linked. After all, as Allen suggests, the isolated individual is "foreign to American Indian thought" because "at base, every story, every song, every ceremony tells the Indian that each creature is part of a living whole and that all parts of that whole are related to one another by virtue of their participation in the whole of being" (*Sacred* 60). Allen's discussion of ceremony engages the same rhetoric of adaptation theory, which argues that all stories and art "are related to one another" and inherently adaptive. If, however, Indigenous peoples often conceive of a collective "we" rather than an isolated "I," then what is the significance of the repeated "I am" declarations in these two plays?[4] Allen's discussion of repetition provides some insight into the function of the "I am" refrain because "Repetition [in Indigenous stories] operates like a chorus in Western drama" that serves to "reinforce the theme" while it "integrates and fuses" (*Sacred* 63).

In this way, the repeated "I am" declarations both announce the theme of individual identity and integrate the speaker within a larger whole.

Princess Pocahontas and *Almighty Voice* respond to stereotypes of the "real Indian" by presenting the "real" self as illusive and transformative. Trinh T. Minh-ha – whose theories also emerged from experiences of colonization – explains that dominant ideologies conceive of the "genuine, original, authentic self" as un-changing or homogenous, which renders difference oppositional to the "real" core self (415). As Minh-ha says, "Identity, thus understood, supposes that a clear dividing line can be made between I and not-I … between depth and surface, or vertical and horizontal identity. The further one moves from the core the less likely one is thought to be capable of fulfilling one's role as the real self, the real black, Indian, or Asian, the real woman" (415). I see Minh-ha's theory of self and difference as a way of explicating Mojica and Moses's use of performance to redefine difference not as antithetical to but as an intrinsic part of the self. Minh-ha re-theorizes the self in order to re-conceive of difference as constructive and constitutive. Comparatively, *Princess Pocahontas* re-theorizes the "I" as multiple and layered, while *Almighty Voice* destabilizes racial boundaries by demonstrating the performativity of race and the relative ease with which one can enact race change. Both plays present the self as multiple, performative, and adaptive because, after all, the "I is not unitary" (Minh-ha 415).

For Allen, the differences between the First Nations and Inuit "I," or, more accurately, a holistic "we," and the European concept of an individual autonomous "I" has not only been responsible for the colonial focus on ownership but has also fuelled earlier stereotypes of the primitive Indian. Colonial stereotypes set up the so-called "primitive Indians" as a threat to industrial society's values of capital growth and individual property (*Sacred* 5). The American dream of wealth and progress, as Allen describes it, cast First Nations and Inuit peoples as savage, and, by extension, as antithetical to a post-industrial society; the characterization of Indigenous people as primitive, and thereby non-capitalistic, has been a rationale for racism and "a root cause of the genocide practiced against American Indians since the colonial period" (*Sacred* 5). Because Canadian history has privileged the colonial "I" or perspective and conceptions of "I" have been used as one of the excuses for the colonizer's investment in the attainment of private property, *Princess Pocahontas*'s and *Almighty Voice*'s "I am" statements accrue weighty cultural significance as they respond to the civilizing claims and genocide of colonial conquests.

Building on the argument in chapter 2, that performative utterances and political adaptations announce a citational history of previous usages of a name or past tellings of a story, I argue that *Princess Pocahontas* and *Almighty Voice* emphasize this citationality in order to present the self as transformative, layered, and integrated within a larger collective. Mojica's and Moses's plays feature crises of identity that culminate in self-assertive statements, such as "I am Princess Pocahontas" (Mojica 30) and "I am the wife of Almighty Voice" (Moses 20). In works that seek to reshape earlier versions of the Pocahontas and Almighty Voice myths, these performative utterances resonate with the biblical "I am" and are a key strategy for talking back to colonial legends and a history of enforced Christianity in Canada. By re-appropriating religious rhetoric, Mojica and Moses at once repeat and challenge the antecedent narratives of colonial settlement. This doubleness governs Mojica's and Moses's re-conceptualization of the "I" as layered and performative.[5] The citational history of "I am" declarations at once hinders and facilitates the authority of the speaker, just as the historical source material of the political adaptations simultaneously constrains and constructs the significance of the adaptation. To highlight this connection between adaptation and identification, I turn to the characters' performed "I am" declarations as a model for the disidentificatory dynamics of Mojica's and Moses's political adaptations.

Princess Pocahontas and *Almighty Voice* challenge identity constructions of the Indian princess (Pocahontas) and the vanishing savage (Almighty Voice) through the use of multiple "I am" statements.[6] Integrating performance, identity, and adaptation theories in the following section, I argue that Mojica and Moses harness the form of political adaptation in order to promote the inherently transformative quality of identity: in short, the plays define the self as an adaptation. I then outline four main functions of "I am" statements and how they perform identity in the contexts of political adaptations. After using performative utterances as a model for how identity functions as adaptation, I turn to the plays to show how Mojica and Moses use adaptation and "I am" declarations to transform the preconceived notions of the Indian princess or vanishing Indian, respectively. Ultimately, *Princess Pocahontas* and *Almighty Voice* reveal the potential of political adaptations to transform the source material without reinforcing its cultural significance or validity.

The Adaptive Self

Scholars of performance, literature, race, and gender, among other fields, have come to understand identity in terms of performance, but I propose that we consider identity as a performance of adaptation. Richard Schechner applies performance studies to artistic events as well as cultural rituals and everyday practices, including individual performances of racial, gendered, economic, or sexual identities.[7] As Simone de Beauvoir famously says, "*On ne naît pas femme: on le devient*" (xviii) or "a woman is not born, but rather becomes, woman" (283). Identity is not born; it is constantly in a state of becoming and is always already composed of earlier identificatory iterations. Put another way, the way we construct identity is akin to the way we construct adaptations: self-defining narratives and statements not only narrate one's identity and life but also adapt previous narratives of identity, gender, sexuality, culture, and nationalism that have come before and that layer one's telling and understanding of selfhood. Butler's pivotal definition of identity as a "stylized repetition of acts through time" ("Performative Acts" 2) engages the language and structure of adaptation as a repetition of acts or narratives through time. Theories of identity present identity as performance and also gesture towards identity as a performance of adaptation.

The rules and theoretical approaches to adaptation, and political adaptation in particular, offer strategies for how we can talk about and change identity. The theory of adaptation as a palimpsest – where multiple layers of writing or storytelling are visible at once – provides a language and concept for layered identity.[8] In her theory of adaptation, Hutcheon conceives of both adaptations and the experience of adaptations as "palimpsestuous," asserting that "we experience adaptations … as palimpsests through our memory of other works that resonate through repetition with variation" (8). I argue that Mojica's and Moses's political adaptations are not only palimpsests themselves but also construct a palimpsestic "I."

Princess Pocahontas and *Almighty Voice* conceive of the self as layered and multiple much like the form of adaptation itself. In the process of presenting a layered "I," *Princess Pocahontas*'s and *Almighty Voice*'s self-assertions re-identify the speakers and demonstrate the subject-making function of performative acts. As discussed in chapter 2 in relation to successful or failed self-declarations, J.L. Austin's speech act theory examines performances of language wherein to say something is to do something, such as a curse, a bet, or a marriage ceremony declaration, "I do (take this woman to be my lawful wedded wife)" (Austin 12). Responding to Austin's speech act theory and use of the marriage ceremony, Judith Butler interrogates the power that authorizes this pronouncement and interprets the marriage ceremony as a reinforcement of heteronormativity. Butler argues that "it is through the invocation of convention" and not through the speaking subject that the speech act "derives its binding power" (*Bodies That Matter* 225). Whereas Austin imbues the speaking subject with the power to act through language, Butler emphasizes the authority of the performed convention itself. My analysis combines both approaches by investigating the subject-making and empowering capabilities of performed language: *Princess Pocahontas* and *Almighty Voice* demonstrate a symbiotic connection between the authority of the language itself and the authority of the speaker. To apply Austin's speech act theory, the "I am" declaration performs an action and gains its authority from both the speaker and the speaker's delivery. Yet as Butler's theories of performative identity would suggest, the history of the "I am" statement resounds with each delivery and, as a result, the declaration also invokes authority through citation.

Conceiving of "I am" statements as palimpsestic speech acts provides a theoretical framework – that of performance theory and adaptation theory – for understanding the relationship between individual "I am" declarations and their many echoes. Butler's emphasis on the citationality of performative utterances does not valorize earlier utterances as "original" or as "source" but rather democratizes every performative utterance as one of many. Adaptation theorists, by comparison, have been advocating for scholars, viewers, and critics to adopt this type of a democratic approach to adaptations. Literary adaptations, like speech acts, call attention to their predecessors, but unlike speech acts, they have a history of being denounced for this citationality. Hutcheon, Robert Stam, and Julie Sanders argue for an egalitarian approach to literary adaptation that takes the earlier works into account without blindly valorizing them. Sanders, in particular, argues for the value of contemporary adaptation, asserting that adaptations "make texts 'relevant' or easily comprehensible to new audiences and readerships via the process of proximation and updating" (19). The "I am" declarations of *Princess Pocahontas* and *Almighty Voice* call up a citational history of culturally loaded "I am" statements from announced intertexts that range from the Bible, to colonial history, to contemporary literatures. Using speech acts as a way of adapting earlier works helps to avoid the pitfalls of adaptation as a seemingly parasitic form because the citationality of speech acts is widely accepted as a democratic process. In Mojica's and Moses's particular integration of speech acts and intertextuality, the two plays avoid the subservient worship of older works and critique many of the source materials.

Integrating adaptation studies with theories on performative identity suggests the highly adaptive nature of the self. According to Butler's conception of speech acts, all language, whether it references the dominant or the marginal, cites earlier instances of naming and the "historically revisable possibility of a name" or of an "I" that precedes, exceeds, and creates the speaker (*Bodies* 226). Butler suggests that "the 'I' only comes into being through being called, named, interpellated … and this discursive constitution takes place prior to the 'I'" (*Bodies That Matter* 225). This emphasis on the definitive power of citation and historicity should not be confused with a celebration of fidelity or a valourization of the earlier utterance since Butler herself seems to take it for granted that "reiterations are never simply replicas of the same" (*Bodies* 226). The inherent variation within replication is actually the premise of Butler's theories of linguistic performance and citationality. For Butler, as with recent adaptation theorists, the history of a performative utterance further "decenters the presentist view of the subject as the exclusive origin or owner of what is said" (*Bodies*, 227). In this way, the multiple echoes of "I am" statements destabilize the notion that an identity or self can be traced back to a single originating source.

Allen points to a similar overarching assumption of intertextuality in Indigenous literature, explaining that "It is reasonable, from an Indian point of view, that all literary forms should be interrelated, given the basic idea of the unity and relatedness of all the phenomena of life" (*The Sacred Hoop* 62). This citational history of the plays and of "I am" statements reinforces the performance of the "I" as layered and multiple. Allen's conception of the self begins where Butler's ends: with the theory that the self is transformative and connected to earlier performances. While Austin and Butler outline the constitutive powers of speech, Allen describes the constitutive force of Indigenous peoples' ceremonies. Allen's *The Sacred Hoop* contributes to a theorization of performative identity by conceiving of life in terms of a transformative ritual: "the ritual cycle of dying, birth, growth, ripening, dying, and rebirth" is a "transformative process" (80). Unlike Butler's sequential ordering of language as a predecessor of the self, Allen does not assume that ritual ceremonies precede the self. For Allen, ritual "means transforming something from one state or condition to another" because performative ceremonies involve "the power to make, to create, to transform" (*Sacred Hoop* 29). Approaching the plays as performed ceremonies, then, replaces a linear, hierarchical structure of source above adaptation or of language before selfhood with a cyclical and eternal form. In *Princess Pocahontas* and *Almighty Voice*, by extension, the "I am" statements and performative acts manifest what they state or perform. Allen's discussion of ceremonies contributes an emphasis on change: the performative utterances simultaneously constitute and transform the self. In this way, the repetition of "I am" statements draws attention to the transformative, cyclical act of political adaptation as a form that invites further artistic creation and political response, a form that promotes rebirth and continued change.

Four Functions of "I Am" Statements

"I am" statements are a microcosm for the way that political adaptation's citationality functions and the impact of its layered narratives. *Princess Pocahontas* and *Almighty Voice* dramatize four main functions of "I am" statements: (1) to describe and thereby constitute the self; (2) to forge belongingness to a community; (3) to assert ownership over identificatory categories; and (4) to emphasize individuality as distinct from yet simultaneously connected to a group. The first function describes the "I am" statement's effect on the speaker's identity, the second and third functions describe the speaker's relation to the identificatory category, and the fourth function speaks to the individual's participation in communal identity.[9]

To begin with the first function, self-defining utterances describe and create the speaker's identity, as in Austin's speech act theory.[10] Applying Austin's speech act theory – which claims that to say something is to do or create something – to "I am" statements, exposes the constitutive functions of self-assertive declarations. The beginning of Moses's *Almighty Voice and His Wife* demonstrates this self-defining strategy as White Girl and Almighty Voice establish their individual identities and marriage. In the first scene White Girl declares "I am a crazy one" (5) and tells Almighty Voice that "I'm going to be your wife now" (6). When the treaty agent tries to rename Almighty Voice

"John Baptist," Almighty Voice rejects the Judeo-Christian appellation and asserts his own identity, proclaiming "I'm Almighty Voice" (10). Almighty Voice later recalls this self-assertive moment and defines himself as someone "who's not afraid to say his name" (16). In fact, when White Girl struggles with her traumatic memories of residential school, Almighty Voice's name rekindles her self-knowledge:

> VOICE: You married Almighty Voice, who's not afraid to say his name. Let your glass god hear it. Almighty Voice! – who has listened to our fathers and heard what they say. Almighty Voice, who remembers our Creator and our people's ways. Almighty Voice knows how to fight for you. Do you hear what I'm saying? Do you?
> GIRL: Yes. Yes, I do.
> VOICE: Who is saying it?
> GIRL: Almighty Voice.
> VOICE: Remember who you are. Remember what your mother taught you.
> GIRL: Almighty Voice, the husband of White Girl! (16)

Almighty Voice's name acts as a punctuating marker and metonym for their rejection of the Judeo-Christian "glass god," belief in "our Creator," and knowledge of "our people's ways." In order to remember "who you are" and "what your mother taught you," White Girl repeats Almighty Voice's name as she chants, "Almighty Voice […] Almighty Voice" (17). Marking her self-realization, White Girl finally becomes the primary named subject when she defines Almighty Voice as "the husband of White Girl!" (17). In these opening scenes, their empowered self-naming is rooted in agency and self-constitution.

Mojica and Moses engage with the issue of the Christian conversion of Indigenous peoples across North America in part by echoing and challenging the authoritative power of the biblical "I AM" or "I am who I am" (which signals Yahweh or the Judeo-Christian God).[11] The biblical "I am who I am," however, also exemplifies the self-constituting, and occasionally tautological, potential of speech acts. William Franke, for instance, emphasizes the self-constituting powers of "I am" and language in the Bible, asserting, "language becomes the medium of a disclosure of human life" (156). Mojica and Moses reappropriate the "I am" rhetoric of the Judeo-Christian Bible in order to construct alternative versions of Cree identities. "I am" is at once an emblem of White Girl's forced religious conversion and of the constitutive functions of speech acts.

"I am" statements, however, do not always perform self-constitution. I would like to complicate the first function of self-assertions by accounting for speech acts that demonstrate an inner confusion and self-loss. Throughout the play, White Girl's self-identifications as "Marrie" (10), "crazy one" (5), "White Girl" (13), and "wife" (20) exemplify her inner instability as she oscillates between her Judeo-Christian and Cree identities. Because her appellation "White Girl" is rarely spoken in the play, the uneasy irony of her name is thus more pronounced in the dramatic script as a prompt to her lines than on the stage: the text highlights the white-washing of "White Girl" whereas the performance confronts us with her undeniable Indigeneity with actors like Prudat, who identifies as Métis, Cree, and Saulteaux, playing the role of White Girl in Native Earth's 2011 production. The disconnect between White Girl's name and selfhood gestures towards the lack of historical records on Almighty Voice's wives and her absence from the popular legend. Episkenew explains that "the historical Almighty Voice is reported to have had four wives – evidently, he was not a Christian – but nothing is known of them. Those who have authored the documents that form the historical record have rarely considered First Nations women sufficiently important to record their names and stories" (157–8). Speaking to her omission from national records, White Girl tells the audience and Judeo-Christian god, "You don't know my name" because "I'm only a crazy squaw" (20). White Girl's self-naming, then, not only signifies her self-constitution but also her erasure from history. Butler warns that "as much as it is necessary to … lay claim to the power to name oneself and determine the conditions under which that name is used, it is also impossible to sustain that kind of mastery over the trajectory of those categories" (*Bodies* 227). For Butler, the history of the identificatory category also signals the "history of the usages that one never controlled" (*Bodies* 227). Almighty Voice's name, for instance, elicits the history of the Judeo-Christian "Almighty" God just as "squaw" and "White Girl" resound with the history of colonial stereotypes and white settler culture, respectively. Self-naming, then, constitutes the self, but the history of the identificatory category – such as "squaw," "wife," "husband," Virgin Mary (or "Marrie"), and "White Girl" – also signals the previous usages of the label that the speaker did not control. In fact, each "I am" function has both self-affirming and self-effacing potential.[12]

With performative utterances, the speaker lays claim to the identificatory label, yet paradoxically, this very label may also constrain the speaker's autonomy.[13] This same paradox holds true for literary adaptations because an adaptation's connection to a source enriches its narrative layers and market value while simultaneously impeding its originality. Though adaptations benefit from their relation to a known source or popular narrative, Robert Stam explains that critical commentary on adaptations often involves accusations of parasitism.

Marking the second and third functions, self-defining utterances assert a sense of belonging to and ownership of identificatory categories and of the self. In establishing belongingness, Episkenew asserts that self-defining "stories show us that we are not alone" and "can help dislocated 'tribal relations' reconnect with their communities" (16). As a form of self-narration, "I am" statements transform isolated individuals into "members of a larger community" of identificatory categories and of "shared stories" (Episkenew 16). The speaker also stakes a proprietary claim over the identificatory label by at once belonging to and asserting ownership over an appellation. As Miri Albahari argues, thoughts of "'me,' 'mine,' or 'I am'" express "a sense of belongingness" and "possessive ownership" (53). As speech acts that assert belongingness, "I am" statements directly contribute to Mojica's and Moses's project of reviving Indigenous communities.

"I am" declarations, however, can fail to assert the speaker's ownership or belonging to a group, and, as a result, can denigrate the speaker into the property of an identificatory category. In *Princess Pocahontas*, Pocahontas says, "I am Lady Rebecca," and "I am a Christian Englishwoman" (30–1). In the context of the play and the history of colonial rule in North America, the labels "Christian" and "Englishwoman" signify the historical erasure of her Powhatan "Matoaka" and "Pocahontas" identities as well as her perceived status as the property of John Rolfe and Christian England. The same holds true for *Almighty Voice*'s titular character when, as mentioned above, a treaty agent tries to rename Almighty Voice as "John Baptist," which White Girl explains is "the name of one of their ghosts" (10). White Girl's Christian name, which she mars by pronouncing Mary as "*Mar*rie" (10; emphasis added), similarly indexes the Christian school's attempt to convert her. Butler explains that "the expectation of self-determination that self-naming arouses" is undercut "by the historicity of the name itself" and "by the history of the usages that one never controlled" (*Bodies* 228). Pocahontas's and White Girl's "I am" statements, then, simultaneously emblematize and hinder the very autonomy they seek to proclaim due to the colonial historicity of the appellations themselves (*Bodies* 228). The history of the identificatory categories "Christian" and "Englishwoman" as well as the characters' experiences of coerced religious conversion undermine Pocahontas and White Girl's autonomy, thereby suggesting the constraining power of the identificatory labels "Christian" and "Englishwoman" as Pocahontas performs the role of "Lady Rebecca" on behalf of her people. This doubleness of self-identification performs the same paradox that defines political adaptation and its disidentification with source material. In short, the individual characters and the plays as a whole perform disidentification.

Finally, the fourth function of self-assertive statements – to posit individual identity as distinct yet connected to a group – occurs due to repetition. I argue that it is not merely the identificatory category or descriptor, but the first-person singular pronoun "I" and the subject's delivery that has self-defining properties. In repeating "I am" declarations in succession, the individual speaker reinforces the existence of the "I." The third Transformation in *Princess Pocahontas* comes via repetition, one that asserts Malinche's presence and agency despite the fact that she has been widely historicized as an enemy to her own people:

> I am the only one can speak to the Maya, to the Mexica. It is my words that are of value. (*moves downstage right, crosses herself, kneeling with head bowed*) I am christened Doña Maria. They call me "Princess." I am a gift claimed as value by this man in metal. I can change the words. I have power. Now I ride at the side of Cortez, the lady of the conquistador. Smart woman. I am a strategist. (23)

Malinche's "I am" statements reinforce her individuality, while simultaneously conveying her plurality. She corrects what "they call me," and complicates the colonial identificatory label "Princess" by adding multiple identificatory categories, such as "Doña Maria," "gift," and "strategist." For Malinche, the "I" is adaptable; and it is this adaptability that is the source of her power. *Princess Pocahontas*, in this way, is a self-reflexive play that advocates individual acts of political adaptation. "I am" statements, like the mode of political adaptation, simultaneously assert individuality while participating in a larger collective.

Likewise, to return to Djanet Sears's political adaptation *Harlem Duet*, Othello's series of statements – "I am not minor," "I am a middle class educated man," "I am an American," and "I am not my skin" (355–6) – spread his claim over multiple identificatory categories, while also employing repetition to affirm the existence of an "I." In repeating, "I am," both Malinche and Othello erect an oral/aural tower of "I"s that also expands horizontally along different categorical lines of nationality, class, and race. With these statements, Malinche and Othello display ownership over multiple categories of identification, and more importantly, over their "I." The repetition of "I am" statements not only asserts belongingness to and ownership of an identificatory category but also reinforces the existence of an individual self. In Malinche's speech, the four functions coalesce, signalling the racial complexity of intersections between community and individuality during the subject-making process.

The Bible further demonstrates how successive "I am" declarations can give authority to the message while also validating the speaker as truth-teller. Biblical scholars explore the interrelated significance of the narrating "I" and repetition in the Christian epic tradition and the Old Testament. In his analysis of the subject-making powers of language in the Bible and literature, Franke notes that "only in being repeated can revelation be realized and validated" (157). Richard S. Briggs similarly argues that repetition signals reliability and explains that we "hear this testimony to the word of God twice, because it is to be taken as reliable" (110). Applying these theological examples to the contemporary usage of "I am" declarations, therefore confirms that it is not only the "I am" statement but also the emphatic repetition of the performative utterance that can authorize the speaker's selfhood.[14] These examples illustrate how the emphatic repetition of the performative "I" authorizes the speaker's selfhood as much as the descriptor or name.

Whether empowering or disempowering, "I am" statements place the declaration and the speaker in relation to the citational history of the utterance – a history that includes previous "I am" assertions in the play itself as well as in its multiple intertexts and interperformances. In short, "I am" simultaneously asserts the speaker's individuality (singular subject) and multiplicity (history of this linguistic "I"). In keeping with their dramatization of a layered selfhood, Mojica and Moses use multi-generational intertexts (Biblical to contemporary), multiple languages (English, Cree, French, Spanish), various theatrical styles (realism, vaudeville, melodrama, transfiguration), and cross-cultural allusions (American, Latin, Cree, colonial European) in order to expose the dramatic text as a heteroglossic and formally diverse medium. Mojica's and Moses's plays demonstrate that both the political adaptation and the self are layered. These layers reinforce the complexity of the dramatic text, performance, and self while simultaneously referencing past versions that were authored and controlled by others.

Princess Pocahontas and the Blue Spots

Princess Pocahontas advocates the transformative potential of political adaptation as the repetition of a narrative with difference by challenging stasis or repetition of a story without difference. Most critics have, quite rightly, analyzed *Princess Pocahontas* as an attack on popular conceptions of "Indianness" because Mojica, as Knowles explains, thinks of the figures in her play "less as 'actual' figures in history than as subjects of Western colonialist *representation*" ("Translators" 257). "Indianness," as Mark Shackleton writes, is merely "the image of Native people held by non-Natives" (257–8).[15] Mojica, like Moses, adapts earlier tellings of Indigenous legends by non-Indigenous authors. Applying Gerald Vizenor's *Manifest Manners: Postindian Warriors of Survivance* to Mojica's *Princess Pocahontas*, Shackleton's conception of Indianness as "a *simulation*" undercuts popular misconceptions that Indigenous culture is "Indian" culture (Shackleton 258). Participating in political adaptation and what Knowles has called the "ongoing reinvention" of Indigenous subjects, *Princess Pocahontas* parodies simplistic stereotypes of the "real Indian Princess" in order to replace this misconception with a representation of the multiplicity of Indigenous women (21).[16] "I am" declarations are the principal method for challenging these very constructions of "Indianness" in *Princess Pocahontas*. Mojica's play re-identifies the female Indigenous characters as powerful individuals, while simultaneously connecting them to a larger community of women, as the successive "I am" statements reveal a development from performances of simulated stereotypes to self-defining proclamations.

Princess Pocahontas's non-linear structure and organizing Transformations (instead of acts and scenes) are integral to the play's political adaptation of the colonial Pocahontas myth. Distinct from a traditional European dramatic structure with its act and scene divisions, Mojica organizes her play as a nonlinear series of thirteen transformations "for each moon in the lunar year," which also include four transfigurations (*Princess Pocahontas* 16).[17] In the introductory notes to the play, Mojica explains that she refused to impose a structure on her story: "I didn't realize that I had a 'structure' until I went through the process of preparing the manuscript for publication" (16). Mojica's transformative structure, which, as Allen explains, is "common in American Indian lore" (19), and successive "I am" utterances go hand-in-hand as alternative strategies for resisting Western conceptions of the static self and linear historical narratives. The dramatic form (series of transformations), as we have seen in the earlier case studies, again complements the adaptor's goal (to transform preconceptions of Indianness) and the play's content (Pocahontas undergoes a transformation of identity).

Adaptations of Indian stereotypes are plentiful in *Princess Pocahontas* with the "Storybook Pocahontas," the historical "Pocahontas/Lady Rebecca/Matoaka" who experiences symbolic name changes, and the "Cigar Store Squaw."[18] The play opens with the Miss North American Indian Beauty Pageant where Princess Buttered-on-Both-Sides (a reference to the image of a female Indian on the Land O Lakes Butter package) performs the "Dance of the Sacrificial Corn Maiden" in the style of a "*Hollywood 'Injun dance'*" for the talent segment of the competition (19). While Princess Buttered-on-Both-Sides strives to measure up to North American beauty standards, the stage directions and props for the Beauty Pageant comically undercut the credibility of the popular "Miss America" contests.[19] When Princess Buttered-on-Both-Sides is named Miss Congeniality – figuring her as merely another re-articulation of the Pocahontas myth in its celebration of an Indigenous woman as friendly ambassador – the Host crowns her with a headdress covered with small ears of corn in mockery of a conventional crown (see figure 4.1). The headdress lights up after the Host plugs it into an electric outlet, comically performing the modern technological corruption of natural products. Adding another layer to the simulation, the fake crown is made of artificial corn. What we are left with is a proliferation of simulation. The "crowning" moment exaggerates the failure of the colonial quest to capture the authentic or real Indian princess. This scene dramatizes the simulation and assimilation of Indianness in popular culture as interrelated strategies of cultural appropriation, demonstrating Shackleton's punning maxim that "it takes a simulation to fight a simulation [and assimilation]" (259).

Figure 4.1 The 1990 production of *Princess Pocahontas and the Blue Spots* at Theatre Passe Muraille Backspace with Alejandra Nuñez (Host) crowning Monique Mojica (Princess Buttered-on-Both-Sides) as winner of the Miss Congeniality contest.

At first, *Princess Pocahontas* conveys a simulation of Indianness and the struggle to reclaim an Indigenous selfhood distinct from the commodity known as "Indian." Following the Miss North American Indian Beauty Pageant, Transformation 2 rejects the pageant crown and the colonial claim to Pocahontas as an Indian princess. Quoting Chrystos's *Not Vanishing*, Contemporary Woman #1 asserts, "I am not your Princess" (21), but her refusal of colonial ownership overlaps with Contemporary Woman #2's reminder, "She's a savage now remember" (21). The two lines are delivered simultaneously and compete for the audience's attention, dramatizing the battle between the acceptance of the colonial "savage" identity and the rejection of these stereotypes.

Despite Contemporary Woman #1's protestations, Lady Rebecca/Pocahontas/Matoaka embraces the colonial image of herself as the Indian Princess. Mojica, however, disrupts the logical sequence of Pocahontas's re-namings – a strategy of political adaptation that we also see in Sears's *Harlem Duet*, which precedes the narrative events of Shakespeare's *Othello* but is set in the present day. In chronological order, Pocahontas's four names were: Pocahontas (a childhood name that refers to her mischievous character and trickster qualities); Matoaka (named after the white feathers, or Matoaks, in her hair); Amonute ("beloved woman"); and finally, Rebecca Rolfe (wife of the English settler John Rolfe) (Allen, *Pocahontas* 17–18). In "Grandmothers of a New World," Brant investigates the motivations for Pocahontas's historical name change to Lady Rebecca, and argues that "Pocahontas had her own destiny to fulfill – that of keeping her people alive" (166). According to Brant, Pocahontas learned the English language from a missionary, and "her conversion to Christianity was only half-hearted, but her conversion to literacy was carried out with powerful zeal" (165). In *Princess Pocahontas*, Pocahontas's Christian conversion also seems half-hearted, or at very least numbing, as she describes herself as Lady Rebecca in a trance-like state. Mojica's play rejects chronological order and instead shifts from Pocahontas to Rebecca and ends with the Matoaka naming ceremony. In Transformation 6, the Troubadour sings of Pocahontas and how she saved John Smith from imminent death. Pocahontas then transforms into a dutiful wife and colonial product, announcing, "I am Lady Rebecca" (30), and, finally, at the end of Transformation 6, we see Matoaka's face-painting ceremony, which marks her self-identification: "I have to find my own colours and mix my own paint" (32). In concluding Transformation 6 with the young Matoaka's agency, the play reverses the loss of her Powhatan name by restoring her ability to "paint" her own identity. This new non-linear chronology transforms Lady Rebecca back into Matoaka; Mojica uses Matoaka's self-definition to change and challenge the European ending of the Pocahontas story.

Although "I am" statements typically assert a sense of belonging to, or ownership of, a specific identificatory category, the declarations "I am Princess and Non Pareil of Virginia" (30) and "I am Lady Rebecca forever and always" (30) ironically signal Pocahontas's status as colonial property and highlight her distance from New World categories. These re-namings fall into the self-negating potential of "I am" declarations. Albahari explains that "whenever a subject has feelings of personal 'my-ness' towards any object, bodily or mental, then the subject implicitly identifies with [a] group" and stands in a relation of "ownership towards the object in question" (59). When "I am" statements announce a speaker's connection to and ownership of an identificatory category, the declarations in turn suggest a sense of belonging; but it is the identificatory groups "English" and "Christian" that claim Pocahontas in Transformation 6. The Transformation, after all, dramatizes her marriage to John Rolfe who "*claimed* her for his bride-y-O" (30; emphasis added). Marking her English conversion, the stage directions describe Pocahontas "*fitting neck and wrists into collar and cuffs with much resistance*" (30) as the Englishwoman garb imprisons her:

> LADY REBECCA: Now you see here, I wear the clothes of an Englishwoman and will disturb you less when I walk. Here, I am Princess and Non Pareil of Virginia. I am Lady Rebecca. For me the Queen holds audience […] Can I still remember how to plant corn? I'll stay. Never, never go back where anyone might know Matoaka. My name is Lady Rebecca forever and always. I am a Christian Englishwoman!
> TROUBADOUR: (*singing*) Alas for our dear lady,
> English climate did not suit her –
> She never saw Virginia again,
> She met her end at Gravesend. (30–1)

Despite her "*resistance*" to the English uniform, Pocahontas sacrifices her "Matoaka" identity and vows to "Never, never go back where anyone might know Matoaka" (31). Assimilation has very real consequences in this play: the relinquishing of her Powhatan identity marks, as the Troubadour narrates, her death or "end" (31). In this way, Pocahontas is cuffed by her English identity much to her detriment as *Princess Pocahontas* warns audiences of what happens with assimilation and without political adaptation.

The attempts to self-identify as "Lady Rebecca forever and always" (31) also resonate with popular historical accounts of Pocahontas as a romantic heroine who sacrificed her "savage" culture to save John Smith and wed John Rolfe. As Jill Carter says, "the popular legend of Pocahontas around which Mojica has constructed her project chronicles the story of a 'savage' but 'noble Indian Princess' who [... was] paraded in England as an object of conquest and a symbol of the 'civilizing' and 'transformative' power of colonization" (8–9). The audience, therefore, would likely recognize these names and speech acts – "I am Princess and Non Pareil of Virginia" (30), "My name is Lady Rebecca forever and always" (31), and "I am a Christian Englishwoman!" (31) – from mainstream histories about the civilizing power of colonization.[20] Pocahontas's "I am" statements paradoxically announce her identity as both the famous "savage" and the civilized "Christian Englishwoman," but this contradictory doubleness results in Pocahontas/Lady Rebecca/Matoaka's failure to belong to either category of "Indian" or "Englishwoman" fully. The popular legends of Pocahontas render her an outcast, and, as Carter describes, "a besotted nubile who betrayed her people" (9). Just as Pocahontas does not successfully inhabit the identificatory labels of "Englishwoman" or "Christian," so too does she fail to inhabit the label "Indian" because of her perceived betrayal and duplicity. The colonial myth of Pocahontas renders hybridity a betrayal. Pocahontas paradoxically brims with names and narratives although they are emptied of identity.

Whereas Pocahontas's "I am a Christian Englishwoman" signals Rolfe's and England's civilization of the Indian princess, the play's next "I am" statement realigns Indigenous women and men when Contemporary Woman #1 helps a buckling Indigenous man to "Stand up" (39). Transformation 8, in particular, shows the potential for a reciprocal relationship among Indigenous men and women: Contemporary Woman #1 tells the weak Man, "you are my man, I am your woman" (39). This moment replaces a hierarchical relationship that posits European men above Indigenous women with a symbiotic one. In describing her unilateral relationship with John Rolfe, Mojica's Lady Rebecca explains that "*I provided* John Rolfe with the seeds to create his hybrid tobacco plants and *I provided* him with a son, and created a hybrid people" (31; emphasis added). John Rolfe seems to give very little in return with the exception of "a nice fan to hide my face and fan myself in these hot, heavy clothes" (31). Unlike Lady Rebecca's asymmetrical relationship to colonial Europe, wherein she is an unrequited giver as suggested by the repetition "I provided" (31), the "you are my man, I am your woman" statement signals a proprietary symbiosis. She seems to foster a bond when he slowly rises in response to her directive: "stand up" (39). Yet this effort to script Contemporary Woman #1 in a symbiotic relationship with an Indigenous man fails to be realized and instead parallels the colonial narrative. Just as the white colonizers used the helpful Powhatan woman, the Indigenous man "*exits*" as soon as he "*is standing tall*" (40). This scene enacts a gender division in Indigenous culture after colonialism and critiques the popular narratives of Indigenous women, like Pocahontas and Malinche, as helpful agents of colonialism.[21]

Offering a metacommentary on adaptation as a political form, *Princess Pocahontas* privileges transformation or repetition *with* difference, over repetition *without* difference. Just as Transformation 8 dramatizes Contemporary Woman #1's double abandonment, Transformation 9 similarly uses repetition to expose Indigenous women's static role as subordinated other. While repetition is used in political adaptations as a tool for political change, repetition without variation can suggest the difficulty of moving beyond past oppressions.[22] Transformation 9 shifts to Margaret's perspective and highlights a crisis of repetition with the refrain, "I am the third and youngest wife of a captain of the home guard" (44, 45):

> MARGARET: *Putting on a calico apron dress, she is stunned, numb, rum-dumb.*
> My husband didn't have a good hunt this season.
> *Putting on kerchief, ratchet sounds.*
> I am the third and youngest wife of a captain of the home guard.
> My husband didn't have a good hunt this season […]
> I am the third and youngest wife of a captain of the home guard. I have no children of my own. I help care for the children of the other wives. My husband didn't have a good hunt this season, so he brought me into the fort; and he left with flour, sugar and brandy. (44–5)

Performing repetition as stasis, the repeated "I am" statement dramatizes Margaret's stagnancy and confines her to the role of "third wife" (44). In this scene, repetition is not merely emphatic – it perpetuates the absence of change when

Margaret is "*stunned*" (44) by her own refrain, "I am the third and youngest wife of a captain" (44, 45). Even the adaptive form of the play itself – a reclaiming of the Pocahontas legend organized by transformation – critiques repetition without change and promotes repetition with difference as a strategy of resistance.

Drawing attention to political adaptation and its performance of disidentification, *Princess Pocahontas* abounds with transformation and repetition with variation. In addition to the series of Transformations, the play's physical properties and performance elements highlight the possibility for change. Mojica notes that the "theme of the set, costumes and props is also transformation; objects and set pieces appear to be one thing but become something else; they can be turned inside-out to reveal another reality" (17). *Princess Pocahontas* breaks free from the confines of a pre-scripted linear narrative of colonial history by telling the story of Pocahontas through a non-linear multi-vocal performance. The play harnesses political adaptation (repetition with political difference) as a form of critique and as a liberating mode that enables the possibility of transformation.

Princess Pocahontas achieves a transformation of identity by concluding with a climactic "I am" statement that at once reflects and realizes Contemporary Woman #1's agency. The same actor that plays Pocahontas in earlier scenes (Mojica) performs the role of Contemporary Woman #1 in the final scene; she explains that it is "International Women's Day" but resists a feminist sisterhood based on similarities and instead asserts her difference. After "so many years of trying to fit into feminist shoes," she demands custom-made ones that are "crafted to fit these wide, square, brown feet" (58). This moment aspires toward a feminism that recognizes differences among women. Positing herself as an individual within a community of feminists and Indigenous women, she proclaims:

> So, it's International Women's Day, and here I am. Now, I'd like you to take a good look – (*turns slowly, all the way around*) I don't want to be mistaken for a crowd of Native women. I am one. And I do not represent all Native women. I am one.
> *Crosses to tree upstage right; brings empty basin and pitcher of water centre stage.*
> And since it can get kind of lonely here, I've brought some friends, sisters, guerrilleras – the women – "Word Warriors," to help. (59)

The "here I am" and "I am one" utterances emphasize the singularity of the "I" as she reminds the audience that she is not plural, or "a crowd," even though she participates in a group of "friends, sisters." Whereas the earlier "I am" statements linked the characters to stereotypes of Indianness, this final declaration posits the speaker as an individual and refutes assimilationist generalizations. Although Shackleton argues that Mojica fights simulation with simulation, the play's final transformation moves beyond this strategy by asserting Contemporary Woman #1's self-construction. As Contemporary Woman #1 explains, "What I want is the freedom to carve and chisel my own face" (59). In contrast with the play's initial, contested negation – when Contemporary Woman #1's defiant "I am not your princess" overlaps with Contemporary Woman #2's reminder, "She's a savage now remember" (21) – the concluding performance of a Contemporary Woman's interiority goes unchallenged and functions as a positive self-assertion, thereby replacing the reductive colonial source material with a new embodiment of an Indigenous woman.

With "I am one," Mojica does not theorize the "I" as unitary but instead refuses generalizations about Indigenous peoples. "I am one" works outside of racial categories (Indian, Native, squaw) and effectively avoids reducing an Indigenous female "I" to a homogenous collective "we." Instead, Contemporary Woman #1, with her "I am one" statement, simultaneously connects herself to a larger group of "Word Warriors" and asserts her individuality. In working outside of prescribed racial categories, Contemporary Woman #1 offers the alternative label "Word Warriors" to describe her "friends, sisters, guerrilleras – the women" (59). While Contemporary Woman #1 imagines herself as a singular individual or "one," she also connects herself to collective groups, including both the "Word Warriors" or "the women" and the historical figures that make "I am" declarations throughout the play. The play's final Transformation interconnects "one" woman with a nation as both Contemporary #1 and #2 repeat: "*Una nación no sera conquistada hasta que los corazones de sus mujeres caigan a la tierra* […] A nation is not conquered until the hearts of its women are on the ground" (60). While Contemporary Woman #1 may have struggled to forge a symbiotic relationship with an Indigenous man, here she reminds the audience that the hearts of women are an essential component to the subjugation of a culture. There are two immediate consequences to Mojica's presentation of the self as multiple and transformative: difference is no longer antithetical to the "I" and, as a result, the *other* (a subject position defined by its difference from the self) is no longer the threat.

Engaging a popular strategy of political adaptation, *Princess Pocahontas*'s casting reinforces the ever-changing state of the self: two actors perform the entire play. In the only production to date, Mojica played the roles of Princess Buttered-on-Both-Sides, Contemporary Woman #1, Malinche, Storybook Pocahontas, Pocahontas/Lady Rebecca/Matoaka, Deity/Woman of the Puna/Virgin, Marie/Margaret/Madelaine, Cigar Store Squaw, and Spirit Animal; Nuñez acted as Host, the Blue Spots, Contemporary Woman #2, Troubadour, Ceremony, the Man, Spirit-Sister, and Musician. By using two actors to play multiple roles, Mojica's casting strategy further layers the "I" and embodies the connectedness of the "one" to the "many."

Just as an adaptation functions as an independent yet palimpsestic work of art, Mojica integrates all four functions of the self-assertions by constructing an Indigenous selfhood that is simultaneously individual and part of a collective. Pocahontas/Lady Rebecca/Matoaka's earlier failed performances of "I am," of symbiotic relationships, and of belonging to a group draw attention to the success of Contemporary Woman #1's self-declarations in the play's final moments. The play as a whole and its performances of identity argues for the transformative power of difference over repetition, adaptation over assimilation. In *Princess Pocahontas* the individual and by extension the storyteller must enact change or adaptation in order to survive.

Almighty Voice and His Wife

Like Mojica's play, Moses's political adaptation warns against assimilation and reveals the historical source material on Almighty Voice to be little more than a minstrel production of colonial fantasies and redface. Whereas *Princess Pocahontas* moves from stereotypical conceptions of Indigenous identity to self-identification, *Almighty Voice and His Wife* begins with the playful courtship of Almighty Voice and White Girl only to revert to a minstrel performance of Indian stereotypes (see figures 4.2 and 4.3 for a juxtaposition of the first and second acts). Inverting the stereotypical representations of Indians as redfaced savages, Moses uses whiteface together with an abundance of "I am" statements in order to highlight the precariousness of racial identity. The whiteface – an obvious stage trick that calls attention to the artificiality and transparency of race change – reduces whiteness and "Indianness" to flimsy performances that merely involve stage makeup.

From act 1 to act 2, Almighty Voice is reduced to a ghost of himself and an entertaining redfaced Indian. The first act ends with Almighty Voice's ethereal vision of his wife and child as he dies:

> ALMIGHTY VOICE *lies by the dead fire, his leg badly wounded. The spectral tipi appears and the drum goes silent. Inside the tipi are* WHITE GIRL *and her baby, mother and child, a destination.* ALMIGHTY VOICE *rises and uses his Winchester as a crutch to come to the tipi.* WHITE GIRL *comes out and shows him the baby and the baby cries. The moon turns white.* ALMIGHTY VOICE *dies.* (29)

The baby's cry offers a counterpoint to the white moon and Almighty Voice's death by gesturing towards future generations and the continuation of life. This scene, entitled "His Vision," invokes a "spectral" mood, as the moon turns white. In *Almighty Voice*, the only image more ominous than the blood-red moon is the white moon because it corresponds with the whitewashing of the characters' identities. Act 2 begins with a white moon that fades to "reveal the white face that masks WHITE GIRL in her role as the INTERLOCUTOR, a Mountie and the Master of Ceremonies" (3). In his review of the Native Canadian Centre's 1992 production (directed by Marrie Mumford and starring Pamela Matthews and Jonathan Fisher), Liam Lacey emphasizes the surprising shift in style, explaining that the second act "takes a sharp right turn that leaves you grabbing the door handle to hold on" (C6). The play's final moments bring together the two acts by recalling the first act's "*spectral*" (29, 60) tableau and promise of the future when Almighty Voice and White Girl shed their vaudevillian characters and "WHITE GIRL *lifts a baby-sized bundle to the audience*" (61).

The stylistic shift between acts challenges the source material by bringing attention to the artificiality of historical re-tellings of Almighty Voice and Indigenous cultures in Canada. The vaudevillian excess undercuts the credibility of Indian stereotypes as we witness the tragic disconnect between the characters' self-identificatory statements in the first act and the imposed Indian stereotypes in the second act. Moses's play, then, speaks back to the many different versions of the legend including retellings by Johnson, Wiebe, Peterson, and Berton. While Moses concludes his play with the image of Almighty Voice's baby, Johnson ends "The Cattle Thief" with the voice of Almighty Voice's child. Johnson's poem describes the "band of cursing settlers" as they kill "the famous Eagle Chief" (28), and, most poignantly, features Almighty Voice's daughter who demands that the settlers "Go back with your new religion, we have never understood" (28–9). In "Where is the Voice Coming From?," by comparison, Wiebe challenges the historicization of the myth as a celebration of a Cree man's death. Just as Moses responds to the lack of historical record on Almighty Voice's wives, Wiebe questions the validity of the different historical versions and museum artefacts (such as a photo, a piece of Almighty Voice's skull, and the Mounties' canon). Unlike Johnson and Wiebe, Berton is quite critical of Almighty Voice, describing him as "a restless and volatile youth" who indulged in a "consuming but transitory interest in young girls" as evidenced by his four marriages (213). Whereas Johnson blames the settlers and explains that Almighty Voice was "hollow with hunger" (29), Berton critiques this "motive" and suggests that "Almighty Voice and his seventeen-year-old crony, Flying Sound" killed the steer on a whim (214). Moses's depiction of a sympathetic wife (White Girl) responds to Berton's vilifying portraiture of Almighty Voice as much as it does to the lack of historical records on Cree women.

The ordering of the play, which moves from Almighty Voice and White Girl (see figure 4.2) to a white Interlocutor's second-hand version of their tale, enacts a larger narrative of historical adaptation. The second act's minstrel show references the Geronimo legend, Buffalo Bill Cody's Wild West exhibitions, and Mister Tambo as well as colonial versions of Almighty Voice. In particular, Moses's second act parodies Peterson's historical play *Almighty Voice*, which casts children as wild "*chanting and dancing*" Indians (12) and was originally performed by Young People's Theatre of Toronto in August of 1970. The actors in Peterson's *Almighty Voice*, as with Moses's version, play multiple roles and often directly address the audience. Just as Peterson produced his play in a school's auditorium and directed the audience of children to act as "volunteers for our outposts at Duck Lake" (15), Moses sets his second act in a school's auditorium at Duck Lake. The Interlocutor even asks for a performance of Indianness that echoes Peterson's "*dancing*" Indians: "Would you now consider performing, Mister Ghost, for our attentive friends that charming curiosity you called a dance" (41). With this parody and the stylistic shifts between acts, Moses distances the second act's hypertheatrical enactments of Indian stereotypes from the first act's more spectral portrayal of Almighty Voice and White Girl's loving relationship. In this way, Almighty Voice reveals colonial histories and popular Indian narratives to be little more than fictionalized appropriations of a real couple and their story.

The beginning of Moses's *Almighty Voice* offers a set of strategies for reclaiming misleading popular narratives of Indigenous figures as White Girl and Almighty Voice establish ownership over their own identities. Almighty Voice, for instance, adamantly rejects the new biblical names prescribed by the treaty agent:

> GIRL: They called me Marrie. It's the name of their god's mother.
> VOICE: What's wrong with White Girl? White Girl's a good name. They're so stupid. That agent has to call me John Baptist so I can get my treaty money.
> GIRL: John Baptist. That's the name of one of their ghosts.
> VOICE: I'm no ghost. I'm Almighty Voice. Why can't they say Almighty Voice?
> GIRL: I'll call you John Baptist too.
> VOICE: You're not the agent! You're my wife.
> GIRL: It's so he'll kill the ghost instead of you, husband. That god won't know it's us if we use their names.
> VOICE: So I have to call my wife Marrie?
> GIRL: Yes. Their god won't be able to touch us. Just call me Marrie.
> VOICE: My crazy White Girl.
> […]
> VOICE: Crazy Marrie. (10)

In her first "I am" statement of the play, White Girl teases, "I am a crazy one" (5), which here inspires Almighty Voice's playful appellations: "crazy White Girl" and "Crazy Marrie." Although Almighty Voice rejects the biblical pseudonyms, White Girl here interprets her new name as a potential disguise and tool for survival: "Their god won't be able to touch us. Just call me Marrie." This scene uses White Girl to voice assimilation as a strategy of survival. The problematic strategy of donning a colonizer's mask, however, is carried out

Figure 4.2 Derek Garza (Almighty Voice) and PJ Prudat (White Girl) in Native Earth's 2011 production of *Almighty Voice and His Wife* (directed by Michael Greyeyes).

with disturbing results when Almighty Voice and White Girl wear whiteface in the second act.

The play ultimately warns against assimilation and this acceptance of socially prescribed White identities when White Girl confronts the "White God" (20) and her forced Christian name. Moses capitalizes on the Biblical resonance of "I am" when White Girl uses the tools of Christianity – "I AM," a prayer, and the Eucharist – to defy the Judeo-Christian "White God of the ghost men" as she recalls memories of sexual abuse at the residential school (20). "Her 'marriage' to god," as Episkenew explains, "takes on another dimension when god's helper, as husband by proxy, is the one who consummates that marriage" (160). As her hybrid name "Crazy Marrie" suggests, White Girl struggles to harmonize her two identities as the White God's Mary and as Almighty Voice's wife. In a prayer, she further confuses her Indigenous and Biblical names, asking her "husband god" to "see what a little girl I am" (20). This panicked prayer blends Almighty Voice's appellation "little girl" with the Biblical "I am," revealing the tension between her Cree and Christian selves. As with Margaret in *Princess Pocahontas*, repetition signals internal conflict as White Girl repeats, "what a little girl I am" (19, 20) and relives her experiences of sexual abuse at the residential school. In her prayer, however, White Girl signals her conflicted identities and violent memories, but also challenges God, shouting "stupid god, this is what you want!" (20). Her prayer employs epizeuxis, the repetition of a word with no words between, accelerating the rhythm and emphasizing the violence of her speech:

> Great husband god, see what a little girl I am. Great White God of the ghost men, mother is here. Blood blood blood between my thighs. Yes, gimme, gimme, gimme something sweet. Oh yes, yes, you're rotten, rotten meat, but wifey wife will eat you up. Mister God, stupid god, this is what you want! Come on! Come on, don't leave! I'm your little squaw. Eye-eye! See! Eye-eye, Mister God. Eye-eye! (20)

The structural repetition inherent in the act of remembrance frames the stylistic repetition of certain words ("look," "wife," "eye") and phrases ("see what a little girl I am"). As Cathy Caruth argues, there is doubleness to trauma – the traumatic event itself and the memory of it that replays in one's mind and through one's stories of the past. As "*the bloody moon rises*" in the backdrop (19), her repetition of "Blood blood blood" encourages the audience to imagine the blood spreading between her thighs as an emblem of the violent consummation of her marriage to the husband god. The heated repetition of "yes," "Come on," and "Eye-eye" rhetorically climaxes while it signals Mister God's (or the priest's) physical orgasm. Repetition, as a result, at once marks her traumatic memory as well as her strategies to redefine herself as an autonomous "I." Much like Mojica's play, Moses dramatizes the violence of the repetition of colonial myths without difference; in short, *Almighty Voice* advocates for political adaptation over assimilation and repetition.

Showcasing the potential of adaptation as a tool for survival and defiance, the sexual monologue imbues White Girl with power. By adapting the language of the Eucharist, for instance, she "will eat" the White God and reclaim authority. Episkenew suggests that "the result [of her time in residential school] is unresolved trauma that White Girl self-diagnoses as craziness" (160); a look at the resistant potential of repetition with difference, however, reveals that White Girl enacts control over her past traumatic experiences by instigating the memory, confronting the White God, and adapting the self-constituting power of the "I am" declaration. After this speech, she shifts from the god's ocular "eye" to her own individual "I" when she announces that "I am the wife of Almighty Voice," and further separating herself from the Christian God, says, "You don't know my name" (20). Her "I am" declarations effectively rename and re-identify her as White Girl. At the end of this scene, White Girl rejects the paternal White God and symbolically turns towards the maternal moon: "I turn here in the wind toward the river and the moon is there, a woman with better things to do" (2). With White Girl's speech acts, Moses exposes the power of adaptation and performative utterances to reclaim rather than merely retell or describe an identity.

In the second act, White Girl as the Interlocutor exposes colonial history's artificial claims to truth. By presenting the Indian as hyperperformative, *Almighty Voice* further undermines the veracity of colonial history. The Interlocutor presents the colonial "facts" as intentional "lies": "these fine, kind folks want to know the truth, the amazing details and circumstance behind your savagely beautiful appearance … They want to know the facts. And it's up to you and me to try and lie that convincingly" (32). Here, the Interlocutor suggests that theatrical representations of Indigenous peoples do not capture the "real true Indian" but instead create convincing lies and mere "simulation" (Shackleton 259). The second act overtly historicizes the first act, but it also includes whiteface, dance, song, and jokes. This generic blend of history and vaudeville forcefully undermines the believability of colonial history and popular representations of Indians.

Moses demonstrates another common strategy of political adaptation by using metatheatricality to undercut popular representations of the "real" Indian. In act two, the vaudevillian performance and breaking of the fourth wall remind the audience that they are watching a play and highlight the artificiality of institutionalized educational productions of Indigenous culture in schools across Canada. For example, the Interlocutor's characterization of the audience prompts the real viewers to create their own "I am" statements and self-identify. In one of the Interlocutor's direct addresses to the audience, the play characterizes the spectators as a group of un-thinking people who merely want to be "entertained" by the spectacle of the "Indian" (32). Moses provocatively aligns the audience with the racist Interlocutor who addresses the viewers as "dear friends" and expects them to share his concern over the "indigent Indian problem" because all Indians are "bad ones" (40). Enacting the imagined audience's reaction, Ghost responds "Bravo! Bravo, Mister Interlocutor" (40). In this instance, misrepresentations of onstage Indians extend to an uncomfortable misrepresentation of the offstage audience.

Helen Gilbert's article on whiteface in *Almighty Voice* notes that some of the play's "speeches are addressed directly to the spectators, who thus become no longer anonymous consumers, but objects against which the play is enacted" (692). In his review of a 2012 production of *Almighty Voice*, Dickinson describes the audience's reactions to Moses's second act:

> in Act 2 Moses doesn't just break the fourth wall, he explodes it, with both Mr. Interlocutor and Almighty Ghost coming out into the audience at various points, and each strategically playing to and upon our ideological sympathies in order to gain the upper hand. And it is this last point that makes Moses' play at once so groundbreaking and compellingly contemporary, for it accomplishes via its canny structure the double task of exposing both real and representational violence to us, theatricalizing Aboriginal stereotypes and then catching us in the act of succumbing to them. ("Push")

Moses, as Dickinson explains, forces the audience to separate themselves actively from the play's imagined racist audience. The play thus incites the audience to reject (or counteridentify with) the Interlocutor through their own rebellious "I am" declarations. In this moment, the audience joins Almighty Voice and White Girl as subjects of misrepresentation. As a result, the play invokes an uncomfortable audience and leads the viewers to be sceptical of identity constructions. Moses appeals to the complexities of a political adaptation's audience – or dispublic – by avoiding a simple bifurcated relationship between a politically correct, morally upstanding audience and the Interlocutor's detestable performance of political incorrectness, thereby demonstrating the entertaining allure of the very stereotypes he seeks to challenge.

Almighty Voice's dispublic does not get to celebrate their political superiority and are instead reminded of the slippery slope of Indigenous stereotypes as well as minstrelsy.[23] Offering insights into the audience's experience of race change, W.T. Lhamon Jr maintains, "at least three core groups organize themselves around signs of blackface" (34). The first group "deploys its codes to scandalize blacks, believing that the stereotypes they have imputed to blacks deserve scornful laughter" (34). Group two, by contrast, "appropriate[s] those negative codes" of blackness in order "to invert them" and expose their "bigoted condescension" (34). The third group "work[s] to outlaw the scandalized sign of blackness – burnt cork and its gestural surrogates" – and thereby functions outside of the minstrel performance tradition (35). Moses, to apply Lhamon's categorization of minstrel codes to the play's whiteface, participates in the second group's strategies by adopting the minstrel tradition in order to reveal both the prevalence and the uncomfortable entertainment value of the redfaced Indian figure in popular culture; *Almighty Voice* inverts the codes of blackface and redface by using whiteface to expose the "bigoted condescension" of race change. Just as the history of minstrelsy reveals key moments of reversal where "the target was not the actor but the public who cheered what he portrayed" (Lhamon 39), Moses indicts the dispublic as a complicit participant in the reification of the red-faced Indian.

Despite Almighty Voice's and White Girl's defiant "I am" utterances in the first act – such as, "I'm no ghost. I'm Almighty Voice" (10), "I am the wife of Almighty Voice. You don't know my name" (20) – the initial threats to Almighty Voice's and White Girl's identities are realized in act 2. First of all, the re-writing of White Girl as "Marrie" seems to be complete when she appears in act two as the white-faced Interlocutor in a Mountie costume who entertains the audience with stereotypes of Indians (see figure 4.3). Secondly, the appearance of Almighty Voice as "Ghost" in the second act rearticulates his earlier death and demonstrates the ultimate failure of his denial, "I'm no ghost" (10). Ghost's white make-up signals a double erasure: the death of Almighty Voice as well as the death of his Cree self (see figure 4.3). In figuring Almighty Voice as a ghost, the play satisfies and exposes the fantasy of the vanishing or ghosted Indian and the Interlocutor jokes that "the only good Indians are the dead ones" (40). In her definition of two categories of the stereotypical American Indian – noble savage and howling savage – Allen exposes the overarching colonial fetishization of the vanishing Indian, explaining that these stereotypes of the primitive and dangerous Indian are not only the cause but also the "compelling rationale for genocide" (5). In the second act, *Almighty Voice* exposes the Interlocutor's portraiture of Indigenous culture as an ancient relic of an uncivil past as a strategy for reinforcing the deserved elimination, or ghosting, of the Indigenous peoples in Canada. As Allen observes, the "savage" Indians are seen to "deserve extermination" (*The Sacred Hoop*, 5). In the second act, the whiteface fulfills the colonial demand for cultural extermination through the renaming of Almighty Voice as a ghost.

Critics, such as Dorinne Kondo and Gilbert, argue that whiteface references the minstrel tradition and the white oppression of minority groups. I add that Moses's use of whiteface also destabilizes minstrelsy and race as artificial performances. In "How My Ghosts Got Pale Faces," Moses himself explains the subversive potential of whiteface:

> White as a colour only exists because some of us get told we're black or yellow or Indians. I think my ghosts exist to probe this white problem, this tonal confusion, to spook its metaphors. Maybe my ghosts are like mirrors, but from a funhouse.
>
> I want to spin new meanings out [of] the stereotypes or turn it into a cliché trying. Once white itself is a ghost, colour will be just a too-simple beginning of rich and strange complexities. (81)

Almighty Voice is groundbreaking in its implementation of whiteface as a parody of the minstrel tradition that, in Moses's words, turns Indian stereotypes into a "cliché trying."[24] In *Almighty Voice*, whiteface exposes the fallibility of assimilation – as prescribed by the treaty agent in the first act – and only results in the removal of the face paint in the play's final scene: the identity of "white" is "just a too-simple" performance of identity.

Moses's use of whiteface takes part in a revived interest in minstrelsy and has garnered critical attention in its reversal of the minstrel tradition. Susan

Figure 4.3 Derek Garza (Ghost) and PJ Prudat (Interlocutor) in Native Earth's 2011 production of *Almighty Voice and His Wife* (directed by Michael Greyeyes).

Gubar, on the one hand, argues that race change (or what she refers to as "racechange") involves "the traversing of race boundaries, racial imitation or impersonation, cross-racial mimicry or mutability" (5). For Gubar, race change can involve either "white passing as black or black passing as white" (5), which in Moses's case extends to red passing as white. Kondo and Gilbert, on the other hand, each warn against Gubar's over-idealization of whiteface because race change works within a history of racial stratification. Kondo argues that race change is "systematically encoded and maintained in structures of white privilege that persist despite individual intentionality" (100). Gilbert similarly interjects that "racial impersonation often indexes white power" (681). In addition to mimicking racist discriminations against Indigenous culture, however, Moses uses whiteface to expose minstrelsy and redface as strategic exaggerations of culture that index white power and prejudice. Although the historical use of minstrelsy as a strategy for reinforcing racist codes informs the reception of whiteface, Gilbert concedes that whiteface "can also set up opportunities to de-essentialize race" (681). In *Almighty Voice*'s second act, the artificiality of whiteface emphasizes the constructedness of self-defining utterances and the sheer performativity of Indigenous stereotypes.

White Girl as the Interlocutor at once enacts race change and cross-dressing when she pretends to be a White male Mountie disguised as a female Sweet Sioux. Exemplifying the play's metatheatrical complexity as well as the layered nature of the self, Interlocutor and Ghost act out an inset mock-revelation sketch in scene six of act 2, entitled "The Playlet." Just as the Chief Magistrate (Ghost) is about to rape the "Sweet Sioux" (Interlocutor), the "squaw" explains that she is really the "Corporal Red Coat of the Mounted Police ... cleverly disguised as Sweet Sioux in order to tempt the evil Magistrate to show his true colours" (55). In this moment of race change, the audience sees a female Indigenous actor as White Girl/Interlocutor/ Sweet Sioux/Corporal Red Coat. The scene blurs the division of "white" and "red" through performance. The pun on "show his true colours" (55) comically foreshadows the play's final revelation of "red" skin when Ghost and White Girl remove their white masks. Further anticipating the Interlocutor's rediscovery of her Cree self, the Corporal Red Coat (Interlocutor) directs the dying Chief Magistrate (Ghost) to "Call me Red" (55). In the second act, White Girl's insistence that "I'm the Interlocutor" identifies her as the Master of Ceremonies, but the audience's memory of her role as White Girl in act 1 troubles this self-identification. The play and Playlet's layering of cultural performance (Cree/White/Cree) suggests the impossibility of locating "true colours" in one body.

In addition to complicating culture as a layered and performative identity, whiteface also offers the cathartic opportunity to remove a white mask and recall Indigenous appellations. The play ends with Ghost and Interlocutor's racial striptease as they wipe away the white layers from their body and face (see figure 4.4 for a promotional image of this key scene). The stage directions note that White Girl's "*gloved hands begin to wipe the white face off, unmasking the woman inside*" and "becoming White Girl again" (61). Reacting to her rediscovered White Girl identity, the Interlocutor asks, "Who am I?" (61). Ghost offers her the many different conceptions of her Cree self from act 1 and re-names her "White Girl," "crazy little girl," "my wife," and finally, a new appellation in the context of the play, "*Ni-wikimakan [My wife]*" (61). But it is in articulating White Girl's identity that Ghost simultaneously redefines himself as her husband. This renaming enacts Almighty Voice and White Girl's rediscovery of their Cree selves without the framework of a didactic "Indian" showcase.

Figure 4.4 Michael Greyeyes (director) in a promotional photo for Native Earth's 2011 production of *Almighty Voice and His Wife*. Greyeyes depicts the Interlocutor's climactic removal of white face paint in the final moments of the play.

The removal of whiteface and the return to their roles as Almighty Voice and White Girl does not suggest that there is an essential, static Indigenous identity but rather a complex, transformative identity that can be sifted out from the deluge of stereotypes. In "deliberately refusing to satisfy the settler audience's desire" for a "real," authentic Indian, Episkenew asserts that "Moses characterizes Almighty Voice as a mere mortal, a flawed human being like the rest of us" (162). Moses, according to Episkenew, rejects the characterization of Almighty Voice as the "almighty Native voice" and as a "homegrown super-hero" with "the realism of Act 1" (162). Building on Episkenew's reading, I argue that Moses further critiques the mythic characterization of the cattle thief when Almighty Voice and White Girl struggle to return to their identities as wife and husband in the closing moments of the play. Moses's treatment of the self parallels his representation of the Almighty Voice legend: just as the characters' self-identifications underscore and restrict the speakers' autonomy, the earlier versions of the Almighty Voice legend at once reinforce Almighty Voice's historical significance and distort him into a man of mythic proportions.

Delivering the final lines in Cree, Ghost and Interlocutor respond to earlier non-Indigenous stories of Almighty Voice and call attention to Moses's own use of the English language throughout much of the play:

> GHOST: *Piko ta-ta-wi kisisomoyan ekwo. [I have to go finish dancing now.]*
> INTERLOCUTOR: *Patima, Kisse-Manitou-Wayou. [Goodbye, Almighty Voice.]* (61)

Here, White Girl calls Almighty Voice by his Cree name for the first time. Reflecting on his first encounter with the Almighty Voice legend in school, Moses says that he "hadn't realized how much space there might be between the lines of such [historical] documents, hadn't seen the difficulties in translation between the language of English and, for instance, Cree, between the respective cultures and sets of values, between, for instance, what each community thought was the definition of human" ("How My Ghosts" 70). The ending of *Almighty Voice* responds to this space between the languages of English and Cree.[25] With the last line of Moses's play, White Girl re-identifies Almighty Voice as *Kisse-Manitou-Wayou*, which, in turn, helps them confront and grapple with their Cree identities.

Moses's use of Cree also offers a response to Wiebe's short story "Where Is the Voice Coming From?" As the title of the short story suggests, Wiebe questions the narrativization of Almighty Voice's history. Beginning with an announced awareness of the history-making process of narration and identification, Wiebe declares that "The problem is to make the story" (78). While the short story poeticizes Almighty Voice as "an incredible voice that rises from among the young poplars ripped of their spring bark, from among the dead somewhere lying there" (86), it ends with a pronounced and regretted distance between the narrator and subject. The narrator can only describe Almighty Voice's poetic cry as "wordless" because, unfortunately, "that is the way it sounds to me … For I do not, of course, understand the Cree myself" (12). As a response to this difficult untranslatability, the final lines of *Almighty Voice* call attention to this difference in language while still retaining Cree as a rich signifier of cultural identity. By introducing Cree as a mode of expression at the end of the play, Moses participates in a school of criticism that refutes the normative image of an English-speaking white Canada and the "previously assumed standard" of English or French literature and drama (Coleman 4). As Daniel Coleman explains, "many commentators have celebrated the veritable explosion of multicultural or minority writing over the past thirty years in Canada, because they see in it the potential to pluralize what had been a bicultural image of Canada" (4). Moses exemplifies the potential to pluralize the "normative concept of (English) Canadianness" through his complex characterizations of Almighty Voice and White Girl as well as his use of the Cree language (Coleman 4).

The play's final scene marks yet another shift in theatrical form as Almighty Voice and White Girl transition from the minstrel tradition to a freeing dance. Ultimately, Almighty Voice and White Girl can only respond to the question "Who am I?" in the Cree language and through a ritual dance. Signalling future growth and continued transformation of self, White Girl "*lifts a baby-sized bundle to the audience*" as Almighty Voice "*continues to dance in the fading lights*" (61) of the play's final moments. The baby-sized bundle gestures towards future generations' inheritance of the Almighty Voice legend and of adaptation strategies. The play ends not with a return to their earlier Cree identities but with the creation of a renewed life and of future promise as symbolized by the fire, dance, and child.

Throughout the play, the strategies of political adaptation reclaim the colonial myths by giving Almighty Voice and White Girl authority over their own names, re-appropriating Biblical rhetoric, challenging the truth-claims of colonial history, and exposing the theatricality of racialized identities. Yet the final pursuit of identification – "Who am I?" – leaves the audience with more questions than answers. The political adaptation, then, has transformed the colonial source material by revealing its fictionalization of Almighty Voice as a vanishing Indian but the play also gestures towards the work that still needs to be done as it holds up a child, a symbol of future stories that need to be told and adapted.

Why Adapt?

Mojica's and Moses's political adaptations may retell stories of the past, but they also end with a nod to the future generations of storytellers, activists, and performers. The endings – with Contemporary Woman #1 (*Princess*

Pocahontas) and a "*baby-sized bundle*" (*Almighty Voice*) – suggest the impact that past stories can have on future generations. Mojica and Moses are not only fighting to transform how the past is understood, they are also working to change how Indigenous peoples navigate the future. These goals speak to political adaptation's propensity for at once telling stories of the past and recontextualizing them for present and future audiences.

Performative utterances are a microcosm for the genre of political adaptation. In the context of *Princess Pocahontas* and *Almighty Voice*, the "I am" statements have a complex lineage, including Indigenous legends, contemporary works, colonial histories, and the Bible. Both the individual "I am" statements as well as each play as a whole are connected laterally to the intertexts and interperformances because Mojica and Moses refuse to privilege a singular work as the authoritative source. In contributing yet another narrative variation (or layer) to the Almighty Voice myth, Moses's narrative creates a palimpsestic identity of the mythic figure: the "I am" statements' intertextuality and interperformativity highlight Almighty Voice's layered, transformative identity. The literary form of political adaptation, therefore, simultaneously parallels and contributes to the re-theorizing of the self.

Both plays' adaptive forms, intertextuality, and interperformativity reinforce the plurality of the "I." The plays' narratives, after all, are not singular and immutable but multiple and permeable. Carter approaches the many layers of Mojica's play as a *mola*, that is, a hand-woven cloth used to dress Kuna woman of Panama: "each story – each fragment of female experience – selected for inclusion in Mojica's play becomes a layer in the performative *mola*" (12). Similarly, Moses's use of whiteface literally layers the characters' bodies with white paint, which symbolically places white on top of red, but also exposes the Indigenous actor's skin beneath the surface. This racial layering is one of the play's methods for interconnecting what Minh-ha calls the "I and not-I," thereby challenging the bifurcations of "red" and "white" as hierarchal racial categories. Adaptations, I argue, are akin to the re-theorized self – layered, multiple, and varied – because palimpsests have no authoritative, real, or core text.

Princess Pocahontas and *Almighty Voice* pluralize the "I" as a method of reconfiguring cultural difference as no longer antithetical to the real self. With these plays, the "I" is stretched out horizontally through hyphenated identities that extend and deepen the self. In rotating the "I" from a vertical position ("I") to a horizontal position (" – "), the two plays challenge cultural hierarchies by layering racial identities on a horizontal plane and by undermining notions of the "real Indian." Minh-ha calls for a "practice of subjectivity" that is aware of "its own constituted nature" (419), and understanding the self as a layered adaptation responds to this call.

Just as Mojica's Contemporary Woman #1 does not want to forgo her individuality or one-ness while still taking part in a group of Word Warriors, Moses's Almighty Voice is simultaneously a singular "I" and a collective "we" – he belongs to White Girl, the many different versions of the historical legend, and the audience that the play speaks to. Princess Pocahontas and Almighty Voice both end with a consideration of the question, "Who am I?," but this inquiry is not simply replaced but necessarily accompanied by the question of "Who are we?" As with the "I am" declarations and misrepresentations of Indigenous culture, the questioning of identity extends to the audience as we individually and collectively ask: who defines this "we" in Canadian theatre and how can we challenge these inherited notions of identities?

As political adaptations, *Princess Pocahontas* and *Almighty Voice* disidentify with the colonial reiterations of Indigenous histories. In doing so, they work to transform the audience's prior understanding of Pocahontas's willingness to marry John Rolfe and Almighty Voice's stand-off with the mounted police. These plays embrace the layered structure of political adaptation by foregrounding the necessarily layered narrative of adaptation and by extending this narrative structure to the performed identities of the historical figures themselves. The same actors perform the historical figures in multiple time periods; this multiple role-play effectively layers the actors' bodies. The actor playing Almighty Voice's Ghost even wears white face paint – a layering that threatens to whiteout the Cree man beneath the performances of Indian stereotypes. In this way, Moses highlights the layering of stories as a layering of identities: the play promotes political adaptation as a mode of palimpsestuous layering that enables both the Cree man and the white-colonial interpretations to be seen at once.

By the end of both plays, Mojica and Moses successfully transform the source material into derogatory fictions about imagined Indians that fail to give a voice to Pocahontas or Almighty Voice. In this way, *Princess Pocahontas* and *Almighty Voice* call attention to the transformative potential of political adaptation's performance of disidentification by transforming Indian stereotypes from within the context of colonial fantasies. Mojica and Moses show us the ability of political adaptation to retell source material without reinforcing its cultural significance or authority. The power of these plays to replace the source material with more complex retellings of Pocahontas and Almighty Voice gestures towards an answer to an overarching question of this book: how does political adaptation effect change in Canada? Mojica and Moses reveal the power of political adaptation to change the cultural value and relevancy of enduring source material.

Conclusion

> Re-vision – the act of looking back, of seeing with fresh eyes, of entering an old text from a new critical direction … We need to know the writing of the past and know it differently than we have ever known it; not to pass on a tradition but to break its hold over us.
>
> Adrienne Rich

Political adaptations are canon makers and breakers that illustrate the interrelated challenges of Canada's identity, history, and art. As Adrienne Rich says, the purpose of political adaptation, or what she calls "re-vision," is "not to pass on a tradition but to break its hold over us" (369). Political adaptations retell popular narratives in order to break with literary tradition and make space for new voices. If, as Thomas King suggests, "the truth about stories is that that's all we are" (2) then the stakes could not be higher for adaptors working to break inherited stories' hold over us: political adaptations offer a mode of negotiating who we are and whose story survives.

We are experiencing the socio-cultural impacts of political adaptation as the stories we perform are either falling under public scrutiny or becoming more inclusive of the diverse peoples in the nation known as Canada. The cultural significance of retelling or adapting stories is in part why there was a national outcry about Canada's Appropriation Prize scandal in 2017. In a 2017 editorial for *Write* magazine, Hal Niedzviecki imagined an "appropriation prize" that would be given to authors who write from perspectives that are unfamiliar to them, which sparked controversy over what should have been a publication celebrating Indigenous voices.[1] Niedzviecki advised writers to "write what you don't know. Get outside your own head. Relentlessly explore the lives of people who aren't like you"; these directives encourage empathy and consideration of what he refers to as "the other" (8).[2] The editorial, however, begins with Niedzviecki confessing, "I don't believe in cultural appropriation," and recommending a figurative "Appropriation Prize." It is the call for "appropriation" that is contentious and that fails to fully recognize that Indigenous artists are not given the same opportunities to tell their stories as the vanguard of, in Niedzviecki's own words, "white and middle class" authors in Canada ("Winning" 8). As a result of the public outcry, Niedzviecki resigned from his position as editor-in-chief of *Write* and apologized for being insensitive in the magazine to the complexities of retellings and to the Indigenous writers.[3] The Appropriation Prize controversy stirred discussions of the importance of ethical retellings of Indigenous stories.

The controversy over the politics of retellings gestures towards the need for a distinction between acts of cultural appropriation and political adaptation. "There are many ways in which both the practice and the effects of adaptation and appropriation intersect and interrelate," as Sanders says, "yet it is equally important to maintain some clear distinctions between them as creative activities" (26). Cultural appropriation distorts the goals, methodology, and effects of political adaptation because it benefits from the adoption of another person or group's story or culture without their consent, acknowledgement, or benefit. In her account of literary appropriation, Sanders explains that "the appropriated text or texts are not always as clearly signalled or acknowledged as in the adaptive process" (26) with its extended, announced retelling of the source material. While political adaptations give a voice to previously marginalized figures or groups, cultural appropriations benefit from speaking for another figure or group. All too often a dominant culture appropriates a marginalized one and thereby reinforces the existing power structure. As Niedzviecki himself acknowledged in an interview with the *Toronto Star*, "I failed to recognize how charged (the term cultural appropriation) is and how deeply painful acts of cultural appropriation have been to indigenous peoples" (Dundas). Cultural appropriation reinforces those in power; political adaptation amplifies those who are not.

As discussed earlier, the set of circumstances involving one of Canadian theatre's prominent directors and playwrights, Robert Lepage, further illustrates what is at stake in retelling political stories and in understanding the significance of political adaptation's creation process. During the summer of 2018,

Lepage had not one but two shows cancelled because of their creation process, casting, and theatrical strategies for retelling historical source material: *SLĀV* and *Kanata*. The 2018 Montreal International Jazz Festival cancelled Lepage's show *SLĀV* because of its cultural appropriation of slave songs with an "all-white production team, a white lead singer, and a predominantly white cast who were dressed as cotton pickers" (O'Toole 3). Echoing Niedzviecki's rhetoric in "Winning the Cultural Appropriation Prize," Lepage defended his production and exclaimed that "theatre has always been based on a simple principle: that of stepping into the shoes of another person to try to understand them" (Cori-Manocchio). Emer O'Toole, however, emphasizes the importance of the cultural power dynamics in a white production team profiting from slave songs: "First, before you walk in another person's shoes, ask if that person wants you to do so" and "second, where there are histories of exploitation, colonialism, and violence, perpetrated precisely by the culture from which the [artist] comes and against the people he is representing, then you need to meaningfully include the represented community in the process" (17–18). Lepage did not heed the production consultant (hip-hop artist and historian) Aly Ndiaye's advice to include more black actors. By contrast, Djanet Sears's *Harlem Duet*, discussed at length in chapter 2, retells Shakespeare's *Othello* in the contexts of North American slavery and race relations; Sears's play is an example of political adaptation and not cultural appropriation because it is written by an African-Canadian playwright; it cites a range of African artists, thinkers, and activists; and it features an all-Black cast. Cultural appropriation, then, can occur when a political adaptation is not executed with respect for and with the involvement of the marginalized or diverse peoples it represents.

Cultural appropriation is political adaptation gone wrong. The protests over Lepage's theatre productions (*SLĀV* and *Kanata*) magnify the importance of an ethical, informed dramatic adaptation of Canadian history and cultures. With a world premiere planned at Paris's Théâtre du Soleil for December 2018, Lepage's *Kanata* is an epic retelling of Canada's settler-Indigenous history where French actors portray Indigenous Americans.[4] Shortly after *SLĀV's* cancellation, Lepage received an open letter from and met with Indigenous artists, activists, educators, and allies who expressed concern over *Kanata*'s representation of Canada's history, cultural genocide, and Indigenous peoples. In a special opinion piece for the *Montreal Gazette*, Quincy Armorer (artistic director of Black Theatre Workshop), Mathieu Murphy-Perron (artistic producer of Tableau D'Hôte Theatre), and PJ Prudat (Métis actor and writer) explain how power dynamics complicate an act of retelling and can classify it as cultural appropriation: "Lepage, as one of the most powerful theatre creators in the world, should have leveraged his clout … to make space for Indigenous creators on the subject of the colonization of Indigenous lands and peoples in what became Canada. Our communities and our ancestors did not survive this long only to be excluded from telling our own stories" (9). As a result of these protests, co-producers withdrew their support for the production and Lepage officially cancelled the premiere of *Kanata*. Although plans for an international tour were cancelled, a version of Lepage's *Kanata* had a bried run in Paris. His two cancelled shows serve as a reminder that the creation process is fundamental to political theatre and adaptation because who is involved in storytelling and how we perform our canon is just as important as the narratives themselves. As *SLĀV* and *Kanata* illustrate, understanding effective methodologies of political adaptations can help dramatists carry out production processes, casting, and staging that underline rather than undermine their artistic goals.

Political adaptations are an artistic form of activism that reveal the pressing cultural debates of our time. We can see the influence of plays like Monique Mojica's *Princess Pocahontas and the Blue Spots* and Daniel David Moses's *Almighty Voice and His Wife* in the more recent calls for reconciliation. The *Final Report of the Truth and Reconciliation Commission of Canada*, for instance, documents "the establishment and operation of residential schools … which can best be described as 'cultural genocide'" or "the destruction of those structures and practices that allow the group to continue as a group" (1). In their "Calls to Action," the Truth and Reconciliation Commission makes it clear that "federal, provincial, and territorial governments, in consultation with Survivors, Aboriginal peoples, and educators" need to change the way public schools and universities teach Canadian history and Indigenous knowledge. The 2018 Ontario education debate over whether to integrate Indigenous content into school curriculum demonstrates the ongoing need for plays that expose the history of residential schools and cultural genocide. Moses's *Almighty Voice*, for instance, not only targets the memorialization of Almighty Voice but also how Indigenous history is taught in high schools. The study of political adaptation is both important and timely: we are experiencing the effects of Moses's and many other artists' calls to action with current amendments to Indigenous content in school curriculums across Canada. The case studies in *Political Adaptation in Canada* contribute to these ongoing changes by complicating the stories of Canadian theatre in order to include racialized, feminist, and Indigenous perspectives.

Many of the adaptors' source materials in this book – Shakespeare, Homer, Ovid, colonial legends – are themselves retellings or adaptations of earlier works, thereby participating in the continuing cycle of adaptation. "In the workings of the human mind," as Linda Hutcheon says, "adaptation is the norm, not the exception" (*Theory* 177). Despite the popular celebrations of literary and historical firsts, political adaptations like Moses's *Almighty Voice* and Mojica's *Princess Pocahontas* call attention to the pervasiveness of their adaptive mode and encourage an understanding that the adaptation process and change are "the norm, not the exception" when it comes to "the human imagination" (*Theory* 177). If we can accept that the adaptation of familiar stories from diverse perspectives is a necessary part of our national stages, then openness to socio-political change and cultural differences should not be far off.

The Governor General's Award for Drama serves as a cultural barometer of theatre in Canada. Recent awardees reveal the artistic regard for adaptations or spin-offs with a political lens. Some of the latest winners include Hiro Kanagawa's *Indian Arm* (2017 winner), a modern adaptation of Henrik Ibsen's *Little Eyolf* that explores issues of Indigenous land claims and family tensions; Catherine Banks's *It Is Solved by Walking* (2012 winner) uses Wallace Stevens's poem "13 Ways of Looking at a Black Bird" to structure and inspire the journey of a budding female poet reflecting back on marriage, abortion, miscarriage, and gendered academic hierarchies;[5] and Erin Shields's *If We Were Birds* (2011 winner) gives us a feminist adaptation of Ovid's "Tereus, Procne, and Philomela" myth. The list of recent winners is also weighted with plays that adapt historical events with political messages, such as Colleen Murphy's *Pig Girl* (2016 winner), a provocative dramatization of serial killer Robert Pickton that draws attention to the serious issue of Canada's murdered and missing Indigenous women. The 2015 winner, David Yee's *Carried Away on the Crest of a Wave*, is a piece of historical fiction set during the cataclysmic 2004 Indian Ocean tsunami that brings together characters from different nations. In *Age of Minority: Three Solo Plays* (2014 winner), Jordan Tannahill's *Get Yourself Home Skyler James* tells the true story of a queer soldier who defects from the army. Together, these plays gather an audience in order to challenge who gets remembered and how we conceive of national identity.

I want to return to my definition of political adaptation as repetition with political variation by emphasizing the many different forms this political transformation can take. There is, for example, a key difference between reformulating a political issue already present in the source – like Margaret Clarke's *Gertrude and Ophelia*, Erin Shield's *If We Were Birds*, and Margaret Atwood's *The Penelopiad* tackling feminine ideals in Shakespeare or Greek mythology – and adding a new political lens as is the case with Yvette Nolan and Kennedy Cathy MacKinnon's retelling of *Julius Caesar*, entitled *Death of a Chief*, with an all-Indigenous cast and a Brutus who questions his "Indian" identity. My adaptation grid, with its narrative fidelity and political fidelity axes, helps to account for these varying political approaches and exposes the inherent complexities in performing political adaptation.[6] Optative Theatrical Laboratories' *Sinking Neptune* (a retelling of Marc Lescarbot's *Le Théâtre de Neptune en la Nouvelle France* with a postcolonial framework) and Atwood's *The Penelopiad* (a retelling of Homer's *The Odyssey* from female characters' perspectives) may appear at different points along the narrative fidelity axis, but they are both close to the middle of the political infidelity spectrum because they at once repeat and alter existing issues of colonial conquest and gender, respectively, in their source material (see figure 5.1). Mojica's *Princess Pocahontas* and Moses's *Almighty Voice*, by comparison, re-politicize colonial legends as stories not simply about colonialism but also about contemporary Indigenous women and Almighty Voice's family, respectively. Mojica's and Moses's plays expose pre-existing political issues in the colonial legends (colonialism, religious conversions, racism) while also adding their own cultural framework and narrative plot lines (naming ceremonies, blue spots, marriage, family). *Harlem Duet* similarly builds on the political issues in its Shakespearean source material (*Othello*) through a present-day interracial couple as well as twentieth-century racial protests, artists, and intertexts. Because they insert new political narratives and issues, I chart *Princess Pocahontas*, *Almighty Voice*, and *Harlem Duet* closer to the repoliticizing end of the spectrum than *Gertrude and Ophelia*, *If We Were Birds*, and *The Penelopiad* in the grid below (see figure 5.1). Graphing the political adaptations demonstrates the heightened importance of political infidelity over narrative (in)fidelity when assessing the transformative work of a political adaptation.

In comparison to the other political adaptations, *Death of a Chief* is at the highest point on the political infidelity axis because it injects Indigenous issues into the source material. *Death of a Chief*, however, is not more politically

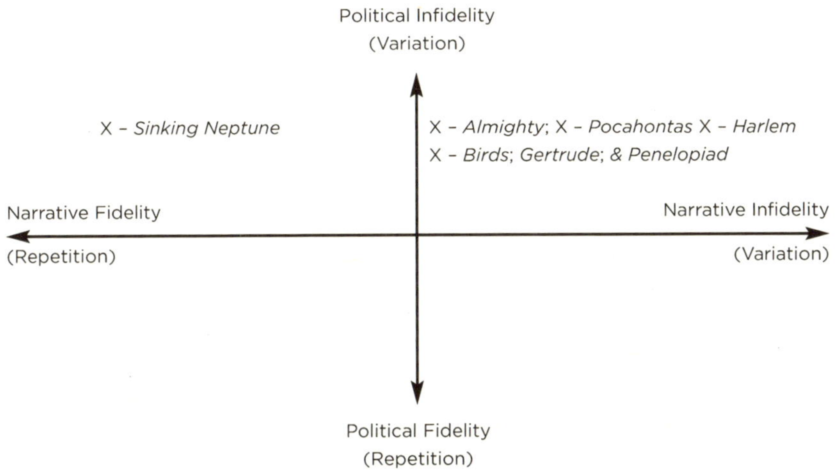

Figure 5.1 Grid of political adaptations with (from top to bottom) Daniel David Moses's *Almighty Voice*; Monique Mojica's *Princess Pocahontas*; Djanet Sears's *Harlem Duet*; Optative Theatrical Laboratories' *Sinking Neptune*; Erin Shields's *If We Were Birds*; Margaret Clarke's *Gertrude and Ophelia*; and Margaret Atwood's *The Penelopiad*.

radical or effective than Mojica's and Moses's adaptations because *Princess Pocahontas* and *Almighty Voice* expose the racism that is at work in the colonial legends and stereotypes. The grid, then, offers a method for comparing the adaptations' relationships to the source material in the context of political change without enforcing an evaluative hierarchy of successful or failed plays. Infidelity with the source material's narrative or politics does not necessarily correlate with a more radical message or effect.

The political adaptations closest to the top of the political infidelity end of the spectrum have changed the original's political messages the most. Phyllis Frus and Christy Williams take account of this change or what they call a literary "move beyond adaptation" when works "transform the source text into something new that works independently of its source" (3). I argue, however, that this transformational potential and effect of political adaptation is not beyond but part of the form of adaptation: adaptation, after all, must involve change and be able to stand on its own as an independent work of art. Political adaptors, in their frequent efforts to displace the source, showcase the potential of adaptation to function as a form and process of metamorphosis when they succeed in changing the original beyond recognition (Frus and Williams, 3). The move "beyond adaptation," as Frus and Williams would describe it, is actually an example of the sheer potential of political adaptation to effect change and offer independent artwork.

At a conference celebrating the four-hundredth anniversary of Shakespeare's death in 2016, Mojica called attention to the problematic doubleness of political adaptations that inevitably perform disidentification by reinscribing the centrality of a source material while also seeking to challenge it. In an effort to elicit adaptations that change current dominant narratives, Mojica asked scholars and artists to "burn it down" because the canon "needs to die" in order for "transformation and regrowth." Political adaptation is a vehicle for this radical "transformation and regrowth." Because of plays like *Princess Pocahontas* and *Harlem Duet*, scholars and theatre artists are no longer approaching historical or canonical figures like Pocahontas and Othello without considering their representation of colonialist and racist narratives, respectively. Mojica, Sears, and other playwrights use political adaptation as way for marginalized perspectives to survive and even thrive within a traditional canon; in the process, the adaptors and their adaptations are transforming inherited national narratives to better represent diverse experiences. The ongoing, inclusive changes to Canadian history, curriculum, and canons are in no small part a result of the efforts of political adaptors and their critiques of an exclusionary literary and theatrical tradition.

Political adaptations at once reveal and reinforce the cultural work being done on stages and in public policy. "In the realm of culture," as Mark Fortier says, "one might postulate that there is nothing beyond adaptation" or beyond the "renovation" of past words and worlds ("Beyond Adaptation" 374, 382). It is, however, not only adaptation that drives Canada's cultural imaginary – it is political adaptation. In this context of cultural and artistic updating, one thing is apparent: political adaptation dramatizes the possibilities of the imagination's and of art's ability to perform change. In Jo-Ann Episkenew's words, these politicized and "personal myths" are relational acts that are key to collective healing in a nation grappling with generations of cultural genocide, slavery, and gender inequality: "Personal myths play a central role in the construction of identity. Without a complete and coherent personal myth, a person is prone to suffer from emotional and mental illness. By reconstructing a complete and coherent personal myth and then sharing that myth with others, one can heal" (15). Political adaptation's reconstructions of personal and popular myths can help alleviate individual and collective trauma.

Political adaptation transforms the stories we tell and the stories we are told in Canada; they change who "we" are as a collective nation of nations. In Canada, political adaptation is more than a theatrical mode of cultural updating – it is a national mode of radical change and survival. If you change a nation's cultural imaginary, you change a nation. The act of retelling and re-performing one's story is at the centre of a radical healing process for the adaptor, actor, audience, and even the collective.

Notes

Introduction

1 King is of Cherokee, German, and Greek descent.

2 Black is capitalized in all references to *Harlem Duet* in keeping with Sears's work.

3 I refer to Canadian theatre and theatre in Canada throughout this study but it is important to note that some playwrights, such as Mojica, resist this national category.

4 See Fischlin and Knowles, *Adapting Shakespeare in Canada*; Brydon and Makaryk, *Shakespeare in Canada*; Knowles, *Shakespeare and Canada*; and Drouin, *Shakespeare in Quebec*.

5 See Pêcheux's *Language, Semantics and Ideology.* Muñoz's analysis of disidentificatory strategies builds on Pêcheux's theories of the "discursive formations on the subject-form" (*Language* 155).

6 See Rabillard, "*Age of Iron*," for an extended examination of how Clements's *Age of Iron* adapts Euripides's *Trojan Women* in a contemporary Canadian context.

7 Since opening its doors in 1982 in "the historic heart of [Vancouver]," the Firehall "strives to produce and present work that highlights and supports Canada's multiculturalism. As the first company focusing on Canadian work with this intent, the Firehall broke through social barriers and helped playwrights, actors, dancers, performers and producers of various cultural backgrounds present work to audiences across the country" ("Our History").

8 For further discussion of Canada's perceived dependence on the United States, see Potter's introduction (x).

9 See Grant's seminal historical text on Canadian nationalism, *Lament for a Nation*.

10 Political scientists, Berdahl and Raney use Canada's "strong sense of internationalism" as a premise to their study of how "the important link between Canada's role on the world stage and its national identity" affects "public opinion attitudes on international issues in Canada" (995). See also Kymlicka's discussion of Canadian national identity in "Being Canadian."

11 There is an established field of criticism on the performance of nationalism in Canada; see, for instance, Filewod, *Performing Canada*; Bociurkiw's *Feeling Canadian* and Hurley's *National Performance* use affect theory as a framework for analyzing performances of nationalism; and Koustas's *Robert Lepage on the Toronto Stage* focuses on one playwright's productions and complications of Canadian nationalism.

12 Amy Green charts a similar trajectory in American theatre over the last century from the use of Shakespeare as a bastion of high culture to an adaptable subject for "fusions of high and popular cultural and multicultural casts" (180).

13 For further analysis on the contexts and effects of multicultural policies in Canada, see Breton's *Ethnic Relations in Canada*.

14 Dobson argues that the postcolonial writings of the 1980s and 90s, or "the proliferation of what has been called 'minority' writing," challenge Atwood's and Frye's articulations of national identity (xiii).

15 *Afrika Solo* was followed by two of Sears's other plays, *Harlem Duet* and *The Adventures of a Black Girl in Search of God*, and her two-volume anthology *Testifyin': Contemporary African Canadian Drama*. For further discussion of African Canadian literature, see also Nurse's *Revival* and Tettey and Puplampu's *The African Diaspora in Canada*. Compton's *Bluesprint* and Clarke's two-volume collection *Fire on the Water* offer regional specific collections of British Columbian and Nova Scotian literature, respectively.

16 Hunt assumes the parasitical nature of literary adaptation in his review of a Canadian stage adaptation of David Adams Richard's novel *Nights below Station Street*.

17 See chapter 4 for further analysis of Mojica's and Moses's plays as well as the potential of political adaptation to divest itself of the source material.

18 For a more detailed consideration of palimpsests and adaptation, see chapter 4.

19 Soulpepper's *Almighty Voice and His Wife* (2019) production was directed by Jani Lauzon and starred James Dallas Smith as Almighty Voice/Ghost and Michaela Washburn as White Girl/Interlocutor.

20 *Beatrice Chancy* premiered in 1997 as a staged reading at Toronto's Theatre Passe Muraille. Clarke created a libretto version of the verse play, which premiered at Toronto's Music Gallery in 1998. For the libretto version, see *Beatrice Chancy: A Libretto in Four Acts*.

21 See King, *The Ethos of Drama*, for a theoretical discussion of direct address and the play-within-a-play's political effect on the audience.

22 *The Penelopiad* challenges the popular view of Penelope as a symbol of a faithful wife. Writers have long celebrated Penelope as a "chaste woman" (Aristophanes) or the "ideal of Roman chastity" (Latin elegiac poets of the first century BC) (Katz 4). Following in this tradition, Marilyn A. Katz provides a comprehensive overview of the critical reception of Penelope and explains that "critics, too, are inclined to underplay the complexity of Penelope's *kleos* in the Odyssey," either "restricting it to her constancy," or "assimilat[ing] her craftiness to it" (5): C. R. Beye portrays Penelope as "the all encompassing stability at the end of man's adventures;" A.T. Edwards attributes her importance to the fact "that she remained faithful to her husband in the face of suitors;" and J. Russo similarly describes Penelope as "renowned throughout Greece for her loyalty and cleverness" (as cited in Katz 6). As Katz says, "Penelope's *kleos* [renown] in this system of meaning, then, is identical with her constancy," and she merely "functions as a stable and unchanging reference point for the adventures of Odysseus" (6).

23 Chapters 2 and 4 examine "I am" declarations as self-defining utterances that not only dramatize the process of self-formation but also re-theorize the self as performative, multiple, and changing.

24 For theories of disidentification, see Pêcheux, *Language, Semantics and Ideology* and Muñoz, *Disidentifications*.

25 See McKinnon's insightful analysis of Stratford's 2006 production, advertising, and reception of *Harlem Duet* in "'Playing the Race Bard.'"

26 For extended analysis of the concept of the dispublic, see Wright, "Dispublics."

27 *Hamilton and Philosophy: Revolutionary Thinking*, edited by Rabinowitz and Arp, collects essays on the hit musical *Hamilton* and its historical

adaptation. For an analysis of *Hamilton*'s genre and production elements, see Schocket, "The American Revolution Rebooted," and McAllister, "Toward a More Perfect Hamilton," respectively.

28 See Helfman, "Why Hamilton Matters."

29 For their theories of publics and counterpublics, respectively, see Habermas, *The Structural Transformation* and Warner, *Publics and Counterpublics*.

Chapter One

1 According to Lescarbot's documents, *Le Théâtre de Neptune* took place on the Annapolis Basin, which is a sheltered body of water attached to the Bay of Fundy, near Port Royal, Nova Scotia. All note references cite Eugene and Renate Benson's 1982 translation. While there are several translations of the play, I have chosen to work with the Benson translation because, as Wasserman aptly notes, it "is more literal … than the others" (Introduction 40). Other English versions include W.L. Grant's 1911 translation, Harriette Taber Richardson's 1926 translation, and R. Keith Hick's 1927 version. For an in-depth comparison of the Richardson, Hick, and Benson translations, see Wasserman's introduction to *The Spectacle of Empire*.

2 A "louable enterprise" translates to a "praiseworthy enterprise" (76).

3 "All we desire / Is to live forever in your favour" (*TN* 78).

4 Although there are many different versions of *Sinking Neptune* – OTL consistently updates their script with new information – all quotations are taken from the online 2006 version because it was repeatedly performed in protest of *Le Théâtre de Neptune's* anniversary celebrations. Along with the online version, *Sinking Neptune* was also published in *Theatre Histories* (edited by Filewod), but this version of the script was never actually performed.

5 See the introduction for a discussion of shared political adaptation strategies.

6 See Wasserman's substantial introduction to *Spectacle of Empire* for an in-depth analysis of the historical contexts and performance conventions of *Le Théâtre de Neptune's* original performance in 1606.

7 As part of the Order of Good Cheer, French colonists appointed each day a chief steward who was responsible for ensuring that the colony's

meals included meat as well as some form of entertainment (Wasserman 23). For further information on Champlain and the Order of Good Cheer, see Litalien and Vaugeois, *Champlain*.

8 "Immortal renown" (75). Wasserman's edition includes significant criticism about *Le Théâtre de Neptune* as a tool of colonialist conquest.

9 The masque's type of boats are also a subject of debate. Wasserman suggests that the six Tritons' boats were "probably canoes" (36); Filewod asserts that Lescarbot "does tell us that the four 'Savages' spoke from a canoe" but "does not identify the watercraft used in the performance," concluding that "it was more likely a longboat with the Tritons at the oars" (xvii).

10 Theatre 400 intended to produce a full re-enactment on the waters where the play originally took place as well as a theatre conference (King, "*Sinking Neptune*: Introduction" 198). These plans, however, were dependent on government funding that never materialized. Musique 400, under the direction of Phil Roberts, managed to execute a re-enactment on 12 November 2006, on the shores of the Annapolis Basin. As Michael Posner explains, "An audience of about 50 people attended. Actors mimed the various parts, including Neptune, Roman god of the sea, and six tritons, while other actors read the French-language script" (R1).

11 OTL performed *Sinking Neptune* at the Anarchist Theatre Festival and the Montreal Infringement Festival before the November 2006 tour (OTL, "About the Project"). From December 2007 to July 2008, it was performed to protest the four-hundredth anniversary of Quebec and Champlain's involvement in Lescarbot's masque at McGill University, CEGEP Montmorency, and the Montreal infringement Festival.

12 In "'Verbatim Theatre,'" Derek Paget explains that words from "'ordinary' people" are collected and performed "in the context of research into a particular region, subject area, issue, event or combination of these things" (317). Paget's emphasis on the use of "ordinary people" as sources gestures towards the democratizing elements of OTL's theatrical process.

13 Paul is a Mi'kmaq elder and columnist; Mayo co-founded Spiderwoman Theatre (based out of New York) in 1976 and is of Kuna and Rappahannock ancestry; Cree theatre director, playwright, and writer Favel is a member of the Poundmaker First Nation.

14 Gilbert and Tompkins's introduction to *Postcolonial Drama* lists four essential features of postcolonial drama that apply to and define *Sinking Neptune*'s response to *Le Théâtre de Neptune*: (1) "acts that respond to the experience of imperialism, whether directly or indirectly"; (2) "acts performed for the continuation and/or regeneration of the colonized (and sometimes pre-contact communities)"; (3) "acts performed with the awareness of, and sometimes the incorporation of, post-contact forms"; and, finally, (4) "acts that interrogate the hegemony that underlies imperial representation" (11).

15 For an examination of these two plays in terms of revisionist drama and theatre historiography, see Wright, "Politicizing Difference."

16 Together, *Le Théâtre de Neptune* and *Sinking Neptune* complicate two distinct approaches to the project of historicizing theatre in Canada – what Filewod refers to as the "recuperation" and "deconstruction" of master-narratives. The "first generation of self-identified Canadian theatre historians," according to Filewod, "saw their project as recuperative," generating "performance calendars, lists of plays and bibliographies that began to cohere into connective narratives" (Introduction, viii). *Le Théâtre de Neptune*, for instance, offers a recuperative history of Canadian "origins" and has garnered fame because it is the earliest documented performance and extant dramatic script in Canada. Complicating Filewod's examples, *Sinking Neptune* demonstrates a deconstructive approach to theatre history in Canada by avoiding a linear narrative (through shifts in time) and foregrounding multiple versions (through shifts in perspectives); *Sinking Neptune*, however, is also recuperative in its fidelity to, and preservation of, Lescarbot's masque. *Sinking Neptune* illustrates how postcolonial historiography can be at once recuperative and deconstructive.

17 "The author of the book of Wisdom witnesseth unto us a most true thing, that 'All men have a like entrance into the world, and the like going out.' But each nation hath added some ceremonies, after these things are accomplished: for some have wept, seeing the birth of man upon the theatre of this world, there to be as it were a spectacle of miseries and calamities" (Lescarbot, *Histoire* 2). All English translations of *Histoire* cite Grant's English edition. For original French quotations, u/v and long s have been normalized. Italics and punctuation are retained from the original.

18 In *Performing Canada*, Filewod offers one of the first extended analyses of *Le Théâtre de Neptune*, arguing that the play is an "enactment of nation" that exemplifies "the historical and reciprocal relationship of theatre and nation in Canada" (xvii). Voicing quotations from the real scholar's work, the Filewod character similarly offers provocative explanations of the masque's "fantasy of interculturalism" (*Performing* xvi).

19 First Indian: "Sagamos, if you have any faith / In our services, / Then we will devote ourselves to you / And to your descendants" (TN 78).

20 On behalf of the Indian peoples
Who inhabit these countries,
We come to render their homage
To the sacred *Fleur-de-lis*
In your hands, you who represent
The Majesty of your Prince. (TN 78)

21 "Bring you any gifts" (79).

22 "Our skills … lie only in hunting" (78).

23 Lescarbot's use of the French theatre tradition has been examined in Lelièvre and Baillet, "Une Entrée Triomphale;" Fournier, "Lescarbot's '*Théâtre de Neptune*;'" and, most recently, in Wasserman's critical introduction to *Spectacle of Empire*.

24 For further information on Mi'kmaq culture, see both volumes of *The Mi'kmaq Anthology* (Choyce et al.) as well as Davis, *Micmac*. For the impact of colonial settlement on the Mi'kmaq people and their customs, see Reid and Baker, *Essays on Northeastern North America;* Hornborg, *Mi'kmaq*; and Sullivan, *Native Religions and Cultures of North America*.

25 This technique of announcing multiple intertexts and source materials is also discussed as the first shared strategy of political adaptations in chapter 1.

26 Geiogamah, a Kiowa Tribe member, is a playwright, director, and historian.

27 The Cornwallis statue was removed from a Halifax park in January 2018. A member of Pictou Landing First Nation, Rebecca Moore (Mi'kmaq), called the statue removal "a definite step forward in reconciliation" (as cited in Williams).

Chapter Two

1 As defined in the previous chapters, disidentification is the act of identifying with and against a dominant ideology in order to transform it from within; see Pêcheux and Muñoz. *Gertrude and Ophelia* was performed 30 January to 15 February 1992, at Calgary's Pumphouse Theatre produced by Maenad Theatre Productions, directed by Joyce Doolittle, and performed by Barbara Campbell-Brown (Gertrude/Playwright), Donna Larson (Ophelia/Actress), Trevor Schmidt (Horatio/Actor). *Harlem Duet* premiered at Toronto's Tarragon Extra Space and was produced by Nightwood Theatre, directed by Sears, and performed by Alison Sealy-Smith (Billie), Nigel Shawn Williams (Othello), Barbara Barnes Hopkins (Magi), Dawn Roach (Amah/Mona), Jeff Jones (Canada), Lionel Williams (onstage musician, double bass), and Doug Innes (onstage musician, cello).

2 In Shakespeare's *Hamlet*, Prince Hamlet orchestrates a performance of *The Murder of Gonzalo* and plans to "have these players / Play something like the murder of my father / Before mine uncle" (2.2.595–7) in an effort to arouse Claudius's guilt. As Hamlet says, "the play's the thing / Wherein I'll catch the conscience of the King" (2.2.605–6).

3 Iago's mischievous statement – "I am not what I am" (*Othello*, 1.1.69) – references the Christian Bible as a widely recognized intertext and illuminates the complexities of the biblical "I am who I am" statement (Exodus 3:14). Michael Neill describes Iago's performative utterance as "a blasphemous unspeaking of the biblical name of God" ("Postcolonial Shakespeare?" 165). Although I agree that Iago is a blasphemous figure, I contend that Iago's declaration shares rhetorical nuances with the biblical "I am who I am" because both statements simultaneously reveal and negate the speaker's identity.

4 I investigate "I am" statements and speech acts at more length in the fourth chapter.

5 Thank you to archivist Douglas E. Cass at the Glenbow Museum's archives for helping to uncover the advertising materials for the Maenad production of *Gertrude and Ophelia*.

6 See Knowles, *Reading the Material Theatre*, for his analysis of Stratford's "conservative, affirmative culture" (128).

7 *Cruel Tears*, what Mitchell refers to as a country opera, premiered in

1975 at Saskatoon's Persephone Theatre, written by Mitchell and with music by Humphrey and the Dumptrucks. Having toured nationally, it was published in 1977 and was nominated for a Chalmers award for outstanding Canadian play in 1978.

8 Egervari's adaptation has been performed in both French and English, and was first produced in 1977 by La Comédie des Deux Rive in affiliation with the University of Ottawa's Department of Theatre.

9 *Goodnight Desdemona (Good Morning Juliet)* "began with a joke" in 1985 during a touring performance of *This Is For You, Anna*. As Banuta Rubess (the play's first director and dramaturge) explains, "Ann-Marie MacDonald crammed a pillow on my face and with great hilarity pronounced: 'Goodnight, Desdemona!'" (Introduction xi). Commissioned by Nightwood Theatre, the play premiered there in 1988 and a revised version of the play toured nationally with the Nightwood Theatre Company in 1990; it was also in 1990 that *Goodnight Desdemona (Good Morning Juliet)* won a Governor General's Award for English-Language Drama.

10 Premiering at the Stratford Festival in 2000, *Elizabeth Rex* won the Governor General's Award for English-Language Drama that same year.

11 For more information about the theatre and their mission, see the Pumphouse Theatre's website: http://pumphousetheatre.ca/about-us/.

12 Just as "to die" signalled both death and sexual climax in Shakespeare's time – the *Oxford English Dictionary* explains that "die" was "used as a poetical metaphor in the late 16th and 17th cent." for a "sexual orgasm" – Clarke's play aligns death with sex when Hamlet's "hardened" and "softened" heart, together with Gertrude's "prick" of her pin, contribute to Ophelia's death. *Oxford English Dictionary Online*, s.v. "die," https://www.oed.com/view/Entry/52390?result=1&rskey=xZNJi9&.

13 Newman, "Ophelia Herbal," and Hunt, "Impregnating Ophelia," both explain that Ophelia's flowers, listed in her madness scene in Shakespeare's *Hamlet*, could have acted as abortifacients in the period.

14 See Scarry, *The Body in Pain*, for a theorization of the significance of a "howl."

15 Ophelia's howl connects her with dramatizations of male madness, such as Lear who also voices a "Howl, howl, howl, howl!" (5.3.255).

16 For further discussion of Sears's use of Fanon see Dickinson's "Duets,

Duologues, and Black Diasporic Theatre" and Huebert's "Othello's Testicles, Sybil's Womb."

17 *Gertrude and Ophelia* similarly challenges the all-too-simple dichotomy of separatist and assimilationist strategies in relation to feminist politics. The Playwright, on the one hand, voices a separatist response to patriarchal scholarly traditions in her efforts to focus exclusively on women and separate the genders. Gertrude, on the other hand, exemplifies an assimilationist approach to the patriarchal demands made upon her as Queen to the nation's powerful King. Ophelia straddles these oppositional positions benefitting neither from her assimilationist attempts to obey Hamlet and her father nor from her separatist isolation as a lone "me." Ophelia's resulting madness and death suggest the destructive void of an alternative to separatist and assimilationist strategies. Caught in this binary, Ophelia is collateral damage.

18 The following chapter takes on the role of political adaptation's audiences and their participation in the plays' acts of disidentification

19 *Harlem Duet* contextualizes the controversy of inter-racial marriages and the suppression of Black culture in late twentieth-century society. In addition to the reference to Michael Jackson, the play features sound clips from the OJ Simpson trial, which further emphasizes the modern relevance of Billie and Othello's relationship: Simpson, a Black man, was accused of murdering his white wife and "Othello was often invoked" (Knowles, "Othello" 385).

Chapter Three

1 Atwood wrote two versions of *The Penelopiad* – a novella (2005) as part of Canongate's myth series and a play (2007) – but all discussions of *The Penelopiad* refer to the play version unless otherwise stated.

2 Atwood's and Shields's feminist adaptations of Greek myths participate in an international re-visioning of canonical texts from a feminist (or previously marginalized) perspective. See Friedman, *Feminist Theatrical Revisions of Classical Works* and Foster, *Dramatic Revisions of Myths, Fairy Tales, and Legends.*

3 This chapter concentrates on the 2012 Nightwood production of *The Penelopiad* and the 2011 Tarragon Theatre production of *If We Were*

Birds. The Penelopiad, directed by Kelly Thornton, performed by: Maev Beaty, Christine Brubaker, Raven Dauda, Sarah Dodd, Monica Dottor, Megan Follows, Kelli Fox, Cara Gee, Pat Hamilton, Tara Rosling, Pamela Sinha Sophia Walker, and Bahia Watson (Toronto: Nightwood and Buddies in Bad Times Theatre, 10–29 January 2012). *If We Were Birds*, directed by Alan Dilworth, performed by: Philippa Domville, David Fox, Barbara Gordon, Stephanie Jung, Daniela Lama, Shannon Perrault, Geoffrey Pounsett, Karen Robinson, and Tara Rosling (Toronto: Tarragon Theatre, 14–23 April 2011).

4 *Feminist Theatrical Revisions of Classic Works*, edited by Friedman, offers a comprehensive resource of feminist adaptations of Greek myths; see, in particular, Roth, "The Philomela Myth as Postcolonial Feminist Theatre."

5 Julie Malnig offers an insightful analysis of McLaughlin's *Iphigenia and Other Daughters* in "All Is Not Right in the House of Atreus."

6 Andrea J. Nouryeh examines Zimmerman's feminist process and aesthetic in "Mary Zimmerman's *Metamorphoses*."

7 For further examinations of changing understandings of spectators and spectatorship, see *Theatre Journal*'s special issue on "Spectatorship" (2014) edited by Ric Knowles.

8 Brecht's concept of epic theatre offers a seminal theorization of critically active spectators. See, for instance, *Brecht on Theatre*. My concept of the dispublic considers the role of popular yet political theatre audiences in the context of theories of publics.

9 Creative Trust for Arts & Culture's *The Audience Engagement Survey Report* (2010) collects audience demographics of midsize theatres in Toronto.

10 In her introduction to the play, Atwood is careful to list multiple sources beyond the Homeric version of the Trojan war: "the play you hold in your hands is an echo of an echo of an echo of an echo of an echo of an echo" (v). With this opening line, Atwood underlines the sheer abundance of different versions of the myth from Oral Trojan War material to Homer's *The Odyssey* to "post-Homeric retellings, stretching from Ovid through Dante and Chaucer and Shakespeare and Tennyson to James Joyce and Derek Walcott and Barry Unsworth and Lewis Hyde" to Atwood's own novella and play (v). *The Penelopiad* and its many literary

echoes remind us that Penelope has been created and recreated by male authors in order to serve patriarchal ideals of female silence, patience, and loyalty.

11 Arendt's *The Human Condition* offers an analysis of the public and private realm in the context of ancient Greece.

12 *The Penelopiad*, directed by Josette Bushell-Mingo, performed by Mojisola Adebayo, Jade Anouka, Lisa Karen Cox, Derbhle Crotty, Philippa Domville, Penny Downie, Kate Hennig, Pauline Hutton, Corrine Koslo, Sarah Malin, Pamela Matthews, Kelly McIntosh, Jenny Young was produced by The Royal Shakespeare Company and the National Arts Centre, 19 September to 6 October 2007.

13 The 2009 Nightwood showcase was directed by: Arianna Bardesono; Kate Cayley; Ashlie Corcoran; Audrey Dwyer; Lise Ann Johnson; Esther Jun; Ann-Marie Kerr; Mary-Lou Martin; Sonia Norris; and Emma Tibaldo.

14 Salverson's essay collection *Popular Political Theatre and Performance* examines the continuing prevalence of popular yet political theatre in Canada.

15 As Susan Haedicke points out "more than half of the world's population now live in cities" (643). For examinations of the interrelated development of Toronto and its theatre, see McKinnie's *City Stages* and Knowles's "Multicultural Text, Intercultural Performance."

16 While the plays may seem to pit a female counterpublic (choruses, Penelope, Philomela) against a male-dominated public (Odysseus, Tereus), Atwood and Shields are careful to complicate this gender division. Penelope and Philomela are sometimes joined with the choruses, but this relationship is overtly troubled due to class issues. Atwood casts Penelope as a betrayer of the Maids, and Shields presents Philomela as an upper-class woman who is at first unsympathetic to the sufferings of her female servants. The lead female characters, Penelope and Philomela, are in some ways no better than the male counterparts. The public and counterpublic, as a result, are not gendered as masculine and feminine, respectively.

17 See the introduction for further discussion of political adaptation's common strategies.

18 The repeated use and referral to ropes in *The Penelopiad* not only symbolize the thread of life, as spun by the fates in Greek mythology, but

also remind the audience of the Maids' eventual hanging at the hands of Odysseus and his son.

19 While every production need not employ the same ropes for the weaving and hanging scenes, Atwood's call for "ropes" in both instances invites directors to reuse the same prop. In the 2009 and 2012 Nightwood productions of *The Penelopiad*, the directors did just that.

20 Nightwood Theatre's 2012 production of *The Penelopiad* rented space in Buddies in Bad Times Theatre (a downtown Toronto theatre dedicated to promoting queer art) in order to hold the large audience that they were anticipating. Representatives from both Buddies and Nightwood theatre confirm that *The Penelopiad* attendees were Nightwood audiences, which is why I examine Nightwood audience demographics.

21 Theatre attendees had the highest response rate to the survey with a 57 per cent completion rate, whereas the other discipline audiences had a 4 to 28 per cent response rate.

22 Of the audience respondents, 50 per cent had attended a production at Tarragon Theatre in the last two years – making Tarragon Theatre the most popular venue of the eight theatres listed and beating out Nightwood Theatre for which only 17 per cent of respondents had attended recently (Nightwood, *Sponsor* 8).

23 Tarragon Theatre's 2009–10 season featured plays by canonical Canadian playwrights such as Daniel MacIvor and Michael Healey.

24 The NAC Theatre Company's playbill for *The Penelopiad* describes it as "a refreshingly modern perspective on Homer's enduring epic *The Odyssey*." Tarragon Theatre similarly establishes Shields's play as an adaptation by introducing *If We Were Birds* as "A vivid re-imagining of Ovid's myth" (see the Tarragon Theatre's website for the 9 January 2011 playbill: http://www.tarragontheatre.com). Both playbills go on to compare the adaptations' plots with the source narratives.

25 See Hennig, "The Penelopiad Blog," *katehennig.com/thepenelopiad-blog*, September 2007.

Chapter Four

1 For further examination of Mojica's performance of history in *Princess Pocahontas*, see Walters, "After the Death of the Last."

2 See Knowles's "Translators, Traitors, Mistresses and Whores" for an

in-depth examination of the many "sources, inspirations, genealogies and intertexts" of *Princess Pocahontas* (249).

3 Disney's *Pocahontas* (1995) film postdates the *Princess Pocahontas*'s premiere (1990) and playscript (1991) but adds another intertextual layer for more recent productions and readers.

4 For a focused examination of the different performative effects of "I am" declarations in Moses's *Almighty Voice and His Wife*, see Wright's "Performing Cultural Crossroads."

5 For further discussion of literature and palimpsests, see Genette, *Palimpsests*.

6 See chapter 1 for a discussion of political adaptations' common strategies, which include self-identifications or "I am" statements.

7 For his extended theory of performance studies, see Schechner, *Performance Studies*.

8 Gérard Genette theorizes the palimpsest as a way of conceiving and approaching literature in *Palimpsests: Literature in the Second Degree*.

9 See the introduction for further examples of "I am" utterances in Canadian literature.

10 According to Austin, performative utterances satisfy the following conditions: "they do not 'describe' or 'report' or constate anything at all, are not 'true or false'" and "the uttering of the sentence is, or is a part of, the doing of an action, which again would not *normally* be described as, or as 'just,' saying something" (5). Some examples of performative utterances include "'I name this ship the *Queen Elizabeth*' – as uttered when smashing the bottle against the stern" or "I bet you sixpence it will rain tomorrow" (Austin 5). See chapter 2 for an extended analysis of Austin and Butler's definitions of performative utterances.

11 *The New Oxford Annotated Bible with the Apocrypha* explains that "'I AM WHO I AM' is an etymology of the Israelite name for God, YHWH […]. YHWH is treated as a verbal form derived from 'to be' and formulated in the first person because God is the speaker" (70). Many scholars agree on the mysteriousness and tautology of the self-defining utterances "I AM" and "I am who I am" (from the Old Testament): William R. Arnold notes that the naming "I AM WHO I AM" is "opaque" and "unintelligible" (108), Ee Kon Kim suggests that "Yahweh is the very God who conceals himself" (108), and Jeffrey J. Niehaus explains that "In the very act of revealing himself, God conceals himself" (179). The

biblical "I am" demonstrates the inscrutable enigma of God in that the tautology simultaneously "reveals" and "conceals."

12 In *Richard III* Shakespeare expresses Richard's conflicted self through a series of troubled declarations: "Richard loves Richard, that is, I am I. / Is there a murderer here? No. Yes, I am!" (5.3.184–5). Richard attempts self-constituting rhetoric and struggles to define his identity by naming and then un-naming himself: "I am a villain – yet I lie, I am not!" (5.3.192); for Richard, "I am" declarations announce his inner instability.

13 See Stam's *Literature through Film* and Hutcheon's *A Theory of Adaptation* for further discussion of the commercial benefit of adaptation as well as common denunciations of adaptations as second and therefore secondary.

14 A speech act does not always succeed in establishing the authority of the speaker. Repeated self-assertions in *Princess Pocahontas* also communicate the stagnancy of the speaker's identity as wife.

15 See Berkhofer's *The White Man's Indian* and Francis's *The Imaginary Indian* for a contextualization of the noble savage stereotype as the product of European prejudices in popular literature and culture.

16 For a treatment of Métis and Mestizo nations in relation to *Princess Pocahontas,* see Knowles's "Translators, Traitors, Mistresses, and Whores."

17 Moses also marks his scenes by phases of the moon in *Almighty Voice.*

18 For further discussion of Pocahontas's name change, see Carter's "Blind Faith Remembers." Carter explains that "A naming ceremony announces the child to the community, but as the child grows, his/her works announce themselves and new names are bestowed" (14). See also Allen's *Pocahontas* and Brant's "Grandmothers of a New World."

19 Much like Princess Buttered-on-Both-Sides, Mojica's Cigar Store Squaw dramatizes problematic efforts to conform to North American beauty standards. In Transformation 10, the Cigar Store Squaw fantasizes about being "Doris Day, Farrah Fawcett, Daryl Hannah … Christie Brinkley" and "*hums 'Uptown Girl' while putting on white buckskin mini-dress*" (49). The "*white buckskin mini-dress*" (49) emphasizes the North American sexualization involved in the popular images of the Indian woman that combines the Indian "buckskin" with popular culture's "mini-dress."

20 Because *Princess Pocahontas* and *Almighty Voice*'s critique of the theatre

audience changes depending on the spectators' demographics, production choices, and theatre venue, future productions of both plays will enable an enriched analysis and comparison of the plays' audience reception and impact on the spectators.

21 There are many in-depth studies on the gender division in Indigenous communities. In order to theorize the history of gender division in Indigenous communities, Van Kirk's "*Many Tender Ties*" explores the potential allure of the colonialists' domestic offerings to Indigenous women.

22 For an example of political critique in adaptive retellings, see Optative Theatrical Laboratories' *Sinking Neptune* (and chapter 1) because the play retells the colonial source material in its entirety but with a postcolonial lens.

23 I approach the audience of a political adaptation as a dispublic because they identify with, and against, the dominant source material thereby sharing the political adaptation's disidentificatory position. See chapter 3 for my discussion of this concept.

24 Gilbert's "Black and White and Re(a)d All Over Again" gives an overview of whiteface in contemporary drama. Gilbert compares *Almighty Voice* with the 2000 production of *Fountains Beyond* that was directed and updated by Wesley Enoch – as an adaptation of Landen Dann's 1942 script – at QUT Gardens Theatre in Brisbane, Australia. *Almighty Voice* and Enoch's production of *Fountains Beyond* offer the unique use of whiteface as a strategy for combating Indigenous othering.

25 For further discussion of translation between cultures and translation in theatre, see Godard's "Writing Between Cultures" and "Between Performative and Performance," respectively.

Conclusion

1 *Write* is a quarterly magazine by the Writers' Union of Canada.

2 See *The Current*'s 2017 interview where Anna Maria Tremonti discusses the Appropriation Prize controversy with Hal Niedzviecki and Ryan McMahon (Anishinaabe). In defence of Niedzviecki, Jon Kay (who resigned as editor-in-chief at the *Walrus* during the controversy) critiqued "identity-politics fundamentalists" and retweeted fundraising

initiatives for an actual Appropriation Prize, thereby making light of the issue of cultural appropriation and white privilege.

3 In response to the critiques of the Appropriation Prize article, Ken Whyte (former editor of the *National Post* and *Maclean's*) began fundraising for a real Appropriation Prize when he tweeted, "I will donate $500 to the founding of the appropriation prize if someone else wants to organize" (as cited in Kassam). Whyte's tongue-in-cheek fundraising efforts were quickly overshadowed by a crowd-sourcing campaign for a new Indigenous literary prize, entitled Emerging Indigenous Voices, that had raised over C$117,000 as of July 2018. Robin Parker launched the Emerging Indigenous Voices prize in 2017 and explains: "We want the award to ... build community ... To create mentorship opportunities, bring writers together ... After the Truth and Reconciliation Commission Report came out, people's voices began to be freed by the discourse, and more elders are writing down their stories. And those stories are so valuable" (as cited in Robertson). The Emerging Indigenous Voices initiative echoes the arguments made by political adaptations – that stories can forge, heal, and fortify a community. Atwood is also dedicating her Booker Prize (2019) money for *The Testaments* (a sequel to her dystopian novel *The Handmaid's Tale*) to an Indigenous fund, Indspire, that supports the education of Indigenous students.

4 Kanata – the basis for "Canada" – is the Iroquois word for village.

5 Much like Ann-Marie MacDonald's hero who comes to realize her own authority and/as authorship in *Goodnight Desdemona (Good Morning Juliet)*, Banks's protagonist gains agency by discovering her poetic voice.

6 See the introduction for further discussion of the political adaptation grid.

Bibliography

100 Years of Theatre in Canada: Stratford Festival. Ottawa: National Arts Centre, Ottawa, and the Centennial Commission, 1968.

"400-Year-Old Play Stirs Controversy in Nova Scotia." CBC *News*, 14 November 2006. Web. 25 June 2009. https://www.cbc.ca/news/canada/nova-scotia/400-year-old-play-stirs-controversy-in-nova-scotia-1.612130.

Aebischer, Pascale, Edward J. Esche, and Nigel Wheale, eds. *Remaking Shakespeare: Performance Across Media, Genres, and Cultures*. New York: Palgrave Macmillan, 2003.

Albahari, Miri. *Analytical Buddhism: The Two-Tiered Illusion of Self*. Basingstoke: Palgrave Macmillan, 2006.

Allen, Paula Gunn. *Pocahontas: Medicine Woman, Spy, Entrepreneur, Diplomat*. San Francisco: HarperCollins, 2003.

– *The Sacred Hoop: Recovering the Feminine in American Indian Traditions*. Boston: Beacon, 1986.

Anderson, Benedict. *Imagined Communities: Reflections on the Origin and Spread of Nationalism*. London: Verso, 2006.

Anderson, Patrick. *The White Centre*. Toronto: Ryerson Press, 1946.

Anouilh, Jean, Barbara Bray, and E Freeman. *Antigone*. London: Methuen, 2005.

Anzaldúa, Gloria. *Borderlands/La Frontera: The New Mestiza*. 2nd ed. San Francisco: Aunt Lute Books, 1999.

Apocalypse Now. Directed by Francis F. Coppola. Performed by Marlon Brando and Robert Duvall. San Francisco: Omni Zoetrope, 1979.

Appia, Kwame Anthony. "Is the 'Post-' in 'Postcolonial' the 'Post-' in 'Postmodern'?" In *Dangerous Liaisons: Gender, Nation, and Postcolonial Perspectives*, edited by Anne McClintock, Aamir Mufti, and Ella Shohat, 420–44. Minneapolis: University of Minnesota Press, 1997.

Appleford, Rob. "The Desire to Crunch Bone: Daniel David Moses and the 'True Real Indian.'" *Canadian Theatre Review* 77 (1993): 21.

Appleton, Sarah A. *Once Upon a Time: Myth, Fairy Tales and Legends in Margaret Atwood's Writings*. Newcastle upon Tyne: Cambridge Scholars, 2008.

Arendt, Hannah. *The Human Condition*. Chicago: University of Chicago Press, 1998.

Armorer, Quincy, Mathieu Murphy-Perron, and PJ Prudat. "Robert Lepage's Kanata and SLĀV Have the Same Major Flaws." *Montreal Gazette*, Opinion, 20 July 2018, 1–9. https://montrealgazette.com/opinion/opinion-robert-lepages-kanata-and-slav-have-the-same-major-flaws.

Arnold, William R. "The Divine Name in Exodus iii: 14." *Journal of Biblical Literature* 24, no. 2 (1905): 107–65.

Attridge, Derek. "Oppressive Silence: J.M. Coetzee's Foe and the Politics of Canonisation." In *Critical Perspectives of J. M. Coetzee*, edited by Graham Huggan and Stephen Watson, 168–90. London: Macmillan, 1996.

Atwood, Margaret. *The Edible Woman*. Toronto: McClelland and Stewart, 1969.

– "The Myths Series and Me." *Publishers Weekly* 252, no.47 (2005): 58.

– *The Penelopiad*. Toronto: Vintage Canada, 2005.

– *The Penelopiad: The Play*. London: Faber and Faber, 2007.

– *Surfacing*. Toronto: McClelland and Stewart, 1972.

– *Survival: A Thematic Guide to Canadian Literature*. 2nd ed. Toronto: McClelland and Stewart, 2004.

Austin, J.L. *How To Do Things With Words*. 1962. 2nd ed., edited by J.O. Urmson and Marina Sbisà. Cambridge, MA: Harvard University Press, 1999.

Bakhtin, M.M. *Rabelais and His World*. Cambridge, MA: MIT Press, 1968.

Ball, John, and Richard Plant, eds. *A Bibliography of Theatre History in Canada: The Beginnings through 1984*. Toronto: ECW, 1993.

Balme, Christopher B. *Decolonizing the Stage: Theatrical Syncretism and Post-Colonial Drama*. Oxford: Clarendon, 1999.

Banks, Catherine. *It Is Solved by Walking*. Toronto: Playwrights Canada Press, 2012.

Bannerji, Himani. *The Dark Side of the Nation: Essays on Multiculturalism, Nationalism, and Gender*. Toronto: Canadian Scholars' Press, 2000.

Bardesono, Arianna, Kate Cayley, Ashlie Corcoran, Audrey Dwyer, Lise Ann Johnson, Esther Jun, Ann- Marie Kerr, Mary-Lou Martin, Sonia Norris, and Emma Tibaldo, dir. *The Penelopiad Director's Showcase*. By Margaret Atwood. Nightwood Theatre. Dancemakers Studio Theatre, Toronto, Ontario, Canada. 15 November 2009. Performance.

Barker, Francis, and Peter Hulme. "Nymphs and Reapers Heavily Vanish: The Discursive Con-texts of *The Tempest*." In *Alternative Shakespeares*. 2nd ed., edited by John Drakakis, 191–205. London: Routledge, 2002.

Baum, L F. *The Wonderful Wizard of Oz*. New York: Lancer Books, 1968.

Beauvoir, Simone de. *The Second Sex*. Translated by Constance Borde and Sheila Malovany-Chevallier. New York: Vintage, 2011.

Bennett, Susan. *Theatre Audiences: A Theory of Production and Reception*. 2nd ed. New York: Routledge, 2003.

Benson, Eugene. "Marc Lescarbot and 'The Theatre of Neptune.'" *Canadian Drama* 8, no.1 (1982): 84–5.

Benson, Eugene, and Renate Benson, trans. "The Theatre of Neptune in New France." 1982. In *Spectacle of Empire: Marc Lescarbot's Theatre of Neptune in New France*, 73–81. 400th Anniversary commemorative ed. Vancouver: Talonbooks, 2006.

Berdahl, Loleen, and Tracey Raney. "Being Canadian in the World: Mapping the Contours of National Identity and Public Opinion on International Issues in Canada." *International Journal* 65, no. 4 (2010): 995–1010.

Bergren, Ann. *Weaving Truth: Essays on Language and the Female in Greek Thought*. Cambridge, MA: Harvard University Press, 2008.

Berkhofer, Robert F., Jr. *The White Man's Indian: Images of the American Indian from Columbus to the Present*. New York: Knopf, 1978.

Berton, Pierre. *The Wild Frontier: More Tales from the Remarkable Past*. Toronto: McClelland and Stewart, 1978.

Beye, C.R. "Male and Female in the Homeric Poems." *Ramus* 3 (1974): 87–101.

Birdsell, Sandra. *Ladies of the House*. Winnipeg: Turnstone Press, 1984.

Bissoondath, Neil. *The Age of Confession*. Fredericton: Goose Lane Editions, 2007.

– *Selling Illusions: The Cult of Multiculturalism in Canada*. Toronto: Penguin Books, 1994.

Bloom, Harold. *Shakespeare: The Invention of the Human*. New York: Riverhead Books, 1998.

Bociurkiw, Marusya. *Feeling Canadian: Television, Nationalism, and Affect*. Waterloo: Wilfrid Laurier University Press, 2011.

Bramwell, Murray. "Urbane Comedy One Minute." Review of *Goodnight Desdemona (Good Morning Juliet)*, by Ann-Marie MacDonald. *The Adelaide Review* 254 (October 15, 2004): 23.

Brant, Beth. "Grandmothers of a New World." In *An Anthology of Canadian Native Literature in English*, 163–74. 2nd ed., edited by Daniel David Moses and Terry Goldie. Toronto: Oxford University Press, 1998.

Brecht, Bertolt. *Brecht On Theatre: The Development of an Aesthetic*. Translated and edited by John Willet. New York: Hill and Wang, 1964.

Breton, Raymond. *Ethnic Relations in Canada: Institutional Dynamics*. Montreal: McGill-Queen's University Press, 2005.

Brier, Norman. "Grief Following Miscarriage: A Comprehensive Review of the Literature." *Journal of Women's Health* 17, no. 3 (2008): 451–64.

Briggs, Richard S. "The Theological Function of Repetition in the Old Testament Canon." *Horizons in Biblical Theology* 28 (2006): 95–112.

Brontë, Charlotte. *Jane Eyre*. Edited by Richard J. Dunn. New York: Norton, 2001.

Brooks, Nicole. *Obeah Opera*. Directed by ahdri zhina mandiela. Performed by Nicole Brooks, Saphire Demitro, Macomere Fifi aka Eulith Tara Woods, Joni NehRita, Saidah Baba Talibah, Kanika Ambrose, Neema Bickersteth, Sheila Boyd, Jessica Brown, Qwyn Alexis Charter, Najla Edwards, Nickeshia Garrick, Angelique Lazarus, Lisa Michelle McKenzie, and Bemnet Tekleyohannes. Bathurst Centre for Culture, Toronto: b current and Theatre Archipelago, 4 March 2012.

Brown-Guillory, Elizabeth. "Place and Displacement in Djanet Sears's *Harlem Duet* and *The Adventures of a Black Girl in Search of God*." In *Middle Passages and the Healing Place of History: Migration and Identity in Black Women's Literature*, 155–70. Columbus: Ohio State University, 2006.

Brown, Janet. "Feminist Theory and Contemporary Drama." In *The Cambridge Companion to American Women Playwrights*, edited by Brenda Murphy, 155–72. New York: Cambridge University Press, 1999.

Brydon, Diana, and Irena R. Makaryk, eds. *Shakespeare in Canada: A World Elsewhere?* Toronto: University of Toronto Press, 2002.

Buller, Edward. *Indigenous Performing and Ceremonial Arts in Canada: A Bibliography: An Annotated Bibliography of Canadian Indian Rituals and Ceremonies (up to 1976)*. Toronto: Association for Native Development in the Performing and Visual Arts, 1981.

Burnett, Linda. "'Redescribing a World': Towards a Theory of Shakespearean Adaptation in Canada." *Canadian Theatre Review* 111 (2002): 5–9.

Bushell-Mingo, Josette, dir. *The Penelopiad*. By Margaret Atwood. Performed by Mojisola Adebayo, Jade Anouka, Lisa Karen Cox, Derbhle Crotty, Philippa Domville, Penny Downie, Kate Hennig, Pauline Hutton, Corrine Koslo, Sarah Malin, Pamela Matthews, Kelly McIntosh, Jenny Young. Ottawa, Ontario: The National Arts Centre English Theatre Company in Association with the Royal Shakespeare Company (UK), 19 September–6 October 2007.

Butler, Judith. *Bodies that Matter: On the Discursive Limits of "Sex."* New York: Routledge, 1993.

– *Giving an Account of Oneself*. New York: Fordham U, 2005.

– "Performative Acts and Gender Constitution: An Essay in Phenomenology and Feminist Theory." *Theatre Journal* 40, no.4 (1988): 519–531.

The Cambridge Companion to Greek and Roman Theatre. Edited by Marianne McDonald and J. Michael Walton. Cambridge: Cambridge University Press, 2007.

Campbell, Sue. "Inside the Frame of the Past: Memory, Diversity, and Solidarity." In *Embodiment and Agency*, edited by Sue Campbell, Letitia Meynell, and Susan Sherwin, 211–33. Pennsylvania: Pennsylvania State University, 2009.

Carlin, Murray. *Not Now, Sweet Desdemona*. Nairobi: Oxford University Press, 1969.

Carlson, Marvin. *The Haunted Stage: The Theatre as Memory Machine*. Ann Arbor: University of Michigan Press, 2001.

Carson, Anne. *Autobiography of Red: A Novel in Verse*. Toronto: Vintage Canada, 1999.

Cartelli, Thomas. *Repositioning Shakespeare: National Formations, Postcolonial Appropriations*. New York: Routledge, 1999.

Carter, Jill. "Blind Faith Remembers … This Ain't No Love Story, This Ain't No Masque: Princess Pocahontas and the Blue Spots as Transformative Ritual for the Grandmothers, the Ones Who Remain, and for the Ones Who Are Yet to Come." In *Performing Worlds into Being: Native American Women's Theatre*, edited by Ann Elizabeth Armstrong, Kelli Lyon Johnson, and William A. Wortman, 7–28. Oxford: Miami University Press, 2009.

Cawthorne, Jane. *The Abortion Monologues*. Calgary: Jane Cawthorne, 15 March 2012. http://www.abortionmonologues.com/about_play.html.

CBC Radio One. "Interview with Jerry Wasserman." *Sounds Like Canada*. 16 November 2006. Sound recording. http://www.optative.net/neptune/media.htm.

CBC Radio One (Maritimes). "400th Anniversary of The Theatre of New France: Don Connolly speaks with arts producer Phyllis McGregor. Information Morning." 10 November 2006. Sound recording.

CBC Television News. "I ... AM ... CANADIAN!" CBC *Digital Archives Website*. 6 July 2000. https://www.cbc.ca/archives/entry/i-am-canadian-by-molson.

Césaire, Aimé. *Une tempête: d'après "La tempête" de Shakespeare*. Paris: Éditions du Seuil, 1969.

Choyce, Lesley, and Rita Joe. *The Mi'kmaq Anthology*. Vol. 1. Lawrencetown Beach, NS: Pottersfield Press, 1997.

Choyce, Lesley, Theresa Meuse, and Julia Swan, eds. *The Mi'kmaq Anthology*. Vol. 2. Lawrencetown Beach, NS: Pottersfield Press, 2011.

Chrystos. *Not Vanishing*. Vancouver: Press Gang, 1988.

Citron, Paula. "Tarragon Theatre – Erin Shields's If We Were Birds." Review of Tarragon production of *If We Were Birds*, by Erin Shields, directed by Alan Dilworth. *The Classical 96.3 fm*, n.d. http://www.classical963fm.com/arts/reviews/item/if-we-were-birds.

Clarke, George Elliott. *Beatrice Chancy*. Victoria: Polestar, 1999.

– "*Beatrice Chancy*: A Libretto in Four Acts." *Canadian Theatre Review* 96 (1998): 62–77.

– *Fire on the Water: An Anthology of Black Nova Scotian Writing*. 2 vols. Porters Lake: Pottersfield Press, 1991–92.

Clarke, Margaret. "Gertrude and Ophelia: A Play." 1993. *Canadian Adaptations of Shakespeare Project*, edited by Daniel Fischlin. University of Guelph, n.d. http://www.canadianshakespeares.ca/anthology/gertrude_and_ophelia.pdf.

– "An Interview with Margaret Clarke." By *Canadian Adaptations of Shakespeare Project*. *Canadian Adaptations of Shakespeare Project*. February 2004. http://www.canadianshakespeares.ca/i_mclarke.cfm.

Clayton, Barbara. *A Penelopean Poetics: Reweaving the Feminine in Homer's Odyssey*. Toronto: Lexington Books, 2004.

Clements, Marie. "Age of Iron." In *DraMétis: Three Métis Plays*, edited by Greg Daniels, Marie Clements, and Margo Kane, 193–273. Penticton, BC: Theytus, 2001.

Coetzee, J M. *Foe*. Toronto: Stoddart, 1986.

Coleman, Daniel. *White Civility: The Literary Project of English Canada*. Toronto: University of Toronto Press, 2006.

Compton, Wayde. *Bluesprint: Black British Columbian Literature and Orature*. Vancouver: Arsenal Pulp, 2001.

Conrad, Joseph. *Heart of Darkness*. 5th ed. Edited by Paul B. Armstrong. New York: Norton, 2016.

Cori-Manocchio, Valeria. "SLĀV Director Robert Lepage Calls Show's Cancellation a 'Blow to Artistic Freedom.'" *CBC Montreal*, 6 July 2018. https://www.cbc.ca/news/canada/montreal/robert-lepage-reacts-slāv-cultural-appropriation-1.4736219.

Creative Trust for Arts & Culture, *The Audience Engagement Survey Report*. Toronto: Centre for Social Innovation, 2010.

Crew, Robert. "*If We Were Birds*: Blood, rape, anger, revenge make for fine theatre." Review of Tarragon production of *If We Were Birds* by Erin Shields, directed by Alan Dilworth. *The Star*, 21 April 2010. https://www.thestar.com/entertainment/stage/2010/04/21/if_we_were_birds_blood_rape_anger_revenge_make_for_fine_theatre.html.

Davis, Stephen A. *The Micmac*. Halifax, NS: Nimbus, 1997.

Defoe, Daniel. *Robinson Crusoe*. Oxford: Oxford University Press, 2007.

Derrida, Jacques. *Limited Inc*. Evanston, IL: Northwestern University Press, 1988.

Desmet, Christy and Robert Sawyer, eds. *Shakespeare and Appropriation*. New York: Routledge, 1999.

Dickinson, Peter. "Duets, Duologues, and Black Diasporic Theatre: Djanet Sears, William Shakespeare, and Others." *Modern Drama* 45 (2002): 188–208.

– "Push 2012 Review #11: Almighty Voice and His Wife at The Waterfront." *Performance Place and Politics: A Blog About the Local/Global Interfaces of Audience and Event*. 2 February 2012. http://performanceplacepolitics.blogspot.com/2012/02/push-2012-review-11-almighty-voice-and.html.

Dilworth, Alan, dir. *If We Were Birds*. By Erin Shields. Performed by Philippa Domville, David Fox, Barbara Gordon, Stephanie Jung, Daniela Lama, Shannon Perrault, Geoffrey Pounsett, Karen Robinson, Tara Rosling. Toronto, Ontario: Tarragon Theatre, 14 April–23 May 2010.

Dionne, Craig and Parmita Kapadia, eds. *Native Shakespeares: Indigenous Appropriations on a Global Stage*. Burlington, VT: Ashgate, 2008.

Dobson, Kit. *Transnational Canadas: Anglo-Canadian Literature and Globalization*. Waterloo: Wilfrid Laurier University Press, 2009.

Drouin, Jennifer. *Shakespeare in Québec: Nation, Gender, and Adaptation*. Toronto: University of Toronto Press, 2014.

Dundas, Deborah. "Editor Quits amid Outrage after Call for 'Appropriation Prize' in Writers' Magazine." *The Star*, Books, 10 May 2017. https://www.thestar.com/entertainment/books/2017/05/10/editor-quits-amid-outrage-after-call-for-appropriation-prize-in-writers-magazine.html.

Edwards, A. T. *Achilles in the "Odyssey:" Ideologies of Heroism in the Epic.* Königstein: Anton Hain, 1985.

Egervari, Tibor. "'Le Marchand de Venise' de Shakespeare à Auschwitz" ("Shakespeare's *The Merchant of Venice* in Auschwitz"). Translated by Annick Léger. In *A Certain William: Adapting Shakespeare in Francophone Canada*, edited by Leanore Lieblein, 107–84. Toronto: Playwrights Canada Press, 2009.

Eisenstein, Sergei Mikhailovich. *Film Form: Essays in Film Theory, and the Film Sense.* Translated and edited by Jay Leyda. Cleveland: World Publishing Company, 1967.

Episkenew, Jo-Ann. *Taking Back Our Spirits: Indigenous Literature, Public Policy, and Healing*. Manitoba: University of Manitoba Press, 2009.

Euripides. *Trojan Women*. Translated by Alan Shapiro. New York: Oxford University Press, 2009.

Fanon, Frantz. *Black Skin, White Masks*. Translated by Richard Philcox. New York: Grove Press, 2008.

Filewod, Alan. "Between Empires: Post-Imperialism and Canadian Theatre." *Essays in Theatre-Etudes Theatrales* 11, no. 1 (1992): 3–15.

– *Collective Encounters: Documentary Theatre in English Canada.* Toronto: University of Toronto Press, 1987.

– "Colonial Spectacle." Review of *Spectacle of Empire: Marc Lescarbot's Theatre of Neptune in New France. Canadian Literature* 195 (2007): 190–91.

– *Committing Theatre: Theatre Radicalism and Political Intervention in Canada*. Toronto: Between the Lines, 2011.

– "Introduction: The History of Histories." In *Theatre Histories*, edited by Alan Filewod, vii–xi. Vol. 13, *Critical Perspectives on Canadian Theatre in English*. Toronto: Playwrights Canada Press, 2009.

– *Performing Canada: The Nation Enacted in the Imagined Theatre*. Kamloops: University College of the Cariboo, 2002.

– ed. *Theatre Histories*. Vol. 13, *Critical Perspectives on Canadian Theatre in English*. Toronto: Playwrights Canada Press, 2009.

Filip, Raymond. "The Mighty Buck, the Immigrant Fuck, and Melting Pot Luck." In *New and Selected Poems*, 15. Toronto: Guernica, 2001.

Findley, Timothy. *Elizabeth Rex*. Winnipeg: Blizzard, 2000.

– *Not Wanted on the Voyage*. Markham: Viking, 1984.

Firehall Arts Centre. “Our History.” Vancouver: Firehall, 2018. Firehallarts centre.ca.

Fischlin, Daniel. *Canadian Adaptations of Shakespeare Project*. Guelph: University of Guelph, 2004.

– “Nation and/as Adaptation: Shakespeare, Canada, and Authenticity.” In *Shakespeare in Canada: A World Elsewhere?*, edited by Diana Brydon and Irena R. Makaryk, 313–38. Toronto: University of Toronto Press, 2002.

Fischlin, Daniel, and Mark Fortier, eds. *Adaptations of Shakespeare: A Critical Anthology of Plays from the Seventeenth Century to the Present*. London: Routledge, 2000.

Fischlin, Daniel, and Ric Knowles, eds. *Canadian Theatre Review* 111 (2002).

Florby, Gunilla. “Pragmatic Penelope Or Timeless Tales for the Times.” In *Humane Readings: Essays on Literary Mediation and Communication in Honour of Roger D. Sell*, edited by Jason Finch, et al., 135–43. Amsterdam, Netherlands: John Benjamins, 2009.

Fortier, Mark. “Beyond Adaptation.” In *Outerspeares: Shakespeare, Intermedia, and the Limits of Adaptation*, edited by Daniel Fischlin, 372–86. Toronto: University of Toronto Press, 2014.

– “Undead and Unsafe: Adapting Shakespeare (in Canada).” In *Shakespeare in Canada: A World Elsewhere?*, edited by Diana Brydon and Irena R. Makaryk, 339–52. Toronto: University of Toronto Press, 2002.

Foster, Verna A., ed. *Dramatic Revisions of Myths, Fairy Tales, and Legends: Essays on Recent Plays*. Jefferson, NC: McFarland, 2012.

Fournier, Hannah. “Lescarbot’s ‘*Théâtre de Neptune*’: New World Pageant, Old World Polemic.” *Canadian Drama* 7, no. 1 (Spring 1981): 3–11.

Francis, Daniel. *The Imaginary Indian: The Image of the Indian in Canadian Culture*. Vancouver: Arsenal Press, 1992.

Franke, William. “Linguistic Repetition as Theological Revelation in Christian Epic Tradition: The Case of Joyce’s *Finnegans Wake*.” *Neophilologus* 90 (2006): 155–72.

Freud, Sigmund. *The Interpretation of Dreams*. 1913. Translated by A.A. Brill. London: George Allen & Unwin, 1932.

Friedman, Sharon. “The Feminist Playwright as Critic: Paula Vogel, Ann-Marie MacDonald, and Djanet Sears Interpret *Othello*.” In *Feminist Theatrical Revisions of Classic Works: Critical Essays*, edited by Sharon Friedman, 113–34. Jefferson, NC: McFarland, 2009.

– ed. *Feminist Theatrical Revisions of Classic Works: Critical Essays*. Jefferson, NC: McFarland, 2009.

Frost, Mary, and John T. Condon. "The Psychological Sequelae of Miscarriage: A Critical Review of the Literature." *Australian and New Zealand Journal of Psychology* 30 (1996): 54–62.

Frus, Phyllis, and Christy Williams. *Beyond Adaptation: Essays on Radical Transformations of Original Works*. Jefferson, NC: McFarland, 2010.

Frye, Northrop. *Anatomy of Criticism*. Princeton: Princeton University Press, 1957.

– "Conclusion to a *Literary History of Canada*." In *The Bush Garden: Essays on the Canadian Imagination*, 215–53. 1971. Toronto: Anansi Press, 1995.

Fugard, Athol, John Kani, and Winston Ntshona. *Statements: Three Plays*. London: Oxford University Press, 1974.

Gardner, Eric, ed. *Major Voices: The Drama of Slavery*. New Milford, CT: Toby Press, 2005.

Gass, Ken. *Claudius*. Toronto: Playwrights Canada Press, 1995.

– dir. *The Rez Sisters*. By Tomson Highway. Performed by Bill Merasty, Pamela Sinha, Cara Gee, Jean Yoon, Billy Merasty, Jani Lauzon, Djennie Laguerre, Michaela Washburn, and Kyra Harper. Toronto: Factory Theatre, 5 November–11 December 2011.

Gay, Frederick Lewis. "The First American Play." *The Nation* 88 (February 11, 1909) 136.

Genette, Gérard. *Palimpsests: Literature in the Second Degree*. 1982. Translated by Channa Newman and Claude Doubinsky. Lincoln: University of Nebraska Press, 1997.

Gibson, Graeme. *Five Legs*. Toronto: Anansi, 1969.

Gilbert, Helen. "Black and White and Re(a)d All Over Again: Indigenous Minstrelsy in Contemporary Canadian and Australian Theatre." *Theatre Journal* 55 (2003): 679–98.

Godard, Barbara. "Between Performative and Performance: Translation and Theatre in the Canadian/Quebec Context." *Modern Drama* 43, no. 3 (2000): 327–58.

– "Writing between Cultures." TTR: *Traduction, Terminologie, Redaction: Etudes sur le Texte et Ses Transformations* 10, no.1 (1997): 53–99.

Gömceli, Nursen. "Timberlake Wertenbaker's 'Radical Feminist' Reinterpretation of a Greek Myth: The Love of the Nightingale." AAA – *Arbeiten aus Anglistik und Amerikanistik* 34, no. 1 (2009): 77–100.

Grant, George. *Lament for a Nation: The Defeat of Canadian Nationalism.* Montreal: McGill-Queen's University Press, 2005.

Green, Amy S. *The Revisionist Stage: American Directors Reinvent the Classics.* Cambridge: Cambridge University Press, 1994.

Groome, Margaret. "Stratford and the Aspirations for a Canadian National Theatre." In *Shakespeare in Canada: A World Elsewhere?*, edited by Diana Brydon and Irena R. Makaryk, 108–36. Toronto: University of Toronto Press, 2002.

Grotowski, Jerzy. *Towards a Poor Theatre.* New York: Routledge, 1968.

Gubar, Susan. *RaceChanges: White Skin, Black Face in American Culture.* New York: Oxford University Press, 1997.

Habermas, Jürgen. *The Structural Transformation of the Public Sphere: An Inquiry into a Category of Bourgeois Society.* Translated by Thomas Burger. Cambridge, MA: MIT Press, 1991.

Haedicke, Susan. "Co-Performances of Bodies and Buildings: Compagnie Willi Dorner's *Bodies in Urban Spaces* and *fitting* and Asphalt Piloten's *Around the Block.*" *Theatre Journal* 67, no. 4 (2015): 643–61.

Harvie, Jen. *Fair Play: Art, Performance, and Neoliberalism.* Basingstoke, UK: Palgrave Macmillan, 2013.

Heitman, Richard. *Taking Her Seriously: Penelope & the Plot of Homer's Odyssey.* Ann Arbor: University of Michigan Press, 2005.

Helfman, Tara. "Why Hamilton Matters." *Commentary* 141, no. 2 (2016): 37–40.

Helwig, David. *The Glass Knight: A Novel.* Ottawa: Oberon Press, 1976.

Hengen, Shannon. "Staging Penelope: Margaret Atwood's Changing Audience." In *Once upon a Time: Myth, Fairy Tales and Legends in Margaret Atwood's Writings*, edited by Sarah A. Appleton, 47–55. Newcastle upon Tyne: Cambridge Scholars, 2008.

Hennessy, Rosemary. *Materialist Feminism and the Politics of Discourse.* New York: Routledge, 1993.

Highway, Tomson. *Rez Sisters.* Toronto: Fifth House, 1988.

– "Should Only Native Actors Have the Right to Play Native Roles?" *Prairie Fire* 22, no. 3 (2001): 20–6.

Homer. *The Odyssey.* Translated by Alexander Pope. London: Cambridge, 1992.

Hornborg, Anne-Christine. *Mi'kmaq Landscapes: From Animism to Sacred Ecology.* Aldershot, England: Ashgate, 2008.

Howells, Coral Ann. "Five Ways of Looking at the Penelopiad." *Sydney Studies in English* 32 (2006): 1–18.

– "'we can't Help but be Modern': *The Penelopiad*." In *Once upon a Time: Myth, Fairy Tales and Legends in Margaret Atwood's Writings*, edited by Sarah A. Appleton, 57–72. Newcastle upon Tyne: Cambridge Scholars, 2008.

Huebert, David. "Othello's Testicles, Sybil's Womb: The Interracial Child in *Harlem Duet* and Its Progenitor." *English Studies in Canada* 41, no. 4 (2015): 23–50.

Hughes, Langston. "Harlem [1]." In *The Collected Poems of Langston Hughes*, 363–4. New York: Vintage Books, 1995.

– "Harlem [2]." In *The Collected Poems of Langston Hughes*, 426. New York: Vintage Books, 1995.

Hulme, Peter, and William Sherman. "*The 'Tempest" and Its Travels.* London: Reaktion Books, 2000.

Hunt, Maurice. "Impregnating Ophelia." *Neophilologus* 89 (2005): 641–63.

Hunt, Russell H. Review of *Nights Below Station Street*, by Caleb Marshall. NotaBle Acts Summer Theatre Festival, New Brunswick, August 2006. *Russ Hunt's Website*. http://people.stu.ca/~hunt/www/reviews/nights.htm.

Hurley, Erin. *National Performance: Representing Quebec from Expo 67 to Céline Dion*. Toronto: University of Toronto Press, 2011.

Hutcheon, Linda. "From Page to Stage to Screen: The Age of Adaptation." In *Great Minds at the University of Toronto: The University Professor Lecture Series 2002–2003*, edited by Michael Goldberg, 37–54. Toronto: University of Toronto Press, 2003.

– "Performing Modernism: Adaptation and its Discontents." Keynote address, Performing Adaptations Conference, *The Festival of Original Theatre*, Robert Gill Theatre, Toronto, 15 February 2006.

– *A Theory of Adaptation*. New York: Routledge, 2006.

Ingersoll, Earl G. "Flirting with Tragedy: Margaret Atwood's *The Penelopiad*, and the Play of the Text." *Intertexts* 12, no. 1–2 (2008): 111–28.

Johnson, E. Pauline. "The Cattle Thief." In *An Anthology of Canadian Native Literature in English*, edited by Daniel David Moses and Terry Goldie, 28–9. 2nd ed. Oxford: Oxford University Press, 1998.

Johnson, Stephen. Introduction. *Burnt Cork: Traditions and Legacies of Blackface Minstrelsy*, edited by Stephen Johnson, 1–17. Amherst: University of Massachusetts Press, 2012.

– ed. *Burnt Cork: Traditions and Legacies of Blackface Minstrelsy*. Amherst: University of Massachusetts Press, 2012.

Johnston, Denis William. *Up the Mainstream: The Rise of Toronto's Alternative Theatres, 1968–1975*. Toronto: University of Toronto Press, 1991.

Kamboureli, Smaro. Preface. *Trans. Can. Lit: Resituating the Study of Canadian Literature*, vii–xv. Edited by Smaro Kamboureli and Roy Miki. Waterloo: Wilfrid Laurier University Press, 2007.

Kamboureli, Smaro, and Roy Miki, eds. *Trans. Can. Lit: Resituating the Study of Canadian Literature*. Waterloo: Wilfrid Laurier University Press, 2007.

Kanagawa, Hiro. *Indian Arm*. Toronto: Playwrights Canada Press, 2016.

Kaplan, Jon. "Preview: *If We Were Birds*." *Now*. 15 April 2010. https://nowtoronto.com/culture/stage/preview-if-we-were-birds/.

Kassam, Ashifa. "Canadian Journalists Support 'Appropriation Prize' after Online Furore." *The Guardian* May 13, 2017. https://www.theguardian.com/world/2017/may/13/canadian-journalists-appropriation-prize.

Katz, Marylin A. *Penelope's Renown: Meaning and Indeterminacy in the Odyssey*. Princeton: Princeton University Press, 1991.

Kenner, Hugh. *The Elsewhere Community*. Toronto: House of Anansi Press, 1998.

Kidnie, Margaret Jane. *Shakespeare and the Problem of Adaptation*. New York: Routledge, 2009.

– "'There's Magic in the Web of It': Seeing beyond Tragedy in *Harlem Duet*." *Journal of Commonwealth Literature* 36, no. 2 (2001): 29–44.

Kim, Ee Kon. "Who Is Yahweh? Based on a Contextual Reading of Exodus 3:14." *Asia Journal of Theology* 3 (1989): 108–17.

King, Donovan. "A Dramaturgical Toolbox for Sinking Neptune." *Optative Theatrical Laboratories*. Montreal: Optative Theatrical Laboratories, 2006. http://www.optative.net/wp-content/uploads/2012/10/sinking neptune.pdf.

– "*Sinking Neptune*: Introduction." In *Theatre Histories*, edited by Alan Filewod, 198–201. Vol. 13, Critical Perspectives on Canadian Theatre in English. Toronto: Playwrights Canada Press, 2009.

King, Robert. *The Ethos of Drama: Rhetorical Theory and Dramatic Worth*. Washington: Catholic University of America Press, 2010.

King, Thomas. *The Truth About Stories: A Native Narrative*. CBC Lecture Series. Toronto: House of Anansi Press, 2003.

King James Bible. Michigan: Zondervan, 2002.

Klinck, Carl F. *Literary History of Canada: Canadian Literature in English*. Toronto: University of Toronto Press, 1965.

Knowles, Ric. "Adapting to Shakespeare." In *The Shakespeare's Mine: Adapting Shakespeare in Anglophone Canada*, iii–ix. Toronto: Playwrights Canada Press, 2009.

– "Multicultural Text, Intercultural Performance: The Performance Ecology of Contemporary Toronto." In *Performance and the City*, edited by D.J. Hopkins, Shelley Orr, and Kim Solga, 73–91. Basingstoke, UK: Palgrave Macmillan, 2009.

– "Othello in Three Times." In *Shakespeare in Canada: A World Elsewhere?*, edited by Diana Brydon and Irena R. Makaryk, 371–95. Toronto: University of Toronto Press, 2002.

– *Reading the Material Theatre*. Cambridge: Cambridge University Press, 2004.

– *Shakespeare and Canada*. Brussels: Peter Lang, 2004.

– ed. *The Shakespeare's Mine: Adapting Shakespeare in Anglophone Canada*. Toronto: Playwrights Canada Press, 2009.

– ed. "Spectatorship." Special issue, *Theatre Journal* 66, no. 3 (2014).

– "Translators, Traitors, Mistresses, and Whores: Monique Mojica and the Mothers of the Métis Nations." In *Siting the Other: Re-visions of Marginality in Australian and English-Canadian Drama*, edited by Marc Maufort and Franca Bellarsi, 247–66. Brussels: Peter Lang, 2001.

Komporaly, Jozefina. *Radical Revival as Adaptation: Theatre, Politics, Society*. London: Palgrave Macmillan, 2017.

Kondo, Dorinne. "(Re)Visions of Race: Contemporary Race Theory and the Cultural Politics of Racial Crossover in Documentary Theatre." *Theatre Journal* 52, no. 1 (2000): 100.

Koustas, Jane. *Robert Lepage on the Toronto Stage: Language, Identity, Nation*. Montreal: McGill-Queen's University Press, 2016.

Kristeva, Julia. *Black Sun: Depression and Melancholia*. Translated by Leon S. Roudiez. New York: Columbia University Press, 1989.

– *Desire in Language: A Semiotic Approach to Literature and Art*. Edited by Leon S. Roudiez. Trans. Thomas Gora, Alice Jardine, and Leon S. Roudiez. New York: Columbia University Press, 1980.

Kroetsch, Robert. *The Words of My Roaring*. Toronto: Macmillan of Canada, 1966.

Kymlicka, Will. "Being Canadian." *Government and Opposition* 38, no.3 (2003): 357–85.

Lacey, Liam. "Almighty Voice and His Wife Is a Peculiar, Yet Fascinating Romantic Tale of a Young Cree and His Wife That Takes a Wild Turn." *The Globe and Mail*, 15 February 1992. C6.

Laera, Margherita. *Theatre and Adaptation: Return, Rewrite, Repeat*. London: Bloomsbury Press, 2014.

Lambert, Tina. "Performance Review: *The Penelopiad*." *Theatre Journal* 62, no. 4 (2010): 673–5.

Laurence, Margaret. *The Diviners*. Toronto: McClelland and Stewart, 1974.

Lauzon, Jani, dir. *Almighty Voice and His Wife*. By Daniel David Moses. Performed by James Dallas Smith and Michaela Washburn. Soulpepper Theatre. Toronto, Ontario: Young Centre for the Performing Arts, 11 October–10 November 2019.

Lavoie, Laurent. "Le Théâtre de Langue Française au Nouveau Brunswick." *Le Théâtre Canadien-Français*, 451–66. Archies des Lettres Canadiennes. Vol. 5. Montreal: Fides, 1976.

Lawson, Guy. "North Star." *New York Times*, 13 December 2015, MM88. https://www.nytimes.com/2015/12/13/magazine/trudeaus-canada-again.html.

Lelièvre, Renée, and Monique Baillet. "Une Entrée Triomphale en Acadie en 1606." *Revue d'Histoire du Théâtre* 21, no. 2 (1969): 134–41.

Lescarbot, Marc. *Histoire de la Nouvelle-France* (*History of New France*). Vol. 3. Translated by W.L. Grant. Toronto: Champlain Society, 1914.

– "Le Theatre de Neptune en la Nouvelle-France." 1606. In *Spectacle of Empire: Marc Lescarbot's Theatre of Neptune in New France*, edited by Jerry Wasserman, 47–57. 400th anniversary commemorative ed. Vancouver: Talonbooks, 2006.

Levinas, Emmanuel. *Otherwise than Being or Beyond Essence*. 2nd ed. Translated by Alphonso Lingis. Dordecht, Netherlands: Kluwer, 1991.

Lhamon, W.T., Jr. "Turning Around Jim Crow." In *Burnt Cork: Traditions and Legacies of Blackface Minstrelsy*, edited by Stephen Johnson, 18–50. Amherst: University of Massachusetts Press, 2012.

Lieblein, Leanore. *A Certain William: Adapting Shakespeare in Francophone Canada*. Toronto: Playwrights Canada Press, 2009.

Lightstone, Michael. "Altering the Course of History: Two Theatre Productions Re-enact Lescarbot's 400-Year-Old Play; One with a Slice of Political Correctness and a Postcolonial Bent." *The Halifax Chronicle Herald*. 11 November 2006, C13.

Lisk, Dean. "Finding Neptune: Theatre Troupe Revisits Legacy of Controversial Early Play." *The Daily News*. 14 November 2006.

Litalien, Raymonde and Denis Vaugeois, eds. *Champlain: The Birth of French America*. Montreal: McGill-Queen's University Press, 2004.

Loomba, Ania. "Sexuality and Racial Difference." In *Shakespeare: An Anthology of Criticism and Theory 1945–2000*, edited by Russ McDonald, 794–816. Malden, MA: Blackwell, 2004.

Loomba, Ania, and Martin Orkin, eds. *Postcolonial Shakespeares*. London: Routledge, 1998.

MacDonald, Ann-Marie. *Goodnight Desdemona (Good Morning Juliet)*. Toronto: Vintage Canada, 1998.

Maenad Theatre Productions. "Newsletter." 1991. Maenad Theatre Productions Fonds. File 18. Glenbow Archives, Calgary.

– Maenad Theatre Productions Fonds. Glenbow Archives, Calgary.

Makaryk, Irena R. Introduction to *Shakespeare in Canada: A World Elsewhere?*, 3–41. Edited by Diana Brydon and Irena R. Makaryk. Toronto: University of Toronto Press, 2002.

Malnig, Julie. "All Is Not Right in the House of Atreus: Feminist Theatrical Renderings of the *Oresteia*." In *Feminist Theatrical Revisions of Classic Works: Critical Essays*, edited by Sharon Friedman, 2–41. Jefferson, NC: McFarland, 2009.

Marshall, Hallie Rebecca. "Greek Drama in Canada: Women's Voices and Minority Views." In *The Oxford Handbook of Greek Drama in the Americas*, edited by Kathryn Bosher, Fiona Macintosh, Justine McConnell, and Patrice Rankine, 671–82. Oxford: Oxford University Press, 2015.

Massai, Sonia, ed. *World-Wide Shakespeares: Local Appropriations in Film and Performance*. New York: Routledge, 2005.

McAllister, Marvin. "Toward a More Perfect *Hamilton*." *Journal of the Early Republic* 37, no. 2 (2017): 279–288.

McDonald, Russ, ed. *Shakespeare: An Anthology of Criticism and Theory 1945–2000*. Malden, MA: Blackwell, 2004.

McKinnie, Michael. *City Stages: Theatre and Urban Space in a Global City*. Toronto: University of Toronto Press, 2007.

McKinnon, James. "'Playing the Race Bard': How Shakespeare and *Harlem Duet* Sold (at) the 2006 Stratford Shakespeare Festival." In *OuterSpeares: Shakespeare, Intermedia, and the Limits of Adaptation*, edited by Daniel Fischlin, 290–320. Toronto: University of Toronto Press, 2014.

McLaughlin, Ellen. *The Greek Plays*. New York: Theatre Communications Group, 2005.

McLuhan, Marshall. *The Crack in the Rear-View Mirror*. Montreal: Faculty of Education, McGill University, 1966.

Miller, Arthur. *The Crucible*. New York: Penguin Books, 2003.

Milne, W.S, ed. *Canadian Full-Length Plays in English: A Preliminary Annotated Catalogue*. Ottawa: Dominion Drama Festival, 1964.

Minh-ha, Trinh T. "Not You/Like You: Postcolonial Women and the Interlocking Questions of Identity and Difference." In *Dangerous Liaisons: Gender, Nation, and Postcolonial Perspectives*, edited by Anne McClintock, Aamir Mufti, and Ella Shohat, 415–19. Minneapolis: University of Minnesota Press, 1997.

Mitchell, Ken, and Humphrey and the Dumptrucks. *Cruel Tears*. 1975. Vancouver: Talonbooks, 1977.

Mojica, Monique. "'From the Spine': A Conversation about Shakespeare, Indigenous Theatre, and *Death of A Chief*." Conference Presentation at *Shakespeare + Canada Symposium*. University of Ottawa, 22 April 2016.

– *Princess Pocahontas and the Blue Spots*. Toronto: Women's Press, 1991.

Mojica, Monique, and Ric Knowles, ed. *Staging Coyote's Dream: An Anthology of First Nations Drama in English*. 2 vols. Toronto: Playwrights Canada Press, 2003, 2009.

Montgomery, Lucy Maud. *Anne of Green Gables*. Toronto: Tundra Books, 2014.

Monteiro, Lyra D. "Review Essay: Race-Conscious Casting and the Erasure of the Black Past in Lin-Manuel Miranda's Hamilton." *The Public Historian* 38, no. 1 (2016): 89–98.

Morrow, Martin. "Milestones: Celebrating 50 Years of the Mirvish Vision." *The Globe and Mail*. 1 October 2013. https://www.theglobeandmail.com/arts/theatre-and-performance/celebrating-50-years-of-the-mirvish-vision/article14608096/.

Moses, Daniel David. *Almighty Voice and His Wife*. Toronto: Playwrights Canada Press, 2001.

– "How My Ghosts Got Pale Faces." In *Pursued by a Bear: Talks, Monologues, and Tales*, 52–81. Toronto: Exile Editions, 2005.

Moss, Laura F.E., ed. *Is Canada Postcolonial?: Unsettling Canadian Literature*. Waterloo: Wilfrid Laurier University Press, 2003.

Muñoz, José Esteban. *Disidentifications: Queers of Color and the Performance of Politics*. Minneapolis: University of Minnesota Press, 1999.

Munro, Alice. *Lives of Girls and Women: A Novel.* Toronto: McGraw-Hill Ryerson, 1971.

Murphy, Colleen. *Pig Girl.* Toronto: Playwrights Canada Press, 2015.

Murray, Leah A. "Introduction: Hollywood Politics: Popular Culture Factor in 21st Century Politics" In *Politics and Popular Culture*, vii–xii. Newcastle upon Tyne: Cambridge Scholars, 2010.

National Arts Centre. *National Arts Centre English Theatre 2007–08 Season.* Ottawa, Ontario. https://nac-cna.ca/en/englishtheatre.

Neely, Carol Thomas. "Women and Men in *Othello*: 'What should such a fool / Do with so good a woman?'" In *The Woman's Part: Feminist Criticism of Shakespeare*, edited by Carolyn Ruth Swift Lenz, Gayle Greene, and Carol Thomas Neely, 211–39. Urbana: University of Illinois Press, 1980.

Neill, Michael, ed. *The Oxford Shakespeare: Othello.* Oxford: Oxford University Press, 2006.

– "Post-Colonial Shakespeare? Writing Away from the Centre." In *Postcolonial Shakespeares*, edited by Ania Loomba and Martin Orkin, 164–85. London: Routledge, 1998.

Nestruck, J. Kelly. "*If We Were Birds*: A Stunning New Play." Review of *If We Were Birds*, directed by Alan Dilworth. *The Globe and Mail.* 23 April 2010. https://www.theglobeandmail.com/arts/theatre-and-performance/if-we-were-birds-a-stunning-new-play/article4189251/.

– "Review: Fine female cast makes for a magical *Penelopiad*." Review of *The Penelopiad*, directed by Kelly Thornton. *The Globe and Mail.* 13 January 2012. https://www.theglobeandmail.com/arts/theatre-and-performance/fine-female-cast-makes-for-a-magical-penelopiad/article630458/.

The New Oxford Annotated Bible with the Apocrypha: Revised Standard Version. Edited by Herbert G. May and Bruce Manning Metzger. Oxford: Oxford University Press, 1973.

New, W.H. *Among Worlds: An Introduction to Modern Commonwealth and South African Fiction.* Erin, ON: Press Porcépic, 1975.

Newman, Lucile F. "Ophelia's Herbal." *Economic Botany* 33, no. 2 (1979): 227–39.

Niedzviecki, Hal, and Ryan McMahon. "I Invoked Cultural Appropriation in the Context of Literature and Writing Only: Hal Niedzviecki." By Anna Maria Termonti. *The Current.* CBC Radio. 15 May 2017. https://www.cbc.ca/radio/thecurrent/the-current-for-may-15-2017-1.4112604/i-invoked-

cultural-appropriation-in-the-context-of-literature-and-writing-only-hal-niedzviecki-1.4112618.
– "Winning the Appropriation Prize." *Write* (Spring 2017): 8.
Niehaus, Jeffrey J. *God at Sinai: Covenant and Theophany in the Bible and Ancient Near East.* Grand Rapids: Zondervan, 1995.
Nightwood Theatre. *The Penelopiad: by Margaret Atwood.* Playbill. Toronto: Nightwood Theatre, 2012.
– *Sponsor a Performance.* Toronto: Nightwood Theatre, 2016.
Nolan, Yvette and Kennedy Cathy MacKinnon. *Death of a Chief: February 2006 version. Canadian Adaptations of Shakespeare Project.* 10 April 2008. http://www.canadianshakespeares.ca/anthology/the_death_of_a_chief.pdf.
Nouryeh, Andrea J. "Mary Zimmerman's *Metamorphoses*: Storytelling Theater as Feminist Process." In *Feminist Theatrical Revisions of Classic Works: Critical Essays*, edited by Sharon Friedman, 61–78. Jefferson, NC: McFarland, 2009.
Nurse, D. Bailey. *Revival: An Anthology of Black Canadian Writing.* Toronto: McClelland & Stewart, 2006.
O'Brien. Michael. *Mad Boy Chronicle.* Toronto: Playwrights Canada Press, 1995.
Optative Theatrical Laboratories. "About *Sinking Neptune*." Montreal: Optative Theatrical Laboratories, n.d. http://www.optative.net/about-sinking-neptune/.
– "Mandate." *Optative Theatrical Laboratories.* Montreal: Optative Theatrical Laboratories, n.d. http://www.optative.net/mandate/.
– *Sinking Neptune. Optative Theatrical Laboratories Library.* Montreal: Optative Theatrical Laboratories, November 2006. http://www.optative.net/neptune/.
– "Sinking Neptune." *Theatre Histories*, edited by Alan Filewod, 202–15. Vol. 13, Critical Perspectives on Canadian Theatre in English. Toronto: Playwrights Canada Press, 2009.
Orgel, Stephen. *The Jonsonian Masque.* Cambridge, MA: Harvard University Press, 1965.
O'Toole, Emer. "White Actors Singing Slave Songs? It's Right That This Play Was Cancelled." *The Guardian.* 30 July 2018, 1–21. https://www.theguardian.com/commentisfree/2018/jul/30/white-actors-slave-songs-play-cancelled.

Ouzounian, Richard. "Playwright Erin Shields Nurtures Two New Creations." *The Toronto Star*. 14 April 2010. https://www.thestar.com/entertainment/stage/2010/04/14/playwright_erin_shields_nurtures_two_new_creations.html.

– "Review: *The Penelopiad* is stunning theatre." Review of *The Penelopiad*, directed by Kelly Thornton. *The Star*. 12 January 2012. https://www.thestar.com/entertainment/2012/01/12/review_the_penelopiad_is_stunning_theatre.html.

Ovid. "Tereus, Procne, Philomela." In *Metamorphoses*, 134–42. Translated by A.D. Melville. Oxford: Oxford University Press, 1998.

Oxford English Dictionary Online. 2nd ed. Oxford: Oxford University Press, 2009.

Paget, Derek. "'Verbatim Theatre': Oral History and Documentary Techniques." *New Theatre Quarterly* 12 (1987): 317–36.

Parker, Robin. "Emerging Indigenous Voices." *Indiegogo*. 23 July 2018. https://www.indiegogo.com/projects/emerging-indigenous-voices#/.

Pêcheux, Michel. *Language, Semantics and Ideology: Stating the Obvious*. Translated by Harbans Nagpal. London: Macmillan, 1982.

Peene, Vida H. Foreword. *Canadian Full-Length Plays in English: A Preliminary Annotated Catalogue*. Ottawa: Dominion Drama Festival, 1964.

Perkyns, Richard. *The Neptune Story: Twenty-Five Years in the Life of a Leading Canadian Theatre*. Hantsport, NS: Lancelot Press, 1989.

Peterson, Leonard. *Almighty Voice*. Agincourt: Book Society of Canada, 1970.

Philip, Marlene Nourbese. *Coups and Calypsos: A Play*. Toronto: Mercury Press, 2001.

Posner, Michael. "Is It Racist Screed or Legitimate History?" *The Globe and Mail*. 14 November 2006: R1–2.

Potter, Andrew. "Introduction to the 40th Anniversary Edition." In *Lament for a Nation: The Defeat of Canadian Nationalism*, ix–lxiiix. Montreal: McGill-Queen's University Press, 2005.

Rabillard, Sheila. "*Age of Iron*: Adaptation and the Matter of Troy in Clements's Indigenous Urban Drama." *Theatre Research in Canada/Recherches Théâtrales au Canada* 31, no. 2 (2010): 118–42.

Rabinowitz, Aaron, and Robert Arp, ed. *Hamilton and Philosophy: Revolutionary Thinking*. Chicago: Open Court Books, 2017.

Redbird, Duke. "I Am Canadian." In *An Anthology of Canadian Native*

Literature in English, edited by Daniel David Moses and Terry Goldie, 120–1. 2nd ed. Oxford: Oxford University Press, 1998.

Reid, John G, and Emerson W. Baker. *Essays on Northeastern North America, Seventeenth and Eighteenth Centuries*. Toronto: University of Toronto Press, 2008.

Reilly, Kara, ed. *Contemporary Approaches to Adaptation in Theatre*. London: Palgrave Macmillan, 2017.

Rhys, Jean. *Wide Sargasso Sea*. New York: Norton, 1966.

Rich, Adrienne. "When We Dead Awaken: Writing as Re-vision." 1971. In *Feminisms: A Reader*, edited by Maggie Humm. Hemel Hempstead: Harvester Wheatsheaf, 1992.

Richards, David Adams. *Evening Snow Will Bring Such Peace*. Toronto: McClelland and Stewart, 2003.

– *Nights below Station Street*. Toronto: McClelland and Stewart, 1988.

Richardson, Harriette Taber, trans. "The Theatre of Neptune in New France." 1927. In *Spectacle of Empire: Marc Lescarbot's Theatre of Neptune in New France*, edited by Jerry Wasserman, 59–69. Vancouver: Talonbooks, 2006.

Ridout, Nicholas. *Theatre & Ethics*. Basingstoke: Palgrave Macmillan, 2009.

Robertson, Becky. "Crowdfunded Emerging Indigenous Voices Prize Surpasses $90,000, Receives Endowment." *Quill & Quire*. 25 May 2017.

Rose, Richard, Maggie Huculak, Duncan Ollerenshaw, Rick Roberts, and Maria Vacratsis. *Hysterica. Canadian Adaptation Project*. Guelph: University of Guelph, 2000.

Roth, Maya E. "The Philomela Myth as Postcolonial Feminist Theatre." In *Feminist Theatrical Revisions of Classic Works: Critical Essays*, edited by Sharon Friedman, 42–60. Jefferson, NC: McFarland, 2009.

Rubess, Banuta. Introduction to *Goodnight Desdemona (Good Morning Juliet)* by Ann-Marie MacDonald, xi–xiii. Toronto: Vintage Canada, 1998.

Rubin, Don, ed. *Canadian Theatre History: Selected Readings*. Toronto: Copp Clark, 1996.

Russo, J. "Interview and Aftermath: Dream, Fantasy, and Intuition in Odyssey 19 and 20." *American Journal of Philology* 103 (1982): 4–18.

Saddlemyer, Ann. Introduction to *Early Stages: Theatre in Ontario 1800–1914*, 3–17. Edited by Ann Saddlemyer. Toronto: University of Toronto Press, 1990.

Salter, Denis. "The Idea of a National Theatre." In *Canadian Canons: Essays in Literary Value*, edited by Robert Lecker, 71–90. Toronto: University of Toronto Press, 1991.

– "On Native Ground: Canadian Theatre Historiography and the Postmodernism/Post-colonialism Axis." *Theatre Histories*, edited by Alan Filewod, 115–23. Vol. 13, Critical Perspectives on Canadian Theatre in English. Toronto: Playwrights Canada Press, 2009.

Salverson, Julie, ed. *Popular Political Theatre and Performance*. Toronto: Playwrights Canada Press, 2010.

Sanders, Julie. *Adaptation and Appropriation*. London: Routledge, 2006.

Sanders, Leslie. "Othello Deconstructed: Djanet Sears' *Harlem Duet*." In *Testifyin': Contemporary African Canadian Drama*, edited by Djanet Sears, 557–9. Vol. 1. Toronto: Playwrights Canada Press, 2000.

Scarry, Elaine. *The Body in Pain: The Making and Unmaking of the World*. New York: Oxford University Press, 1985.

Schaffeld, Norbert, ed. *Shakespeare's Legacy: The Appropriation of the Plays in Post-Colonial Drama*. Trier: Wissenschaftlicher Verlag, 2005.

Schechner, Richard. *Performance Studies: An Introduction*. Abingdon: Routledge, 2002.

– *Performance Theory*. London: Routledge, 2003.

Schocket, Andrew M. "The American Revolution Rebooted: *Hamilton* and Genre in Contemporary Culture." *Journal of the Early Republic* 37, no. 2 (2017): 263–9.

Schwartz, Stephen, and Gregory Maguire. *Wicked: A New Musical*. Milwaukee: Hal Leonard, 2004.

Sears, Djanet. *The Adventures of a Black Girl in Search of God*. Toronto: Playwrights Canada Press, 2003.

– *Afrika Solo*. Toronto: Sister Vision, 1990.

– "Harlem Duet." In *Modern Canadian Plays*, edited by Jerry Wasserman, 337–69. Vol 2. 4th ed. Vancouver: Talonbooks, 2001.

– "NOTES OF a COLOURED girl: 32 SHORT reasons WHY I WRITE for the theatre." In *Harlem Duet*, 11–15. Winnipeg: Scirocco Drama, 1997.

– ed. *Testifyin': Contemporary African Canadian Drama*. 2 Vols. Toronto: Playwrights Canada Press, 2000.

Sears, Djanet, and Allison Sealy-Smith. "The Nike Method." Interview by Ric Knowles. *Canadian Theatre Review* 97 (1998): 24–30.

Shackleton, Mark. "Monique Mojica's *Princess Pocahontas and the Blue Spots* and Thomas King's *Green Grass, Running Water*: Countering Misrepresentations of 'Indianness' in Recent Native North American Writing." In *Towards a Transcultural Future: Literature and Human Rights in a 'Post'- Colonial World*, edited by Peter H. Marsden and Geoffrey V. Davis, 257–66. Amsterdam: Rodopi, 2004.

– "Tomson Highway: Colonizing Christianity versus Native Myth – From Cultural Conflict to Reconciliation." *Missions of Interdependence*, edited by Gerhard Stilz, 41–54. Amsterdam: Rodopi, 2002.

"Shakespeare." In *Canadian Theatre Encyclopedia*. Athabasca University, 12 August 2009.

Shakespeare, William. *Hamlet*. Edited by David Bevington. New York: Bantam, 1980.

– *Henry VI Part II*. Edited by Roger Warren. Oxford: Oxford University Press, 2003.

– *King Lear*. Edited by Russell Fraser. New York: New American Library, 1987.

– *Othello*. Edited by Louis B. Wright and Virginia A. LaMar. New York: Washington Square Press, 1965.

– *The Oxford Shakespeare: Julius Caesar*. Edited by Arthur Humphreys. New York: Oxford University Press, 2009.

– *The Oxford Shakespeare: Titus Andronicus*. Edited by Eugene M. Waith. Oxford: Oxford, 2008.

– *Richard III*. Edited by John Jowett. Oxford: Oxford University Press, 2000.

– "Sonnets." In *The Unabridged William Shakespeare*, edited by William George Clarke and William Aldis Wright, 1284–1308. Philadelphia: Running Press, 1989.

– *The Tempest*. Edited by Stephen Orgel. Oxford: Oxford University Press, 1998.

– *Twelfth Night*. Edited by Herschel Baker. New York: Penguin, 1987.

– "Venus and Adonis." In *The Unabridged William Shakespeare*, edited by William George Clarke and William Aldis Wright, 1246–60. Philadelphia: Running Press, 1989.

Shastri, Sudha. "Revisi(ti)ng the Past: Feminist Concerns in Margaret Atwood's the Penelopiad." In *Sites of Female Terror/En Torno a La Mujer y El Terror*, edited by Ana Antón-Pacheco Bravo et al., 141–49. Cizur Menor, Spain: Aranzadi, 2008.

Shaw, Helen. "The State of the Play: A Critic Addresses the Theatre Nation." *American Theatre* 33, no. 8 (2016): 30.

Shields, Erin. *If We Were Birds*. Toronto: Playwrights Canada Press, 2011.

– "If We Were Birds." Interview by Medina Hahn. *Summer Works Theatre Festival*. 12 July 2008.

Sloan, Carolyn. "Sinking Neptune: Play Challenges Eurocentric Perspective of 1606 Masque." *NovaNewsNow.com*. 7 November 2006.

Snowdon, Wallis. "Walterdale Theatre Cancels *Othello* Citing Anger over Racial Casting Controversy." CBC *News*. 31 January 2017. https://www.cbc.ca/news/canada/edmonton/walterdale-theatre-race-othello-cancelled-1.3959674.

Sophocles. *Antigone*. Edited and translated by Andrew Brown. Warminster, England: Aris and Phillips, 1987.

Staels, Hilde. "*The Penelopiad* and Weight: Contemporary Parodic and Burlesque Transformations of Classical Myths." *College Literature* 36, no. 4 (2009): 101–18.

Stam, Robert. *Literature through Film: Realism, Magic, and the Art of Adaptation*. Malden, MA: Blackwell, 2005.

Stevenson, Melanie Ann. "Re-Settling the 'Bard': Postcolonial Parody in Canadian and Australian Appropriations of Shakespeare." PhD diss., University of Toronto, 1998.

Stoppard, Tom. *Rosencrantz and Guildenstern Are Dead*. New York: Grove Press, 1967.

Sullivan, Lawrence E. *Native Religions and Cultures of North America*. New York: Continuum, 2000.

Sumi, Glenn. "*If We Were Birds*: Soaring Truths." Review of *If We Were Birds*, directed by Alan Dilworth. *Now*. 29 April 2010. https://nowtoronto.com/stage/theatre/if-we-were-birds/.

Suzuki, Mihoko. "Rewriting the Odyssey in the Twenty-First Century: Mary Zimmerman's *Odyssey* and Margaret Atwood's *Penelopiad*." *College Literature* 34, no. 2 (2007): 263–78.

Tannahill, Jordan. "Get Yourself Home Skyler James." *Age of Minority: 3 Solo Plays*. Toronto: Playwrights Canada Press, 2014.

Tarragon Theatre. *If We Were Birds*. Playbill. 9 January 2011. http://www.tarragontheatre.com/season/0910/ifwewerebirds/.

Taylor, Kate. "Fix the Colour Code in Canadian Theatre." *The Globe and Mail*. 6 December 2003: R2. https://www.theglobeandmail.com/arts/fix-the-colour-code-in-canadian-theatre/article18439961/.

Taymor, Julie, dir. *Titus*. Twentieth Century Fox, 2000.

Tettey, Wisdom, and Korbla P. Puplampu. *The African Diaspora in Canada:*

Negotiating Identity & Belonging. Calgary: University of Calgary Press, 2005.

Thomas, Audrey Callahan. *Blown Figures: A Novel*. Vancouver: Talonbooks, 1974.

– *Mrs. Blood*. Vancouver: Talonbooks, 1970.

Thornton, Kelly. "Director's Message." In *The Penelopiad: by Margaret Atwood*, 3. Playbill. Toronto: Nightwood, 2012.

– dir. *The Penelopiad*. By Margaret Atwood. Performed by Maev Beaty, Christine Brubaker, Raven Dauda, Sarah Dodd, Monica Dottor, Megan Follows, Kelli Fox, Cara Gee, Pat Hamilton, Tara Rosling, Pamela Sinha, Sophia Walker, Bahia Watson. Nightwood Theatre. Toronto, Ontario: Buddies in Bad Times Theatre, 10–29 January 2012.

Tremblay, Michel. *Les Belles Soeurs*. Montreal: Lemeac Editeur, 1972.

Usmiani, Renate. *Second Stage: The Alternative Theatre Movement in Canada*. Vancouver: University of British Columbia Press, 1983.

Van Kirk, Sylvia. *"Many Tender Ties": Women in Fur-Trade Society in Western Canada, 1670–1870*. Winnipeg: Watson and Dwyer, 1980.

Verdecchia, Guillermo. "Fronteras Americanas." In *Modern Canadian Plays*, edited by Jerry Wasserman, 313–32. Vol. 2. 4th ed. Vancouver: Talonbooks, 2001.

Vetter, Lisa Pace. *Women's Work as Political Art: Weaving and Dialectical Politics in Homer, Aristophanes, and Plato*. Lanham, MD: Lexington Books, 2005.

Vizenor, Gerald. *The American Indian and the Problem of History*. Edited by Calvin Martin. New York: Oxford University Press, 1987.

– *Manifest Manners: Postindian Warriors of Survivance*. Hanover: Wesleyan University Press, 1994.

Vogel, Paula. "Desdemona: A Play about a Handkerchief." In *Adaptations of Shakespeare: A Critical Anthology of Plays from the Seventeenth Century to the Present*, edited by Daniel Fischlin and Mark Fortier, 233–54. London: Routledge, 2000.

Wagner, Anton, ed. *The Brock Bibliography of Published Canadian Plays in English: 1766*. Toronto: Playwrights Press, 1980.

– ed. *Contemporary Canadian Theatre: New World Visions*. Toronto: Simon & Pierre, 1985.

Wagner, Anton, and Richard Plant, eds. *Canada's Lost Plays*. 4 Vols. Downsview: Canadian Theatre Review Publications, 1978.

Walcott, Derek. *Remembrance & Pantomime: Two Plays*. New York: Farrar, Straus, and Giroux, 1980.

Walker, George F. "Zastrozzi." In *Modern Canadian Plays*, edited by Jerry Wasserman, 261–88. Vol. 1. 4th ed. Vancouver: Talon Books, 2000.

Wallace, Robert. *Producing Marginality: Theatre and Criticism in Canada*. Saskatoon: Fifth House, 1990.

– *Theatre and Transformation in Contemporary Canada*. Thirteenth Annual Robarts Lecture. Toronto: York University, 15 March 1999.

Walley-Beckett, Moira, dir. *Anne with an E*. CBC and Netflix, Northwood Entertainment, 2017.

Walters, Wendy S. "After the Death of the Last: Performance as History in Monique Mojica's *Princess Pocahontas and the Blue Spots*." In *Crossing Waters, Crossing Worlds: The African Diaspora in Indian Country*, edited by Tiya Miles and Sharon Patricia Holland, 226–59. Durham: Duke University Press, 2006.

Warner, Michael. *Publics and Counterpublics*. New York: Zone Books, 2002.

Wasserman, Jerry, ed. *Modern Canadian Plays*. Vol. 2. 4th ed. Vancouver: Talon Books, 2001.

– ed. *Spectacle of Empire: Marc Lescarbot's Theatre of Neptune in New France*. 400th Anniversary commemorative ed. Vancouver: Talonbooks, 2006.

Welch, Ellen R. "Performing a New France, Making Colonial History in Marc Lescarbot's Théâtre De Neptune (1606)." *Modern Language Quarterly: A Journal of Literary History* 72, no. 4 (2011): 439–60.

White, Richard. *The Middle Ground: Indians, Empires, and Republics in the Great Lakes Region, 1650–1815*. Cambridge: Cambridge University Press, 2011.

Wiebe, Rudy. "Where Is the Voice Coming From?" In *Where is the Voice Coming From?*, 78–87. Toronto: McClelland & Stewart, 1974.

Williams, Cassie, and Anjuli Patil. "Controversial Cornwallis Statue Removed from Halifax Park." *CBC* Nova Scotia. 31 January 2018. https://www.cbc.ca/news/canada/nova-scotia/cornwallis-statue-removal-1.4511858.

Willmott, Glenn. "Canadian Ressentiment." *New Literary History* 32, no. 1 (2001): 133–56.

Woolf, Virginia. "Three Guineas." In *The Selected Works of Virginia Woolf*, 781–924. Ware, Hertfordshire: Wordsworth Editions, 2007.

Wright, Kailin. "Dispublics: Popular Yet Political Spectatorship in Margaret Atwood's *The Penelopiad* and Erin Shields's *If We Were Birds*." *Theatre Journal* 69, no. 2 (2017): 213–34.

– "Performing Cultural Crossroads: The Subject-Making Functions of 'I am' Declarations in Daniel David Moses's *Almighty Voice and His Wife*." *Theatre Research in Canada/Recherches théâtrales au Canada* 35, no. 2 (2014): 80–105.

– "Politicizing Difference: (Re)Claiming Canadian Theatre History and 'Les Sauvages' in *Le Théâtre de Neptune en la Nouvelle-France and Sinking Neptune*." *Studies in Canadian Literature* 38, no. 1 (2013): 8–28.

Wyatt, Jean. *Risking Difference: Identification, Race, and Community in Contemporary Fiction and Feminism*. Albany: State University of New York Press, 2004.

Yachnin, Paul. "Performing Publicity." *Shakespeare Bulletin* 28, no. 2 (2010): 201–19.

Yee, David. *Carried Away on the Crest of a Wave*. Toronto: Playwrights Canada Press, 2014.

Index